AMERICA'S NAVAL ARCHITECTURAL GENIUS

'EAM TURBINE · 24 KNOTS · DESIGN BLOHM & VÖSS

100 FEET · FOUR SCREW STEAM TURBINE · 24 KNOTS · DESIGN GIBBS & COX

SS SANTA ROSA, GRACE LINE (1959), NEWPORT NEWS SHIPBUILDING · 15,400 GRT, LENGTH 592 FEET,
BEAM 538 FEET · TWIN SCREW STEAM TURBINE · 21 KNOTS · DESIGN GIBBS & COX

2 GRT, LENGTH 660 FEET, BEAM 93 FEET

REW STEAM TURBINE · 40+ KNOTS · DESIGN GIBBS & COX

SS UNITED STATES

By the author

The Only Way to Cross

Dark Brown Is the River

S/S Norway

Olympic/Titanic

Liners to the Sun

Tribute to a Queen

From Song to Sovereign

Cunard: 150 Glorious Years

Monarch of the Seas

Majesty of the Seas

Safe Return Doubtful

Crossing & Cruising

Legend of the Seas

Under Crown & Anchor

Splendour of the Seas

Grandeur of the Seas

Grand Princess

Sun Princess

Dawn Princess

Titanic Survivor

Cruise Savvy

Century

Queen Mary 2

Normandie

France/Norway

Titanic Tragedy

JOHN MAXTONE-GRAHAM

SS UNITED STATES

RED, WHITE & BLUE RIBBAND, FOREVER

W. W. NORTON & COMPANY · NEW YORK · LONDON

For Maile Meloy, with eternal gratitude for your generosity, wisdom, and skill

Copyright © 2014 by John Maxtone-Graham

For information about special discounts for bulk purchases, please contact W. W. Norton Special Sales at specialsales@wwnorton.com or 800-233-4830

Manufacturing by RR Donnelley, South China
Book design by Robert L. Wiser, Silver Spring, MD
Production management by Anna Oler

ISBN 978-0-393-24170-9

W. W. Norton & Company , Inc.
500 Fifth Avenue, New York, NY 10110
www.wwnorton.com

W. W. Norton & Company Ltd.
Castle House, 75/76 Wells Street, London, WIT 3QT

1 2 3 4 5 6 7 8 9 0

Display photographs

p. 1: Austin Purves's United States seal adorned first class's main stairwell. (Glenn John Lindholm Collection)
pp. 2–3: Tugs maneuver *United States* alongside a Newport News shipway. (Newport News Shipbuilding Collection)
pp. 3–4: *United States* under way at sea. (Newport News Shipbuilding Collection)
pp. 5–9: The crowded 1952 christening ceremony of *United States*. (Newport News Shipbuilding Collection)

CONTENTS

Preface · 11

Acknowledgments · 12

1. *The Eisenhower Decade* · 17

2. *Postwar Shipboard* · 21

3. *The Remarkable Gibbs Brothers* · 25

4. *Leviathan Restoration* · 33

5. *The Jazz Age, Transatlantic* · 53

6. *SS America and Another War* · 57

7. *Building* United States · 81

8. *Christening, Trials, and Maiden* · 99

9. *The Glory Years* · 135

10. *Withdrawal and Layup* · 217

11. *Dereliction and Reprieve* · 225

Bibliography · 239

Index · 241

PREFACE

There is no escaping it. The saga of SS *United States* is inextricably linked with the man who designed her, William Francis Gibbs; the two are utterly inseparable.

An astonishing self-taught expert, Gibbs became America's most accomplished naval architect—resourceful, determined, and possessed of a steel-trap mind. Without his wisdom and ingenuity America would have had a far more challenging struggle at sea during World War II.

His *United States* was the first American vessel in a century to win the North Atlantic's mythic Blue Ribband. That unforgettable summer of 1952, the *Big U*, her inevitable crew nickname, knocked ten hours off former champion *Queen Mary*'s best crossing time, effectively seizing the prize in perpetuity; no passenger vessel sailing today or conceived in the future will achieve—let alone exceed—her service speed of 35 knots. On that score alone, *United States* demands our admiration and attention.

Gibbs's life, together with the progressively glorious objectives he achieved, serves as a perfect rainbow arc. He died in 1967 before the vessel's withdrawal. Had he lived two years longer, *United States*'s layup and subsequent deterioration would have greatly distressed him. She was withdrawn only seventeen years after her maiden voyage, laid up in early middle age, victim of a familiar American maritime malaise—dwindling passenger revenues and relentless union demands. Thereafter, the vessel entered a long twilit era. The glory years—her design, construction, and service from 1950 until 1969—serve as this volume's undeniable focus.

Additional foci must precede it, among them Gibbs's maiden naval architectural coup of transforming *Vaterland* into *Leviathan*, first as troopship and then American liner; also his work for the Matson and Grace Lines as well as designing SS *America* on the eve of World War II. Another great triumph was standardizing and upgrading America's shipbuilding capability and, glorious finale, creating *United States*, America's largest and fastest liner ever.

Gibbs had other enthusiasms as well, among them firefighting and grand opera, but his greatest loves were ships. He was seldom affable nor did he suffer fools gladly yet no naval architect in the world proved more accomplished.

John Maxtone-Graham
At Sea, 2014

United States arrives in Newport News for her annual maintenance. Tugs maneuver the vessel towards her shipway entrance. (Newport News Shipbuilding Collection)

ACKNOWLEDGMENTS

United States is one of my Norton editor Jim Mairs's favorite ocean liners. It pleases us both that writing this book at his urging has enlisted me as loyal adherent to his cause. I am also pleased that his right-hand colleague, Austin O'Driscoll, remains an irreplaceable occupant of his office. The third of a reliable Norton triumvirate is Jim's superb designer of choice, Robert Wiser of Silver Spring, Maryland, whose talent will enrich this, my fourth consecutive Norton publication. Wayne Mazzotta, an old colleague and friend, has been kind enough to create some more lavish endpapers and Nick Burkett's digital input is saluted with my most gracious thanks. A dear friend in Norway, Bård Kolltveit, has provided, once again, some of his superb ship profiles for those same endpapers.

The name Charles Howland must be a feature of any *United States* acknowledgment list. His apartment, seven blocks away from my half-brownstone, remains a treasure trove, filled with furnishings, artworks, images, memorabilia, and ephemera. That together with his impeccable taste, knowledge, and generosity render him one of this maritime historian's most invaluable allies.

Thanks to Howland, I was introduced to Bill DiBenedetto, a man who is a walking compendium of so many aspects of *United States* lore.

At the library of Virginia's Mariners Museum, now housed in the Trible Library building at Christopher Newport University, I was most ably assisted by librarian Bill Barker and his assistant archivist Bill Edwards-Bodmer. Also helpful were information specialist Patti Hinson and technical services chairman Jennifer Anielski. In addition, the museum's director of photographic services, Claudia Jew, is the able custodian of hundreds of admirable photographs.

Newport News expertise was also provided by Tom Clark, a retired engineering naval officer who spent thirty-five years at the shipyard, for twenty of them as manager of quality assurance. Another retired Newport News employee was Bill Lee, recommended by the maritime historian William A. Fox, who provided marvelous assistance and guidance, most especially about *America/ West Point*.

Final Newport News shipyard assistance was given by Mike Dillard, the shipyard's photograph editor. He has discovered and sorted a wide range of images for inclusion in the book, which he organized and delivered flawlessly.

Michael Jedd, another friend dedicated to the history of *United States*, has been kind enough to volunteer much of his incomparable expertise and collection with me. Fellow maritime historian William Miller has been an invaluable source of Hoboken information as well as illustrations from his peerless collection.

I am particularly indebted to former *United States* passengers, crew, and observers who were kind enough to relate their onboard experiences in depth. I thank them alphabetically and wholeheartedly: Van and Molly Bachman, Bruce Blitz, Frank Faulhefer, David Fitzgerald, John Getz, John Glasscock, Mary Jane and Helen Gore, Yvette Frank Greenspan, Victor and Mimi Mather Jr., Arthur McClean, Dan and Carmen McSweeney, David Townsend, Stephen and Daphne Wassner, and Jessica Weber.

I must also thank Noelle Braynard, Susan Ferris, Susan Gibbs, Andres Hernandez, David Pike, and Roger and Nona Skoyles.

As always, my dear wife Mary has once again championed the cause, hearing every chapter first, solving computer and Internet headaches, and providing the ongoing concern and invaluable support that enable me to complete every manuscript. She shares all my cabins at sea and remains a veritable tower of strength and skill; nothing would be achieved without her.

Right: Just-christened *United States* has been withdrawn from her shipway and tugs are escorting the vessel to her fitting-out pier. (Newport News Shipbuilding Collection)

Overleaf: The Gibbs brothers' two greatest ships pass each other in New York Harbor. *United States* (above) is inbound and *America* headed for sea. In that she is nearer the camera, smaller *America* seems of almost equal dimension as her later consort. (Newport News Shipbuilding Collection)

CHAPTER ONE

THE EISENHOWER DECADE

I LIKE IKE

—1952 GOP election slogan

I once came into Pier 86 on the liner United States, *the fastest ever built, and I watched the faces of the passengers around me, waiting for the gangplank to open as the ship's band subsided into a last medley of patriotism—"America, America," "Dixie," "Star-Spangled Banner" and one or two stirring marches I failed to recognize. Trilly secretarial voices rang, as those grand old tunes reverberated, jewelled spectacles vibrated, stiletto heels tapped the deck; but the expressions on the passengers' faces struck me as sad, as though the hum of the liner's mechanisms, the blaring of those anthems as the vessel docked, were holding the voyagers for a moment in a lost American world—a world encapsulated there still between the decks of the great ship, that would disappear the moment the gangplank doors were opened, and they returned to 46th Street.*

—Jan Morris, Contact!, 2009

Opposite: It was July 3, 1952, sailing day for *United States*'s maiden voyage. The interior of Pier 86 was garlanded with signal flags as well as those almost universally ignored signs advising passengers that porters need not be reimbursed. A band was playing and the press of passengers and their outnumbering visitors unrelenting. (The Mariners Museum, Newport News, VA)

The early 1950s was an exciting and burgeoning era for the United States, both the republic and the

remarkable ocean liner named after it, which would sail on its maiden voyage on July 3, 1952.

A former senator from Missouri, Vice President Harry S. Truman, had been propelled abruptly into the presidency after Franklin Roosevelt's death in 1945. Truman went on to win an upset second term in 1948, dislodging his favored and fully confident opponent, the New York governor Thomas E. Dewey. Grinning triumphantly, the reelected president held aloft the *Chicago Tribune*'s embarrassingly premature headline TRUMAN DEFEATED.

In turn, Truman would be succeeded in the oval office by an overwhelming GOP groundswell. The Republicans had endured twenty years in the wilderness, displaced by two successive Democratic administrations. The Second World War had ensured Roosevelt's unprecedented reelection to a fourth term, followed by seven Truman years.

In November 1952 the Republican nominee, General Dwight David Eisenhower, defeated Adlai Stevenson to occupy the White House to begin two complete terms. He boasted an incomparable track record, marching unassailably from supreme Allied commander in Europe through a brief stint as president of Columbia University before achieving the presidency of the United States.

Vast numbers of the electorate "liked Ike," as his campaign slogan proclaimed. What was *not* to like? Many Republicans did not like Ike at first, a career soldier who had joined the party only in January 1952. But his popular appeal proved legendary: without even appearing in New Hampshire, Eisenhower won 47,000 primary votes to Robert Taft's 36,000.

Though in some ways he might seem to pale in comparison with John F. Kennedy, his charismatic and youthful Democratic successor, elected in 1960, he proved exactly the right man for his time. That famous Eisenhower grin said it all: affable, bland, and conformist, an outlook that seemed somehow a guarantee of prosperity to come.

The choice of his 1952 running mate, Californian Richard Nixon, helped mollify disaffected Republicans because Nixon was an avowed Communist hater. Despite a brush with disgrace after having accepted the gift of a dog called Checkers for his two daughters, he managed to remain on the winning ticket after delivering a maudlin "Checkers speech" by way of excusing his behavior. There

was also a secret $16,000 slush fund provided by Californians that contributed to his discomfort.

I enrolled as a freshman at Brown University in the fall of 1947. Many of my fellow undergraduates were older veterans benefiting from the GI Bill, that government-funded tuition reimbursement scheme that guaranteed millions advantageous entry into what was to become history's most rewarding job market. In fact, one huge economic advantage of the GI Bill was that it prevented huge numbers of demobilized servicemen from overwhelming the postwar job market; instead of swamping employment offices millions entered college classrooms instead.

Those GIs spawned what would come to be called baby boomers: a growing accumulation of Americans, offspring produced by American couples reunited by peacetime. Boomers would mature into a relentless consumer powerhouse, triggering an extraordinary marketing phenomenon. Their parents, those acquisitive young marrieds, would embrace—and furnish—a novel suburban lifestyle, buying up property, cars, and an outpouring of newly manufactured postwar luxuries.

Boomers profited from several turned pages. The Great Depression was over, the war was over, and America's industrial engine was gearing up for a surge of peacetime productivity. Finished with tanks, Detroit returned to automobiles. In fact, that 1950s economy duplicated, in a sense, the incredible production achievements galvanized by the country's war effort. Times were good. For the record, America's national debt in 1952 was just over $4 billion.

Perhaps the most profound irony of the era was that buoyant peacetime coexisted with what had already been christened in the press as the Cold War. Winston Churchill, no longer prime minister since the surprising Labour Party upset of 1945, famously identified the war's boundary in an address he called "The Sinews of Peace," delivered at Westminster College in Fulton, Missouri, on March 5, 1946: "From Stettin in the Baltic to Trieste in the Adriatic, an iron curtain has descended across the continent."

His word would serve as a precursor of ominous confrontation between the world's two rival superpowers. Eventually, a U.S.-Soviet space race would be inaugurated by the launch of Russia's *Sputnik* on October 4, 1957. That worrisome Soviet first spurred work on larger and more efficient American rockets that would not only propel satellites into orbit but also give America the capability of lofting missiles toward targets in the Soviet Union. Of course, Soviet missiles would be zeroed in on American targets as well. Ultimately, nuclear warheads mounted atop intercontinental ballistic missiles would be deployed by both sides, poised and waiting in armored underground silos.

Growing up in that Cold War of unease and fear, America's schoolchildren were drilled to "duck and cover," seeking protection from incoming missiles by hiding beneath classroom desks. Though thankfully no nuclear exchange was ever implemented, conventional hostilities could not be avoided, perceived in Washington as unceasing evidence of a worldwide Communist takeover.

The first such conflict broke out on June 25, 1950, only five years after VE Day and VJ Day, when North Korea's People's Liberation Army surged southward across the Korean peninsula's peacetime dividing line marked by the 38th parallel, coincidentally the exact latitude of Washington, D.C.

Resurgent United Nations forces commanded by General Douglas MacArthur ultimately struck back, landing at Inchon and driving north to occupy Pyongyang, North Korea's capital. That feat of arms prompted further escalation: Chinese battalions massed in Mongolia flooded south into North Korea across the Yalu River, instigating additional months of seesaw combat that degenerated into static trench warfare.

Six decades after the Panmunjom truce of 1953, that armed standoff remains in place. North Korea and South Korea as well as a sizable U.S. military force still face each other across the 38th parallel.

That smoldering postwar conflict was only the first of a series of small wars, none engendering an epic global commitment. Nor did the Korean struggle spawn the bitter antagonism of the war in Vietnam that followed it in the next decade. Nevertheless, throughout both, America's burgeoning economy comfortably embraced a guns-and-butter capability, accommodating the unstoppable baby boomers even as increasing numbers of American servicemen were shipped overseas, first to Korea and later to Southeast Asia.

Despite the national upheaval of that Vietnamese quagmire, which precipitated divisive and bitter homefront confrontations, these earlier postwar conflicts seemed, in retrospect, somehow con-

tainable. Although Washington remained convinced that the domino theory of collapsing regimes was a relentless worldwide Soviet conspiracy, neither the Korean nor Vietnam conflicts ever equaled the post–9/11 free-for-all fomented by today's terrorist jihad, pitting radical Islamic extremism against Western Christianity and destabilizing the entire world order.

The military and political collapse of the Soviet Union as well as its formerly impenetrable iron curtain preceded that Middle East imbroglio. Following military reprisal for Iraq's invasion of Kuwait, the commitment of massive American forces in both Iraq and Afghanistan played out against the ominous nuclear machinations of both Iran and consistently antagonistic North Korea.

Now we are going to turn back the clock to vibrant postwar America, to that peaceful and promising Eisenhower decade that comfortably predates today's spectral threats.

Life rings convey an image of their respective ocean liners. But this one is not a standard life ring that adorned a *United States* railing; it is a decorative one used to indicate a passenger muster station somewhere inside the vessel: the ribbon and composition distinguish it immediately, as do the aluminum brackets suspending it from the bulkhead. (David Pike Collection)

CHAPTER TWO

POSTWAR
SHIPBOARD

Getting there is half the fun.

—Cunard White Star slogan

*You stretch out, relaxed, on a warm deck and suddenly, nothing on earth matters.
You see the sun like you've never seen it before—dazzling across the smooth sapphire
of the sea. And you discover how carefree life can be, surrounded by people who are
actually eager to please you. You're in the world of P&O. And it's like nothing on earth!*

—*Canberra* publicity, circa 1959

Opposite: Mid-ocean, *United States*'s first class passengers throng their deck chairs.
Cabin class passengers occupy chairs behind the class barriers, the starboard side's after docking bridge
silhouetted against *Big U*'s boiling wake. (The Mariners Museum, Newport News, VA)

In the 1950s, despite the advent of increasing numbers of passenger aircraft, ocean liners dominated

intercontinental transportation. On the North Atlantic, Cunard White Star's 1,000-foot consorts *Queen Elizabeth* and *Queen Mary* had inaugurated an enormously successful weekly mail service between Southampton, Cherbourg, and New York. Originally conceived in 1929, that unique two-ship shuttle had to wait seventeen years, including an intervening world war, before its 1946 implementation.

Postwar, the French resuscitated Germany's *Europa* into France's *Liberté* and restored trooper *Ile de France* for peacetime service with two rather than three smokestacks. So, too, immediately after the war, Holland America renovated *Nieuw Amsterdam*, redecorating her from grim trooper to former peacetime glory. In 1959 the company would provide *Nieuw Amsterdam* with a new consort by entering a fifth *Rotterdam* into service.

Elsewhere, under the British flag, the Peninsular & Orient (P&O) and Orient Lines revived passenger trade from Britain to the Far East. *Orion* of 1935 had served as Orient Lines' prewar trailblazer, a vessel designed to combat Red Sea and Indian Ocean humidity with a new tropical deck layout but lacking, alas, the essential weapon of air-conditioning.

That would change in 1960 when those former Far East rivals merged into one shipping line called P&O/Orient. Thanks to that strategic union, the world's largest passenger fleet emerged. From Orient Lines came *Orcades*, *Orontsay*, and *Orsova*, their formerly corn-colored hulls repainted to match P&O white. P&O's *Chusan*, *Arcadia*, *Himalaya*, and *Iberia* were updated as well.

The jewels of the fleet, however, were a pair of newcomers, the largest hulls built in the British Isles since the *Queens*. *Oriana* was a fast ship that reduced passage time to Australia from four to three weeks. The other was *Canberra*, entering service in 1959, just a year before the merger. With twin funnels mounted astern, she provided enormous open deck space for increased numbers of passengers.

P&O/Orient's revamped fleet heralded an inevitable change of service. Former exclusively emigrant carriers gradually morphed into air-conditioned cruise liners, with extensive sunning decks, open-air pools, and, by night, increasingly lavish entertainment. The historic route connecting Britain with her most distant colony catered to both outbound emigrants and ongoing cruises thereafter. Once new Australians had disembarked in Sydney, they were replaced by cruising passengers as the ships continued eastbound across the Pacific, either to America's west coast or through the Panama Canal to the Caribbean before returning transatlantic to Great Britain. The vessels had completed a global circumnavigation with two contrasting passenger loads.

Former Axis partners were slower to regroup. Germany's two prewar record breakers were no more. In March 1941, fabled *Bremen*, ostensibly under conversion to a troopship as part of Operation Sea Lion, Hitler's planned invasion of Great Britain, was destroyed by fire at her pier. Arson was suspected, allegedly the work of a "mentally deficient" sixteen-year-old cabin boy who was later executed. *Europa* became a prize of war, sailing for the French Line as *Liberté*.

The Italians, despite the wartime loss of both *Rex* and *Conte di Savoia*, returned to the transatlantic fray with gusto, launching a series of midsized vessels starting with a (second) 27,000-ton *Giulio Cesare* in 1951, together with sister ship *Augustus*. That same year, *Andrea Doria* entered service, to be joined three years later by sister ship *Cristoforo Colombo*. And in 1961 *Leonardo da Vinci* appeared, the company's first black-hulled liner since *Rex*.

That sequential production of dashing midsized vessels would be climaxed by a pair of memorable liners, *Michelangelo* and *Raffaello*, of 1965. The two served, alas, as finales for Italy's postwar maritime surge, fast vessels equipped with long forecastle heads, their twin funnels housed within novel steel cages. They were also the first Italian liners to sport white-painted hulls.

Steaming between Genoa and New York and offering four classes each, *Michelangelo* and *Raffaello* were the last transatlantic liners Italy produced. Additional victims of the inevitable diminution of Atlantic crossings, they remained in service for only ten years before withdrawal in 1975. Unlike *France* of 1962, there would be no cruising reprieve; they were sidelined forever, chartered as floating barracks for the Iranian army.

In America, shipbuilding would never recover the same vigor it had known during the war. And the inspiration and dedication of that memorable national effort would be due to the remarkable impetus provided by two Philadelphians, William and Frederic Gibbs.

Opposite: Images of the two *Queens*—distant three-funneled *Mary* on the left, two-funneled *Elizabeth* closer—rejoice in Cunard White Star's boast "Fastest Ocean Service in the World"; after July 1952, the slogan disappeared. (Cunard White Star Collection)

CHAPTER THREE

THE REMARKABLE GIBBS BROTHERS

Gibbs is a very peculiar man, you see. I mean, he is like an artist. He likes his work.

—Sam Carp, a Soviet representative testifying before the Special Committee Investigating Un-American Activities, 1939

Gibbs is a genius.

—Vice Admiral Emory Scott Land, U.S. Maritime Commissioner

Opposite: It is the morning of June 16, 1952. The Gibbs brothers are perched atop the bridge of *United States* as she departs her Newport News fitting-out pier for the first day of her trials. Frederic sits overlooking the railing while William squats comfortably on deck. Typically, he has turned to direct a somewhat forbidding glance at the photographer. (**The Frank Braynard Collection**)

In the twentieth century's third year, two brothers made transportation history. On December 17, 1903,

at Kitty Hawk, North Carolina, Wilbur and Orville Wright, bicycle repairmen from Ohio, achieved man's first aerial flight. However brief—only twelve seconds—its ultimate global impact was, appropriately, earth-shattering. Offering an equivalent maritime accomplishment, less well known but, to my mind, equally influential, were two Philadelphia brothers named Gibbs.

William Francis, born in 1886, was the elder son of financier William Warren Gibbs, a man who repeatedly accrued and then lost multimillion-dollar fortunes. One of those fortunes was apparently intact during the summers of 1907 and 1912 because the family crossed to Europe and back each of those two summers. Their first return was the historic, maiden voyage of Cunard's brand-new *Mauretania*, the world's fastest steamer.

William and his two-years-younger brother, Frederic, graduated from Philadelphia's DeLancey School (today's Episcopal Academy). William went on to Harvard but a failure in Latin prevented him obtaining a degree. He left after three years, concluding his education, at his father's insistence, as a law student in New York.

A self-made millionaire, Gibbs père was reputed to have served on more corporate boards than anyone in the country. He was determined that his namesake should have a similar industrial and manufacturing background rather than devote his life to what he—the father—considered the "second-rate pursuit" of engineering. Engineers, he opined, had a pronounced shortcoming: no business ability as a result of inarticulacy in business conversations.

After graduating from Columbia Law School in 1913, William returned to Philadelphia for two years' practice of real estate law. Up to that point his career had seemed predictable, if essentially mundane. But an exclusively legal life was not in the cards. A practicing lawyer by day, William pursued naval architecture nocturnally. Quite simply, he and Frederic were besotted with ocean liners.

Aged nine and seven, respectively, the boys had watched steamship *St. Louis* launched from Philadelphia's William Cramp and Sons shipyard on November 12, 1895. Christened by America's first lady, Mrs. Grover Cleveland, the vessel was one of two 11,629-tonners built for the American Line; her sister ship *St. Paul* would emerge from

the same yard the following spring. They were the first and largest American liners built since the 1850s. Ironically, while it was in existence, Cramp's famous yard was located not far from the slip where derelict *United States* currently awaits redemption today.

The contagious excitement of that *St. Louis* ceremony, no less than the sight of her hull thundering down the ways and plunging into the Delaware River, moved both boys profoundly. William would suggest years later that their fascination with ships dated from that moment.

In truth, a fervid maritime predisposition had existed long before then. William began sketching ships at the age of three. For fun, he and Frederic used to redesign the Royal Navy's battleships. Willie, as he was known, not only was intrigued by ships, he was also intrigued by their interior design and how they worked. One boyhood hero was Isambard Kingdom Brunel, the English railway and shipbuilding genius who produced *Great Britain*, *Great Western*, and especially giant *Great Eastern*.

Willie Gibbs also absorbed reams of maritime esoterica like a sponge, information of a complexity and sophistication that few other readers his age could possibly comprehend. An engineer calling at the Gibbs manse one day asked the preoccupied seven-year-old what he was reading; when William showed him *Cassier's Magazine*, a highly abstruse engineering periodical, the man's incredulous response was "Good Lord!"

Naval architectural theory was only one enthusiasm; the boy exhibited a full-blown mechanical practicality as well. The fortuitous gift of a toy British steam engine when William was eleven led to construction of an entire miniature fire department with which he and Frederic extinguished increasingly elaborate garden conflagrations. Both brothers were hooked on firefighting because the family coachman had formerly been a member of Philadelphia's Fire Department. Whenever neighborhood blazes broke out, thanks to the coachman's firehouse contacts, Willie and Freddie sometimes climbed aboard local fire engines and raced to the blaze.

The family's summer home at Spring Lake, New Jersey, boasted a view of Sandy Hook. The profiles of every steamer entering New York through the Gedney Channel were subject to highly critical and informed review by young William, perched on a front porch aerie with binoculars and a stack of shipping journals at the ready.

In 1915, despite America's neutrality while Europe's war escalated, now twenty-nine and twenty-seven, Willie and Freddie shared a rented cottage outside Philadelphia where they drew up plans for the North Atlantic's first two 1,000-foot (305 meters), 30-knot ocean liners, fourteen years before either *Normandie* or *Queen Mary* was conceived. Although Panama's canal had just been completed and opened the year previous, apparently the thought of having either of their projected sister ships sail through it did not occur to them. Panama's lock dimensions were such that the passage of 1,000-foot hulls was impossible.

Most incredible was that neither brother was a qualified naval architect and, amazingly, never would be. Though some of William's Harvard syllabus had included science and engineering courses, naval architecture did not exist as a graduate school option. However, the study of it flourished sub rosa. William spent many Cambridge evenings continuing his analysis and occasional upgrading of the Royal Navy's battle fleet, his goal the provision of additional watertight compartmentation so that a damaged warship would remain afloat longer. But his maritime enthusiasm remained a secret; whenever William left his dormitory room, plans and drawings were concealed under lock and key. Frederic never attended a university; perhaps his graduation from DeLancey coincided with one of his father's financial crises.

Given what one would have thought a crucial educational omission, it is astonishing that the two young men embarked on such a challenging career, youthful hobby metamorphosing seamlessly into adult livelihood. These were neither starry-eyed amateurs writing the great American novel nor novices standing for political office or devising useful inventions; they were intent solely on designing oceangoing vessels. Although naval architecture may not be rocket science, it is nevertheless a métier demanding multiple talents, including extensive mathematical and geometric skills, familiarity with hull lines and strength of materials, mechanical drawing, and knowledge about all manner of maritime machinery, from main engines to a bewilderment of pumps and compressors, arcana that, one assumes, could be absorbed only after years of instruction and training.

But nothing of the kind happened. There was neither academic enrollment nor diplomas indicating any. Their training was entirely self-generated enthusiastically since childhood. William and Frederic Gibbs doubtless remain among the world's few if only autodidactic naval architects.

William Le Roy Emmet, General Electric's chief engineer, pronounced Gibbs's engine specification for his pair of liners perfectly feasible. Conception of those trail-breaking ships was combined with an innovative docking option. Each would embark and disembark passengers not from Manhattan or Hoboken but at a purpose-built terminal out at Montauk on Long Island's easternmost tip. Boat trains, familiar steamship adjuncts for Europeans but unknown in America, would deliver passengers there from Manhattan, shortening crossing time significantly. The two ships and terminal were not only innovative but also expensive. According to the brothers' scrupulous calculations, construction of a pair of four-class vessels would cost $60 million and their Montauk terminal an additional $15 million.

Their plans complete, whom to approach? The Gibbs brothers decided on Ralph Peters, chairman of the Long Island Rail Road. The LIRR was owned by the Pennsylvania Railroad, America's largest and most prestigious railroad network. Frederic had discovered that Peters was also cogitating about enlarging the Pennsy's international influence by implementing its railway clout with a Montauk-based transatlantic steam service.

Laden with plans and notebooks crammed with supportive data, and masking their inexperience behind sober, professional deportment, the brothers walked unannounced into Ralph Peters's outer office. When his receptionist temporized, suggesting that the head of the company was too busy to see them, Frederic announced: "Tell him some men want to talk to him about ships from Montauk Point to England." Moments later, they were ushered into the man's inner sanctum.

Peters listened to a persuasive sales pitch and examined their drawings with growing excitement. So impressed was he that he immediately telephoned J. P. Morgan, whose ambitious holding company, the International Mercantile Marine, or IMM, had recently co-opted nearly every North Atlantic shipping company. Shortly thereafter, Morgan would hire the Gibbs brothers to work at his firm. They also submitted their ships' plans to no less an eminence than Secretary of the Navy Josephus Daniels. U.S. Navy Admiral David W. Taylor, esteemed naval architect and inventor of the bulbous bow to come, was impressed enough to order a model of their proposed hull wrought for tank testing.

It was an extraordinary achievement, the showbiz equivalent of an unknown, untried actor bearding Louis B. Mayer in MGM's head office. That two unqualified young men, however well bred, polite, and seemingly knowledgeable, could impress high-powered titans of Morgan's and Daniels's stature says a great deal about their convincing expertise.

Those two 1,000-footers never came to fruition, at least in their original guise. After America entered the war in April 1917, the U.S. Navy was understandably more preoccupied with warships than passenger vessels. Regardless, the brothers Gibbs found Washington employment in their chosen field. In 1917 both became members of the Shipping Control Committee that General Philip Franklin, former IMM vice president, had formed as a wartime outgrowth of the Shipping Board. The body was charged with the monumental task of allocating merchant ship assignments worldwide.

After the war, encouraged by their exposure to both naval architecture and the Byzantine maze of Washington's maritime bureaucracy, the two decided to go into business for themselves as Gibbs Brothers Inc. They hung out their shingle on New York's lower Broadway in 1922. Seven years later, that first corporate name would be expanded to Gibbs & Cox, Inc., signaling entry into the fraternal partnership of successful yacht designer Daniel Hargate Cox, whose track record lent the brothers credibility. The division of labor was easy. William and the new partner worked exclusively on ship design while Frederic handled the business side; this earliest corporate pigeonholing endured for as long as both brothers lived.

Most striking about the Gibbses entry into such a challenging field was how a combination of chutzpah and knowledge augured so auspiciously from the start. One advantage both shared was their background. The Gibbs family was initially perceived as nouveau riche, arrivistes who fell woefully short of acceptance within mainline purviews. But over the years, thanks to well-chosen moves from the wrong to the right side of the tracks and, even more important, an abiding sense of how things were done, the Gibbs family managed to establish itself as both decent and well respected.

And whatever their father's volatile financial ups and downs, his two sons managed to cultivate what seemed a patrician, wellborn demeanor. Neither William nor Frederic was tainted by snobbism; both the partnership and its dealings seemed blessed with a blue-blooded imprimatur. Whatever airs they affected were not to impress but merely typified both Gibbs boys' personae since birth.

Cast into the rough and tumble of the shipping world and its sometimes abrasive negotiations, three instinctive qualities never deserted them: an adamantine adherence to principle, demonstrably responsible behavior, and, perhaps most important, utter dedication to their jobs. Throughout their careers, it would be safe to say that William and Frederic Gibbs worked longer and harder hours than any colleagues, subordinates, or rivals. As a result, the brother/partners seemed to rise above the fray, coping with life's vicissitudes, doing the right thing, doing it briskly, and never giving offense.

Those inherent predilections obviously honed the firm's and its partners' irreproachable reputations. Despite scant experience, the brothers always completed their contracts, and their confidence and expertise invariably won the day. During Gibbs & Cox's long wartime expansion, standards were maintained to William's demanding measures. One overriding Gibbs rule was "Make sure that's done today and, remember, today ends at midnight."

William and Frederic remained inseparable, a supportive fraternal stance that never wavered. Years later, during World War II when Gibbs & Cox's naval responsibilities expanded the firm into a vast, largely naval establishment, William's daily post was at an elevated drafting table set up at one end of the firm's huge main hall. It had four stools surrounding it and William Francis was always perched on one of them, intent on drawings but also omnisciently aware of everything around him.

As vice president, Frederic worked just as hard but out of sight in his office. Sitting conspicuously and symbolically on his desk was a large adding machine. He became the firm's conscience, serving, in maritime parlance, as William's anchor to windward; it was he who kept the Gibbs & Cox business affairs in correct perspective. If, as occasionally happened, his older brother upset anyone or spent too freely, it was Frederic who inevitably returned matters to an even socio/financial keel.

Their incredible first commission in the early 1920s was being charged by the Shipping Board and United States Lines with the task of converting interned ocean liner *Vaterland* into trooper *Leviathan* and, postwar, back into ocean liner *Leviathan*, to be discussed in the next chapter.

Three remarkable commissions followed, starting in 1924. Gibbs & Cox was asked to design a yacht for Philadelphia's Emily Cadwalader, the 85-foot (26 meters) *Sequoia*. A year later, the company undertook a 104-foot (32 meters) successor, also named *Sequoia*. A year after that, Mrs. Cadwalader commissioned even larger *Savarona*; at 185 feet (56 meters) overall, she too would later be rechristened *Sequoia*.

Emily Cadwalader sold the vessel, now renamed *Allegro*, to Eugene McDonald, founder of Zenith Radio. He would ultimately rechristen her *Mizpah*. Shortly after Pearl Harbor she was donated to the U.S. Navy, becoming PY-29; ultimately, she served as flagship for the Atlantic Fleet's Destroyer Force until 1946. Retired from the navy, she became briefly a banana boat under Honduran registration. Then, in October 1967, she was bought by McDonald's nephew Eugene Kinney. Sadly, he never renovated the vessel but, the following year, donated it as part of an artificial reef established below water off Palm Beach, Florida.

On the eve of World War II, Gibbs was asked by the Soviet navy to design a battleship with a suggested displacement of 35,000 tons. He went to work on his first officially commissioned warship, ultimately delivering to the Soviets plans for a giant aircraft carrier displacing 85,000 tons, which could carry and launch sixty aircraft. Impressed but overwhelmed, the Russians rejected it. That same year, Gibbs also started designing tonnage for the Grace Line, four *Santa*-class South American passenger/cargo vessels.

In 1938 New York City's Fire Department commissioned Gibbs & Cox to design *Firefighter 1*, which became its largest and latest fireboat. It was a splendid creation, bristling with nine nozzles, that could deliver 75 tons of water on demand; its bow nozzle alone churned out 6,000 gallons a minute. One observer compared its deluge to an artillery barrage. But *Firefighter 1* was only a foretaste of Gibbs's extraordinary land-based Super Pumper to come, created for the same department in the mid-1960s.

After World War I Gibbs & Cox was asked to design a liner for Matson's Hawaiian service. Built in

Philadelphia by William Cramp and Sons, the same yard from which young William and Frederic had seen *St. Louis* launched, *Malolo* carried two classes, 457 in first and 163 in cabin. In the first class, many cabins boasted private bathrooms and Matson's first indoor swimming pool. The largest passenger vessel produced in any American yard, *Malolo* would prove the Pacific's fastest ship.

Her sea trials off Nantucket in May 1925 included an unanticipated trial, a near-fatal collision with the Norwegian freighter *Jacob Christensen*, which, in thick fog, had inadvertently rammed *Malolo*'s port flank at the junction of two compartments; she immediately began taking on water.

William Gibbs was on the bridge and, after activating the vessel's watertight doors, he raced down to the engine room. Torrents of green water were flooding the space but, as he watched, the doors closed, confining the ingress. Engulfed by

The Gibbs brothers in the office of Gibbs & Cox. Their division of labor, which would last a lifetime, was that William designed the vessels while Frederic looked after finances.
(The Frank Braynard Collection)

7,000 tons of sea water, *Malolo* listed alarmingly. But thanks to Gibbs's rigorous compartmentation she stayed afloat. Salvage tugs towed the disabled steamer back past New York to Philadelphia for repair. *Malolo* remained in service for half a century under successive names and flags. She served as prototype for three additional Gibbs & Cox Matson newbuilds: *Mariposa*, *Lurline*, and *Monterey*.

Gibbs was understandably gratified by *Malolo*'s resiliency. He had always been haunted by eastbound *Empress of Ireland*'s 1914 nighttime foundering off Rimouski Point in the St. Lawrence. Coincidentally, she was also rammed by a Norwegian vessel, the collier *Storstadt*. Full of newly embarked passengers, the *Empress* was pierced mortally on the starboard side at the junction of neighboring compartments. The Canadian Pacific liner capsized, flooded, and went to the bottom in twenty minutes, with the loss of more than twelve hundred lives.

The downside of William Gibbs's mainline assurance was a curious obstreperousness. One wonders, did he cultivate it or merely surrender to it? He looked forbidding—tall, thin, and invariably black clad, his wing collar cradling a black tie. He once said about himself: "Beneath this rough exterior beats a heart of granite." He had thin hair and always wore silver-rimmed round spectacles. His voice tended to rasp and his manner was consistently brusque; he was once attributed the gloom of an undertaker.

The New Yorker described Gibbs in a 1964 profile as a "thin, hungry, slightly rakish and very excitable archbishop in baggy civilian clothes." When something displeased him, he was like a terrier with a bone. He hated waste and confusion and had no patience with the constant political maneuvering that was endemic throughout Washington's bureaucracy. "If there's anything I dislike," William Francis Gibbs once remarked, "it's big shots," despite the fact that in his chosen field he had become, indubitably, the biggest shot of them all.

One unlikely obsession was his all-consuming fear of bad luck. However unsentimental and dictatorial, Gibbs tried avoiding every possible superstition, even refusing to read letters with thirteen paragraphs. Gibbs was also a fervent patriot, deeply in love with his country, President Lincoln, and the American way. In an article he wrote for *Management Engineering*, in May 1923, discussing the successful conversion of *Leviathan* into a peacetime liner, he stated unequivocally: "The spirit of the workmen is significant.... The familiar excuse—it can't be done—was brushed aside.... When backed by preparation, initiative, enthusiasm and faith, seemingly nothing is impossible in America."

William Gibbs was married in 1927 at the age of forty-one. His wife was the former Vera Cravath Larkin, daughter of Paul D. Cravath, prominent New York lawyer and patron of the arts. Though brief, their courtship was both high pressure and highly unusual. They met at a New York dinner party in the summer of 1927, very soon after she had divorced her first husband. She remembers her dinner partner's compelling persona, summing up his appeal years later to a reporter: "I thought him rather strange but fascinating."

Vera sailed the following day for Europe, accompanied by her young son, Adrian. During their overseas tour, she received a cable from Gibbs in London, asking if he could come and see her in Rome. He brought with him a bag full of dirty laundry and treated both Vera and Adrian to a carriage ride around the city.

"I was impressed, you know, that he came all the way down there to see me," she remembered. "It set me to thinking." After both had returned to New York, Gibbs's courtship continued at such a frenetic rate that they decided to marry a fortnight later, quickly and without a word to either of their families, an impulsive decision that continued to surprise her for months afterward.

The couple produced two sons, Francis and Christopher, who became stepbrothers of Adrian Larkin. Though Francis became an enthusiastic horseman, it was a beast his father never tolerated, always feeling, he confessed, that horses were somehow out to get him.

He and Vera took up residence in a Fifth Avenue apartment on East 75th Street. It had no view of the park but a patchwork of Manhattan rooftops instead. Intensely religious, Gibbs had long been a vestryman at St. Thomas Church farther south on Fifth Avenue and a generous contributor to the structure and the work of the church. One of his gifts was a glass door so that passersby could glimpse the splendors of the nave's interior. He and his wife were also devotees of the Metropolitan Opera. Gibbs particularly relished the works of Wagner and Puccini. Indeed, he was captivated by all classical music, perhaps not surprisingly especially the glorious intricacies of a Bach fugue.

Gibbs lived and ate frugally. Weak tea, heavily sugared, accompanied a breakfast composed exclusively of Uneeda biscuits. At the drawing table in his office, he would have another cup of tea and a biscuit at 11 A.M. "The only real meal he eats is dinner," Vera confided to a *Fortune* reporter in 1957. It was invariably taken in a nearby restaurant, preceded by an old-fashioned cocktail, its main course usually beef and spinach, concluding with an indulgent but simple dessert: scoops of chocolate and vanilla ice cream accompanied by canned peaches.

Like most affluent New Yorkers, he and Vera built a weekend getaway, choosing a spot along the rugged coast north of Boston at Rockport. Gibbs was very familiar with those offshore waters because they were frequently used for timed trials of the navy's latest destroyers; in fact, flagship of the destroyer force happened to be PY-29, the former yacht *Savarona* that he had designed for Mrs. Cadwalader. The Rockport lot the Gibbses particularly admired had a projecting cape, offering an uninterrupted view of the ocean save for a single rocky island a mile or so offshore.

They bought both the lot and the island—to prevent anyone else building on it—and, in 1960, had their house erected to a plan that William and Frederic jointly designed. Only one story high, it had immensely solid granite walls. The only wood used anywhere were exterior porch columns. It had a large central living room with a huge fireplace and four bedrooms, two to either side, each with its own bathroom. As taut and strong as a battleship, its roof was anchored by concealed cables linked immovably to the bedrock on which it had been erected. Typically, having completed that impregnable seaside retreat, Gibbs was seldom there for more than the occasional weekend. It was Vera who loved the place dearly and tended to stay throughout summer weeks, enjoying long swims in the cold sea.

Benign separations typified the Gibbses' menage. However ardently—nay, *frantically*—Gibbs had pursued Vera Cravath, their marriage was one of consistent flexibility. Husband and wife often adhered to their own schedules; utterly devoted, both did their own thing. She was heavily involved, as her father had been, with the Metropolitan Opera, whereas Gibbs, despite a similar love of opera, often retired early because he was an inveterate early riser. He would sometimes be found by his staff on

Sunday afternoons, still clad in the formal striped trousers and cutaway of a St. Thomas Church vestryman, perched at his Gibbs & Cox drafting table, hard at work.

He worked doggedly and, five years after *United States* was in service, was already fretting about how best to design a sister ship. His diligence was unrelenting. He once remarked to a colleague that, like the French president Georges Clemenceau, he planned staying in harness to the end of his life. "When *I* retire, I'll be dead," he was often prone to suggest.

A word about the Gibbs brothers' frequent employer is in order. The history of the United States Lines is checkered, having been cobbled together from the remnants of a failed predecessor, the United States Mail Steamship Company. Assembled just before *Leviathan* would be delivered to Newport News, the newly formed U.S. Lines' three-ship fleet included two former German liners, *Amerika* and *George Washington*, among the seven HAPAG vessels interned at Hoboken. Postwar, their names would remain unchanged, save for the anglicized spelling of *America*.

German shipping companies, eternally anxious to attract American clientele, routinely plundered America's history books. The names of Hamburg America vessels such as *George Washington*, *Amerika*, *President Lincoln*, and *President Grant* offered surefire appeal to peripatetic Americans that names such as *Kaiser Wilhelm der Grosse*, *Deutschland*, or *Vaterland* never would.

It says something about patriotism, pride, and vulnerability that American passengers were made comfortable aboard vessels whose names conveyed an unmistakable American aura. In the early 1920s a fleet of U.S. Lines vessels were named after American presidents. Additionally, the number of passenger vessels whose names incorporated the preliminary word *American* was notable.

It was the United States Lines that, after the war, would be charged by the U.S. Shipping Board to run the huge German liner *Leviathan*-ex-*Vaterland*. This marked the Gibbs brothers' pivotal entry into their chosen field. That daunting career path, leading inevitably to *America*, *United States*, and American naval immortality, unquestionably began with *Leviathan* in 1917. It was the Gibbs brothers' infallible aptitude, patience, diligence, and resourcefulness that brought their first commission to extraordinary fruition.

CHAPTER FOUR

LEVIATHAN RESTORATION

*The ship, when reconditioned, probably in the spring of 1921,
will be the finest in the world.*

—William Francis Gibbs, quoted in the *New York World*

Arriving after a westbound crossing, *Leviathan* reenters her home port.
Manhattan berthing would continue until the Depression, beginning in late 1929,
precipitated successive Hoboken exile. (Newport News Shipbuilding Collection)

General Philip Franklin of the International Mercantile Marine, William and Frederic Gibbs would become involved with converting interned HAPAG liner *Vaterland* into American troopship *Leviathan*. Not surprisingly, when it came time to implement her third incarnation into a proper American liner after the war, the Gibbses firsthand knowledge of her intricacies was perceived as an enormous plus by U.S. Lines. The vessel's fortunes and misfortunes alike constitute the bedrock of the Gibbs brothers' naval architectural baptism.

Originally called *Vaterland*, she was the second of the *Imperator* class, a three-stacker that Albert Ballin had ordered from Blohm & Voss's Hamburg yard. Blohm & Voss hull no. 212 was slightly larger than her predecessor: 912 feet (278 meters) overall, with a beam of 64 feet (19.5 meters) and a 35½-foot (10.8 meters) draft.

In addition to *Vaterland*'s increased dimensions, a revolutionary design wrinkle was incorporated below. For the first time aboard any steamship, uptakes from the boiler rooms to the first and second funnels had been divided. In other words, the chimneys connecting boilers to *Vaterland*'s two forward stacks were not sited along the keel line but had been divided into two separate uptakes moved outboard toward either side of the vessel.

This permitted an exhilarating central vista extending for more than half of B Deck's length. From atop the stage at the after end of the Social Hall (Teutonic sobriquet for Main Lounge), one could absorb the entire public room, then the adjacent Winter Garden and all the way to the Ritz-Carlton restaurant's forward wall. Without uptakes as midship stumbling blocks, the most elegant and festive of *Vaterland*'s major passenger spaces flowed one into the other. Similar divided uptakes would be essayed on only six subsequent liners: *Bremen*, *Europa*, *L'Atlantique*, *Normandie*, *Nieuw Amsterdam*, and present-day *Queen Mary 2*.

Vaterland first arrived in New York with much fanfare on May 20, 1914, though berthing at Hoboken's Pier 2 proved a suspenseful four-hour ordeal. The German vessel sailed into the harbor slightly late and, as a result, Commodore Hans Ruser missed slack water. As more than a dozen tugs chivvied the inbound monster toward her New Jersey slip, a solitary tug towing several barges crossed her path and then suddenly lost way. The

tug and its barge train drifted ominously toward *Vaterland*'s bow.

On the bridge, Sandy Hook pilot John F. McCarthy ordered engines stopped to avert a collision, an ill-advised command: a strong downriver thrust of combined wind and tide propelled *Vaterland* helplessly back south, approaching the 28-foot-deep Lackawanna ferry channel, its waters too shallow for her considerable draft. Her propellers began churning up clouds of mud, and it was only thanks to the fortuitously swift assembly of, some said, fifty tugs that the giant newcomer was finally coaxed into her Hoboken slip.

Once secured, *Vaterland*'s after end projected 25 feet beyond the pier. With ambitious Edwardian tonnage mooring in New York in those days, every city pier was too short. Since *Vaterland*'s propellers could have been damaged by passing traffic, a cordon of lighters, like Conestoga wagons in Indian country, was circled protectively around the stern.

Still *Vaterland*'s maiden arrival had a happier ending than one of her successive departures for Hamburg. Starting her fourth eastbound crossing in July, she backed from Pier 1 with a preliminary burst of speed; given her notorious sensitivity to wind and tide it seemed a prudent strategy. But because of a sudden astern turbine malfunction, that rearward surge could not be checked. Commodore Ruser and the pilot tried doing so repeatedly, to no avail, even ringing down for full ahead power. Nothing worked. Undeterred, the giant ship plowed sternfirst at ruinous speed all the way across New York Harbor, precipitously backing into the occupied slip between Manhattan Piers 50 and 51 down at Jane Street.

Chaos ensued. Morgan Line freighters *Topila* and *El Vale* were torn from their moorings and the coal barge *Ulster*, laden with hundreds of tons of anthracite, capsized. Railroad barge *Freeport* was also overturned, her engineer hurled into the water; his body would later be recovered from the North River. As *Vaterland* resumed forward power to exit the slip, she wreaked further havoc, driving the two freighters against their respective piers, crushing railings and snapping scantlings like matchwood. It was all hideously embarrassing and gave New York's tabloids a field day.

When World War I broke out in August 1914 *Vaterland* was seized by the United States, together

Opposite: Rainbowed with flags and ready for her maiden voyage, SS *Vaterland* at anchor off the shipyard where she was built, Hamburg's Blohm & Voss. At 912 feet (278 meters) overall, not only was she slightly larger than first of the class *Imperator*, she was also more stable and boasted several interior refinements.

(Newport News Shipbuilding Collection)

with seven other Hamburg America liners. All spent three years moldering alongside in neutral Hoboken. Over the first months, wildfire rumors abounded: first, that captive *Vaterland* would be bombed and then also that German cruisers were awaiting her outside the three-mile limit. A huge net was draped over *Vaterland*'s stern to thwart bombers and two American cruisers were alerted.

When America finally did enter the war, on April 6, 1917, the vessel, at the recommendation of President Woodrow Wilson, was renamed *Leviathan*. She became America's most commodious troopship, carrying thousands of doughboys eastbound, first to Liverpool and later to the French port Brest, where they could entrain directly for the trenches.

Although most of her original German crew had long since deserted, the three hundred or so remaining were ferried to Ellis Island. Her lower decks were filthy and neglected, and boarding Americans discovered that all instruction manuals, plans, and blueprints had disappeared. Worse, the astern turbines were badly damaged, hundreds of their rotor blades stripped.

Before departing, German engineers had inflicted minor sabotage, more annoying than dangerous. Random pistons and connecting rods were severed with hacksaws. Some steam pipes had been cut apart, obstructed with brass plugs, and rejoined. Additionally, several steam pipe flange bolts had been backed off and had most of their threads filed off before being replaced; undetected, reactivated steam pressure would have ruptured them.

It cost the U.S. Navy a million dollars to fit out troopship *Leviathan*. Peacetime furniture and decor were removed, stacks of cork life rafts came aboard, hull, funnels, and masts were painted gray. All but three hundred first class cabins (reserved for officers and nurses) were stripped and filled with three-high "standee" bunks. The pool was drained, to become a storage pit for doughboys' canvas gear.

Recruited American civilian workers proved scarcely more cooperative than the departed Germans. Unsupervised men toiled all over the vessel. They stole any fixtures that were not already broken or destroyed and their work ethic was deplorable: it was easier to break a mirror than to remove it. Many bathtubs were heedlessly smashed and the portrait of Prince Rupprecht, regent of Bavaria—assumed to be the kaiser—was savaged.

All that would change on July 25, 1917, when *Leviathan* became officially a U.S. Navy Armed Transport. Trained service personnel supplanted the lackadaisical civilians as sixty-eight officers and 2,240 other ranks, divided between deck and engine, came aboard. Officers and nurses would eat in the Ritz-Carlton; enlisted men would eat two daily meals standing at steel tables in what had been the first class Dining Room, made over into a mess hall.

Engineering priority was quite naturally given to restoration of full astern service. Replacement brass turbine blades, manufactured in Connecticut, were installed on damaged astern rotors; then, uncoupled from propellers, all turbines were, in effect, bench tested successfully alongside.

Completed troopship *Leviathan* sailed on November 17, 1917, departing her Hoboken slip for the first time in three years. All harbor traffic was stopped and forty-six tugs were in attendance. Once through the Narrows, the vessel anchored beyond Quarantine. Engines were once again checked and all eight deck guns test fired, aimed at floating targets. Although some targets survived, several promenade windows did not, shattered from proximity to muzzle blast. Later, en route south, further evidence of German sabotage surfaced as 14 inches of water flooded into officers' quarters forward on the starboard side. Water pipes had been cut and rejoined sloppily, allowing them to break once pressure was resumed.

With the flood contained and promenade windows patched, *Leviathan* headed south for a shakedown cruise that would conveniently deliver a detachment to Guantánamo, Cuba; the first servicemen she carried were marines rather than doughboys. Then the vessel returned to New York, embarked her first full load of army personnel, and, on December 17, 1917, set off eastbound.

There were only two dry docks in Allied hands that could accommodate *Leviathan*—Boston's Navy Yard and the Gladstone Dock in Liverpool. So the vessel's first European destination was Liverpool. The troops disembarked at the landing stage and entrained south to Winchester for transfer to France. The crew remained in Liverpool.

The visit seemed so long that German rumormongers suggested that *Leviathan* had been dispatched to the bottom of the Atlantic. She was temporarily parked at the landing stage until the Gladstone Dock became available. Then high

crosswinds prevented her from entering. Not until January 14 did she finally succeed; the hull had such a vast beam that tugs could not accompany her inside.

Twenty-seven days passed as three years' worth of growth was scaled from underwater plating. At the same time, a dazzle paint scheme was applied above the waterline to confuse German submarines.

Leviathan seemed to linger in Liverpool forever. Her navy crew were both reviled and welcomed into the port's bars and public houses. As in both world wars, overpaid Yanks were greeted with suspicion and mistrust by the British. Girls who fell in love with them were grateful for the same wages that so annoyed their male friends. They were also grateful for the odd sugar or tea rations smuggled ashore from *Leviathan*'s galley.

There would be one additional Liverpool call before the decision was taken to transfer operations to the Breton port of Brest. A huge buoy, secured to the bottom by nine anchors, would serve as offshore tether in the French port. Arriving for her first Brest disembarkation, *Leviathan*'s doughboys

On one of her final calls at Brest in 1918, USS *Leviathan* is moored to her giant buoy, secured by no fewer than nine anchors. This is the second and final dazzle paint scheme that adorned her flanks. (Newport News Shipbuilding Collection)

were offloaded into lighters on the port side and marched to the railhead. Simultaneously, coal barges tied up to starboard. Within forty-eight hours, *Leviathan* had been emptied and refueled and was ready to sail westbound.

Although *Leviathan* was once stalked by a submarine, she sustained no damage from enemy action. But hundreds of her wartime passengers suffered horrendously during the Spanish influenza outbreak of 1918. The 57th Pioneer Infantry, destined for passage to France after assembling at Camp Merritt in nearby Cresskill, New Jersey, was only one of those that were struck by the deadly pandemic. As they tramped toward *Leviathan*'s Hoboken mooring, sick men began dropping out of rank, falling incapacitated by the roadside. Though increasing numbers of casualties were retrieved by ambulances, the route march continued. Once at Hoboken's River Street piers, remaining companies were hastened on board.

Yet the insidious toll continued. Before sailing time that evening, 120 more desperately sick men had to be disembarked. Crowding the vessel's gangways and lobbies, soldiers terrified of being confined in what seemed lower deck charnel houses refused descent to assigned cabins. All over *Leviathan*, bleeding invalids were losing consciousness.

The vessel sailed regardless. Of the more than two thousand flu victims recorded during that crossing alone, seventy perished and dozens more lost their lives en route overland to Flanders. One typical dilemma for *Leviathan*'s sick soldiers was staggering from assigned cabins to the hospital only to find every bed occupied; then, unable to find their way back to their cabins, they collapsed, lost in a confusion of alleyways.

Spanish influenza was a rapacious killer. Casualty reports from the 88th Combat Division tell the tale: 99 men succumbed to enemy action but 444 lives were taken by the flu.

Leviathan completed her trooping duties shortly after the armistice. For her final eastbound crossing in August 1919, only thirty-one passengers rattled around those huge interiors. After a weeklong stay in Brest, *Leviathan* sailed westbound, bringing home thousands of doughboys, together with the American Expeditionary Force commander, General John J. "Black Jack" Pershing, and his chief of staff, ramrod-straight Brigadier General Douglas MacArthur.

For that final New York entry, Secretary of War Newton Baker himself came down to Quarantine to greet General Pershing. There followed a celebratory procession upriver, enriched by dozens of ferries and chartered vessels escorting *Leviathan* to Hoboken's Pier 4, festively adorned with bunting and flowers.

William and Frederic Gibbs's task was updating 1914's traditional Louis Seize decor for American tastes of the 1920s. The job was less conversion than restoration, essentially reviving her German configuration.

The definitive demarcation between prewar and postwar transatlantic tonnage would not emerge until June 1927 when *Ile de France* first steamed into New York Harbor. Incredulous visitors discovered that, with one deft stroke, the French Line had discarded every prevailing concept of interior design afloat.

What the French Line defined proudly as its *style paquebot* (steamship style) transformed everything. Decorative inspiration from Paris's seminal International Exposition of 1925 reigned supreme. Implementation of the first entirely art deco schema aboard an ocean liner established a pivotal moment in transatlantic history, a decorative pinnacle from which shipboard designers started looking forward rather than back.

Until *Ile de France*, all ocean liner public room decor had been restricted to replication of well-known originals ashore. Famous chateaux, palaces, and even reproductions of department stores or hotels were slavishly churned out. Then the French Line instigated a long overdue decorative challenge: why should cutting-edge engineering marvels have interiors devoted to plodding simulacra of shoreside conceits? Why not create anew? Walls, ceilings, and columns no less than carpeting, sculpture, paintings, staircases, and furniture should adhere instead to a specific shipboard ethos.

That modernity from 1925's clean Parisian dream brushed away countless shipboard cobwebs. All shoreside influence was relinquished. Whether art deco or not was immaterial; essential was observance of sound Bauhausian principles. Aboard *Ile de France*, refreshing functional simplicity ruled, clean surfaces defined by unadorned margins. Traditional paneling framing silk-covered bulkheads, egg-and-dart molding, bobbles, and fringes as well as conventional furnishings sometimes described as "upholsterart" were out; a novel decorative serenity was in. There were no other rules. Though one might be hard-pressed to define the new transatlantic vernacular, Hollywood's set designers learned quickly. Starting in the early 1930s, films depicting Atlantic crossings conveyed accurate and apropos ocean liner resonances.

Two even more modern German vessels, *Bremen* and *Europa*, debuted in 1929 and 1930. These were veritable postwar ships and looked it, inside and out. In a show of German unity both were launched on the same day in August 1928, *Bremen* from Bremen's Weser Yard and *Europa* at Blohm & Voss in Hamburg. They were identical with a broad beam of 102 feet (31 meters).

Inside, both vessels adhered if not quite to France's *style paquebot* them at least to wholesale rejection of ostentation. Conventional excesses of what has been termed "Potsdam rococo" were rejected. Inspired by a cadre of young designers, refreshing modernity prevailed aboard both; boldly presented, flat geometric surfaces were the order of the day. In the social halls, rows of tall round-headed windows had been adorned with polished brass rims, typifying the aura of "shippiness"—John Malcolm Brinnin's expressive invention—infusing the vessel. Abandoned was the country house look espoused by the Brits. But not all was consistent: too prominent in *Bremen*'s ballroom was a kitschy fountain equipped with lights that changed colors as couples two-stepped by.

Bremen sailed first from the Columbus Pier on July 16, 1929, racing across at 28 knots and seizing the Blue Riband from aging *Mauretania*. *Europa* had suffered a devastating fire alongside the pier while fitting out and could not enter service until 1930. The two vessels, it was hoped, might establish a weekly mail service between Bremerhaven and New York but they were not able to overcome the geographical limitations. That enviable state of grace would be achieved postwar by Cunard White Star's two *Queens*.

That trio of 1920s exemplars would foreshadow *Rex, Conte di Savoia, Normandie, Queen Mary, Statendam,* and *Nieuw Amsterdam* to come in the 1930s. These latter were unmistakably postwar vessels, sporting squatter funnels, cleaner profiles, updated public rooms, and, long awaited, more cabins with bathrooms attached.

Leviathan would never join the ranks of legitimate postwar vessels. Her every aspect adhered to 1920s tonnage of necessity, Edwardian hulls

dispatched to sea as soon as possible after the Treaty of Versailles. There was neither time, budget, nor the inclination to rejigger steel infrastructure. Available funds were spent adapting existing bunkers to hold oil rather than coal.

Remaining monies superficially revamped suddenly redundant immigrant quarters. In 1921 Congress passed an immigration restriction act, a patently isolationist rejection of mass immigration from Europe. The move effectively reduced prewar's steerage hordes to a trickle. Immediately, British shipping lines beat the bushes all over America in quest of American tourists to take their place. That new clientele was offered inexpensive passage to Europe booked in a special new class identified as tourist third cabin: *tourist* promised adventure, *third* economy, and *cabin* respectability.

In truth, tourist third cabin class cabins delivered only marginally. There was a cotton company bedspread and sinks boasting one faucet with four thin towels suspended on hooks to either side. A spiky potted palm adorned the sink's glass shelf and a tatty carpet stool occupied floor space, leaving room for no more than two occupants to dress at the same time. Nevertheless, tourist third cabin proved a winner; its contented occupants referred to themselves humorously as "white collar steerage."

The vessels dominating postwar's North Atlantic were all 1914 holdovers: *Olympic, Aquitania, Mauretania, France,* and *Paris,* together with four reflagged German prizes: *Berengaria* (ex-*Imperator*), *Leviathan* (ex-*Vaterland*), *Majestic* (ex-*Bismarck*), and *Homeric* (ex-*Columbus*). However dated—vessels grown "long in the funnel"—they served as the most fashionable ships of the 1920s.

Though Gibbs easily could have updated *Leviathan*'s public rooms into the sleek modernity of the 1930s, budget constraints forbade it. Despite those interruptive years of internment and transporting soldiers, she was still comparatively new, having completed only five voyages prewar. Whatever Gibbs might have wished to do, his U.S. Lines' mandate was specific: refashion *Leviathan*-ex-*Vaterland* into what she had been in 1914. Her initial design scheme, redolent of Louis XVI, was deemed acceptable. All the competition—British, French, Italian, Dutch, and German—were fielding the same dated interiors.

Another period of idleness began in Hoboken as *Leviathan* awaited transformation. It seemed that the ex-German giant was forever marking time in

Preparatory work in progress. Bereft of her dazzle paint, former USS *Leviathan* alongside her Hoboken pier. Hundreds of civilian workers are aboard, starting transformation of her wartime interiors. The second view shows further progress: the bridge screen is cleaner and brighter while the foremast has been pruned of wartime additions. (Newport News Shipbuilding Collection)

the New Jersey port between deployments. Shipyard bids to complete the work would have to be solicited and tendered. Regardless of who would take on the conversion, Gibbs began his task at a bruising disadvantage. The only existing plans for *Vaterland* were the property of the builder, Hamburg's Blohm & Voss. When Gibbs requested a set of those drawings, the yard's asking price was a prohibitive million dollars.

Had his timing been better, such a slap in the face might not have occurred. When, in November 1918, the victorious Allies seized *Bismarck*, incomplete third of the *Imperator*-class trio, she was found at her Hamburg pier partially fitted out but abandoned. The same shipyard, in the wake of the country's defeat, had completed the vessel *at their expense* and delivered her to a waiting White Star crew downriver at Cuxhaven. After crossing to Southampton, paint crews were dispatched aloft to daub black tops around the three buff German stacks, rendering the vessel instantly into RMS *Majestic* at no cost whatsoever to White Star.

Four years later, still smarting from that painful precedent, Blohm & Voss refused to be bulldozed again. Hence, its million-dollar demand. Terming it "piracy," Gibbs refused to pay. The vessel was in his possession and his unique solution was creating a new set of blueprints by remeasuring *Leviathan* inside and out. Gibbs would determine the dimension of every interior space, from boiler room to bridge deck, from galley locker to regal suite, from broom cupboard to tiller flat.

He mustered one hundred draftsmen on board, issuing them white coveralls, notebooks, tape measures, and pencils. They were divided into three teams: the first would track and plot all electrical wiring and piping, the second would determine the volume of all onboard machinery, while the third and largest contingent would measure every dimension of the hull's huge interiors.

The first team worked under the most arduous conditions, lying on their backs inside *Levitathan*'s claustrophobic double bottom tanks, locating and measuring every pipe and cable they saw overhead. The other two teams swarmed throughout echoing *Leviathan* with tapes and notebooks, measuring and recording the height, length, and width of all interiors, including the thickness of their dividing bulkheads and every machine.

Each team established its own shipboard headquarters. Machinery documenters regrouped in the ship's library while their hull colleagues did likewise in the Smoking Room. Only after newly gathered measurements had been checked and rechecked were they allowed onto Gibbs's master plan. The Ritz-Carlton restaurant had been temporarily filled with long drafting tables, manned by senior draftsmen equipped with T-squares and mechanical drawing pens. Thousands of measurements were entered onto the appropriate rolls of paper at the rigorous scale of one sixteenth inch to the foot.

Blank hull lengths were slowly adorned with accurate footage. Deck by deck, cabin by cabin, public room by public room, the dimensions of every galley and pantry cranny together with the size of hundreds of blowers, ventilators, telemotors, ash ejectors, and pumps were documented.

After two months' toil, Gibbs's duplicate plans were complete. There were, as always, critics who argued that the million-dollar price tag would have been a bargain compared with the laborious task Gibbs had undertaken. But he countered that the $300,000 cost of his drafting teams delivered him not only the coveted plans but also a complete *Leviathan* survey.

He went on to add several additional features to his new *Leviathan*. Installed in first class was a stock exchange room, furnished comfortably with rows of leather-covered armchairs. Wireless dispatches from New York were chalked onto a wall-mounted blackboard, allowing passenger investors to tweak portfolios from mid-ocean.

Gibbs also correctly assessed that 1920s American travelers would want more sophisticated merchandise than that offered by shipboard's traditional mid-ocean franchisee the barbershop. In fact, enterprising transatlantic barbers offered far more than basics such as razor blades, toothbrushes, and cigarettes. Aboard *Adriatic*, for instance, barbershops were stocked with novelty dolls, pipes, purses, gloves, caps, collars, shirts, motor veils, slippers, tennis balls, pocketknives, saltwater soap, chewing gum, and perfume. But Gibbs's handsomely redesigned three-chair barbershop remained devoid of merchandise. Formal shops, staffed by uniformed personnel, were instituted instead.

In the Pompeiian Bath, abused and displaced tiles were replaced and the marble benches separating Charles Mewès's mosaic columns were restored. *L'enfant pissant*, the urinating bronze cherub that had stood between the curved staircases, had disappeared, probably stolen by one of the original civilian workers. Gibbs replaced it with an arrangement of potted geraniums.

When tenders were sought for the restoration contract, only two responded, Todd Shipyard and the Boston Navy Yard. Both bids were high—$10,740,000 and $8,939,000, respectively; Gibbs rejected them as unacceptable and halted all onboard work. Down in Washington, the Shipping Board was inert, as a lame-duck administration seemed unable or unwilling to achieve anything.

Two high-risk dangers to *Leviathan*'s existence followed, the first a serious if preposterous diversion. The Shipping Board suggested that the liner be anchored off northern Manhattan as a floating apartment house. Tenants would be tendered ashore on demand and $2 million, it was estimated, would permit installation of sufficient bathrooms. Nothing ever came of the scheme.

A second and more flagrant danger occurred on the stifling summer night of August 25, 1921. While the vessel was moored at Hoboken's Pier 6 a fire broke out on Pier 5 just to the south. It burned ferociously. Hundreds of firebrands—fragments of blazing wooden detritus—were wafted aloft by the intense heat, and dozens of those lethal incendiaries descended onto captive *Leviathan*, setting numerous fires. The port bridge deck, several lifeboats, and, incredibly, even the crow's nest started burning. That aerial assault notwithstanding, Pier 5's incredible heat alone scarred and blistered *Leviathan*'s portside hull plating, shattering countless portholes as well.

At work in their Broadway office, the Gibbs brothers were alerted and immediately raced across harbor aboard a commandeered tug. The prospect of a burning liner inflamed the brothers' second childhood passion, firefighting. Their overriding hobbyist devotions—ocean liners and fire engines—were suddenly conjoined in hideous actuality, betrayed by an ominous orange glow as their tug approached Hoboken's waterfront.

When they disembarked and raced aboard partially burning *Leviathan*, William and Frederic set about methodically quelling the flames. Fortunately, sixty recalled crewmen were in place and a dozen fire hoses were already laid out, fed by the ship's pumps at a reliable 150 pounds of pressure per square inch. In fact, those pulsating canvas conduits were the only working hoses anywhere in Hoboken that night. Municipal fire mains had been drained by battling Pier 5's devastating blaze; as a secondary emergency legacy, every Hoboken streetlamp was without power.

Under the Gibbs brothers' leadership, shipboard crews systematically extinguished every onboard conflagration. Arcs of plentiful hose water doused bridge deck and crow's nest flames. Additionally, blazing portside lifeboats were systematically extinguished.

Incoming fireboats tried operating from the slip between the liner and burning Pier 5 but they were dwarfed beneath *Leviathan*'s towering port flank. Their hoses, deployed of necessity pointing straight up, proved hopelessly ineffectual. It was Gibbs's onboard fire teams that prevented *Leviathan*'s destruction. Some aboard urged that she be pulled away from the pier but Gibbs forbade it; maneuvering without sufficient tugs would be catastrophic.

Pier 5's fire spawned additional hazards. A magazine of thirty thousand small arms rounds stored in a shed between Piers 5 and 6 caught fire. As flames consumed the structure, rounds started cooking off. For several hours it seemed as though the area were under siege by random machine-gun fire. Miraculously, no casualties resulted from those intermittent fusillades.

There was further drama just to the north of *Leviathan*. Stacked the length of Pier 6 were 4,600 war dead, recently repatriated from France and offloaded by a freighter. Each body was encased in a lead coffin, then crated within a pine box. The weight of each was a staggering 650 pounds. Providentially shielded by *Leviathan*'s steel bulk, however, all the deceased were successfully removed from harm's way. The total cost of Hoboken's pier fire was a staggering $15 million.

Thanks to the Gibbs brothers and their fortuitously reembarked crews, *Leviathan* survived and the conversion work resumed. Walker & Gillette were hired by Gibbs as a redesign firm, and John Wanamaker offered the lowest bid for stewards' supplies, $587,303.20.

On October 27, 1921, Albert Lasker, chairman of the Shipping Board, solicited bids for the conversion. Tenders were addressed to Gibbs's office at 9 Broadway, the latest submission day December 29, 1921.

Newport News offered an astonishingly low bid of $5,595,000, plus an additional half million dollars to implement oil conversion. His company in

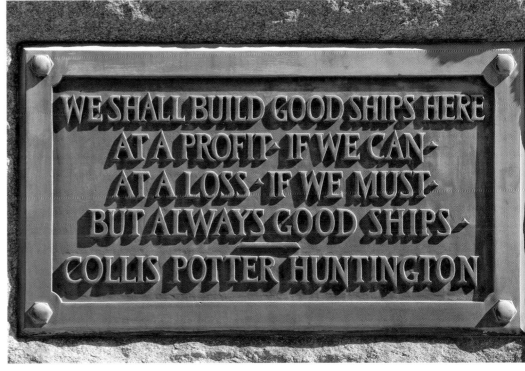

parlous condition, yard president Homer Ferguson had faced facts. His payroll was down from a wartime high of 12,000 to 2,200 and his only current newbuilding was the battleship USS *West Virginia*; by deliberately underbidding, Ferguson hoped to snare *Leviathan* as well. He succeeded and the contract was signed on February 15, 1922. At the end of the month the government turned over *Leviathan* to Gibbs Bros Inc. of Delaware. Six months later, William and Frederic formally resigned from Morgan's International Mercantile Marine.

Newport News Shipbuilding and Drydock Company had been started in 1886 by Collis Potter Huntington. Raised in Connecticut, he crossed the country to California during the 1849 gold rush and became a railway tycoon. Returning to New York, Huntington built a rail connection south via his Chesapeake and Ohio Railway, crossing the mountains into West Virginia. Thus were railroad connections brought to Newport News, Virginia. As Huntington put it in a historical booklet published in 1904: "It was my original intention to start a shipyard plant in the best location in the world and I succeeded in my purpose. It is right at the gateway of the sea. There is never any ice in the winter and it is never so cold but you can hammer metal out of doors."

Hull no. 1 produced by his shipyard was the tug *Dorothy*, named after the four-year-old daughter of Secretary of the Navy William C. Whitney. First yard president was A. L. Hopkins, to be followed by an Annapolis graduate, Homer Ferguson, who remained in charge from 1915 until 1946.

It is 271 sea miles from Sandy Hook to Virginia's Cape Henry. Five weeks remained to prepare for the eighteen-hour passage. Captain W. J. Bernard, marine superintendent of the Army Transport Service, would command a 670-man crew. Another spell of *Leviathan* idleness finally ended after twenty-eight months. Early Sunday morning, April 9, 1922, *Leviathan* left her Hoboken berth at the high-water slack.

Once the hull had cleared pier's end, four tugs swung the bow downstream in seven minutes and she was on her way. Twelve additional tugs held in reserve were not needed, though Captain Bernard reported her steering was "balky" without a great deal of way on. Six minutes after 6 A.M., *Leviathan* steamed past the Statue of Liberty.

Passage south would not be easy. With all engines full ahead on a course of 180 degrees, an impenetrable fog suddenly descended. Captain Bernard stopped the vessel and anchored. An hour later the fog cleared and passage resumed. But at 1815 hours

Leviathan en route to Newport News for conversion. The vessel maintained an overall speed of just over 15 knots, even though fog patches, floods, and steering failures made for successive delays. (Newport News Shipbuilding Collection)

engines had to be used to steer because *Leviathan's* steering gear suddenly became inoperable. There was little sleep that night for either Gibbs brother.

In the approaches to Newport News on the morning of April 10, other vessels had been put on notice not to obstruct the channel. Four Coast Guard vessels enforced the order. At Old Point, four tugs assisted *Leviathan* into the Newport News Channel. With pilot James Peake aboard, she cleared the channel and was alongside Old Point Comfort. There, after a shipyard launch delivered a Newport News representative and the docking pilot, *Leviathan* entered Newport News Channel and tied up at Newport News dockyard's Pier no. 1. With bow and stern lines secured, Captain Bernard rang down "finished with engines." Fog and steering problems notwithstanding, *Leviathan* had averaged a speed of 15.62 knots.

Formal conversion began. It was the last time stokers would fire the vessel's forty-six boilers.

When she departed Newport News *Leviathan* would be oil-fired. For a single crossing, she would be bunkered with 9,503 tons of 11° Beaume Mexican fuel oil. Peabody Engineering company burners would produce a vigorous steam supply at 248 pounds per square inch. Interestingly, all burning grates and doors were removed and inventoried, stored ashore against the remote possibility that coal firing might be reestablished in the future. One unforeseen expense for poor President Ferguson was removing all unused coal from *Leviathan's* bunkers, a cumbersome chore that became a shipyard cost.

Newly built deep water tanks increased *Leviathan's* freshwater capacity to 3,476 tons. A total of seventy-two lifeboats would be aboard, forty of them the Germans' red-painted originals. Gibbs's additional thirty-two were white metallic boats with squat bows, designed specifically for heavy weather. Six groups of three stacked boats were

nested, three per side, along Boat Deck. Each could accommodate fifty persons. Other exterior marine hardware included the largest anchor ever made in the United States. Forged at American Steel Foundries of Chester, Pennsylvania, it weighed in at 33,000 pounds.

William Francis Gibbs commuted by train from New York, snooping around in overalls and a slouch hat. Later, his shipyard nickname became "Old Iron Hat" because over Virginia's humid summer he took to wearing a derby.

One symbolic order of business was grinding the name *Vaterland* from the ship's bell and replacing it with *Leviathan*. The German engraving proved so deep that its replacement had to be shallow. Meanwhile, from all over America, inbound crates materialized. From Schumacher's mill in Paterson, New Jersey, came bolts of crimson silk for lining social hall curtains. Magicoal Electric Fires were installed in the public rooms and Brentano's

supplied the library's every book. Irish linen was used for first class bedding, Scottish linen for second, third, and steerage. The Onondaga Pottery Company of Syracuse, New York, provided 102,000 pieces of china for humbler passengers while 119,278 plates, platters, soup bowls, cups, and saucers arrived for first class from Lenox, Inc., of Trenton, New Jersey. The vessel's cutlery supply— 71,798 pieces—was delivered from R. Wallace and Sons of Wallingford, Connecticut, and the United States Glass Company of Pittsburgh shipped 48,084 assorted glasses. Eleven new Otis elevators were hung and a special ice-making machine installed; the 24-pound blocks it produced could be delivered by special elevator to the upper decks.

All passenger staircases were reinforced with steel girders and strapping, their newly installed steel elements braced by attachment to the ship's frames. Once completed, they were tested by crowds of men standing atop them to ensure that

Fast alongside Newport News Shipway no. 1 and beneath the looming bulk of one of the yard's largest jib cranes, ex-trooper USS *Leviathan* starts her renovation into ocean liner SS *Leviathan*. (Newport News Shipbuilding Collection)

no deflection occurred. Within B, C, and D Deck staterooms, German doorknobs and locks were reused. But according to Gibbs's scrupulous instructions, "Wherever German inscriptions appear on latches, these parts shall be replaced by parts with English inscriptions."

Gibbs's renovations were more far reaching than Cunard's conversion work aboard *Imperator*. Fittings and ashtrays aboard emerging *Berengaria* were left as was, shamelessly adorned with German directions. All bathtub drains had *Auf* and *Zu* (open/closed) signage on them and countless ship's ashtrays were still adorned *Zigarren*.

Leviathan's final crew count was 1,115: 15 deck officers, 135 deck crew, 46 engineering officers, 226 engineer crewmen, and 693 in the stewards and pursers department. All officers were issued engraved napkin rings. As for passengers, *Leviathan*'s final count was 3,398 with 976 in first, 542 in second, 944 in third, and 936 in steerage. Total souls aboard—4,513.

As on *Vaterland*, the Ritz-Carlton restaurant was modeled after the New York original, its galley equipped with the very latest electrical equipment: six of the first ever electric ranges at sea, an ice cream maker, several waffle irons, and a pastry mixer.

Throughout *Leviathan*'s Virginia stay, it was not clear how Prohibition would affect American ships. So in the Ritz-Carlton bar, and indeed for every onboard bar, shakers, stirrers, and mixers were lavishly if optimistically distributed.

Every first class cabin boasted a closet safe, and two framed lithographs, costing $7.50 apiece, adorned the walls. One decisive benchmark was that *Leviathan* would be the first liner with a telephone in every cabin.

Gibbs saw to it that special clock faces and dials were designed for the children's playroom. Curtains for the Social Hall were made up as on *Vaterland*—red European damask interlined with black cambric and lined with Parma satin. Additionally, Gibbs ordained lighter summer replacement curtains. Much as he admired *Vaterland*, he did not retain every German appointment. The Smoking Room's Teutonic decor was replaced by American fixtures and glass. Regardless of national origin, everything was of superb quality.

As the interiors neared completion and potted palms dressed up the Palm Court, Gibbs enriched photo shoots by recruiting fifteen models from

New York. Dressed as passengers, they posed in every public room. Two of the fifteen became famous: a young Canadian actress called Norma Shearer, the other Fred Bickel, who would later change his name to Fredric March. Another finishing touch was music. Gibbs's choice for orchestra leader was the violinist/conductor Richard Kraetke of Syracuse.

In March 1923 yard president Homer Ferguson told a *Journal of Commerce* reporter, "The end is in sight. Only nine more miles of pipes have to be installed." But Gibbs did not want to rush completion. To that end, he refused to have the funnels painted until all onboard work had been completed.

Appointed master of the vessel was Captain Herbert Hartley, his selection counter to a Washington preference for a U.S. Navy captain. Another key figure in Gibbs's future materialized that winter. A young Newport News native named William Kaiser had been told that he worked well in hot places; when he applied for a job aboard *Leviathan*, he was immediately assigned to the engine room. Later, he became a runner for Gibbs. Obviously, his reputation for doing well in hot places bore fruit; Bill Kaiser would become chief engineer aboard *United States*.

Finally, as completion neared, Gibbs sent crews aloft to paint the stacks. Blue topping was daubed on first, then white banding below it and, for the supporting shafts, what Gibbs described as "brick red." Her funnel trio gleaming, *Leviathan* was ready to sail north for dry docking at the Boston Navy Yard. It is worth remembering that everything the Gibbs brothers did during that yearlong Virginia refit, they were doing for the first time. It says something about their talent that, however untrained and inexperienced, they learned early on to run a taut ship.

On May 15, 1923, *Leviathan* departed for Boston. At one in the morning of the eighteenth, the vessel arrived off Boston Lightship in the teeth of a northwest gale and low tide. After the flood, fifteen tugs escorted the vessel inside. Before the dock was pumped dry, American Bureau of Shipping surveyors embarked; they would stay aboard for a month.

It was in that dock that a stooped Gibbs walked under the length of *Leviathan*'s hull for the first time. The vessel would stay for three days; next on the docket was a shakedown cruise for which hundreds had already booked.

On June 18, 55 million gallons of seawater flooded the dock. Just before 1 P.M. *Leviathan* emerged and anchored off Finn's Light, near the Boston Lightship. Trial trip guests were embarked via the tender *King Philip*. Another load would arrive from New York by train the following day. Albert Lasker, chairman of the Shipping Board, was hustled aboard quietly to avoid the possibility of an injunction that Congress had threatened to prevent the shakedown cruise. It was considered unnecessary and, because only men would embark, a sexist outing.

Leviathan raised anchor at 1520 hours on June 19. She would sail down to Cuba and back. Gibbs was everywhere, wearing a tall collar and high button boots. He drank tea with Captain Hartley on the bridge and chatted with Lasker, who came out of hiding once it was known he was on board.

There were so many reporters aboard that cables backed up in the wireless shack. One passenger, former wireless operator David Sarnoff, rolled up his sleeves and got to work. He and the wireless chief Elmo Pickerell devised a superior antenna and the two telegraphers made short work of the backlog, Sarnoff thrilled to be back doing the work he loved.

During the run south, continuous tests and trials were effected. D Deck lifeboats were swung out to verify the strength of their davits, watertight doors were closed from the bridge, whistles, sirens, engine room telegraphs, and steering machinery were checked exhaustively. Auxiliary generators roared into life, implementing emergency lighting. For boat and fire drills, crew and passengers assembled with life preservers in the public rooms.

Occasionally, fog was so thick that Captain Hartley could not see all his funnels. But on the clear night of June 22, engine revolutions were steadily increased from 150 to 182, for a fast trial run. *Leviathan* achieved a sustained speed of 28.4 knots, bettering Cunarder *Mauretania*'s fastest on the Atlantic.

Reporters surged to the wireless shack to advise their editors. When the vessel entered New York Harbor early on June 24 the Gibbs brothers stood on the flying bridge. Lashed to the foremast was an upended broom, symbolic shipboard icon of a clean sweep.

The practice had originated in 1652 when the enterprising and aggressive Dutch admiral Maarten Tromp first hoisted an upturned broom

Opposite: Funnels gleaming, this upper deck view reveals some of Gibbs's broad steel lifeboats, stacked three high.
(Newport News Shipbuilding Collection)

atop his flagship's mainmast, displaying it defiantly down-Channel to alert Royal Navy rivals that the Hollanders were determined to outgun them, hoping to perpetuate, in effect, history's first naval clean sweep.

That symbolic broom would be flaunted from *Leviathan*'s masthead for entry into New York. The city's reception was frenetic. Passing ferries listed as craning passengers lined the railings and whistled salutes shrieked from every harbor vessel. Avoiding an immovable offshore rocky ledge that could not be removed, *Leviathan* docked smoothly on the south side of Manhattan's Pier 86 at 0700, allowing her shakedown passengers to disembark. Across the slip lay the battleship USS *Colorado*.

Leviathan's maiden voyage was booked solid, and on sailing day, July 4, fifty-five hundred visitors surged aboard, carrying books, flowers, candy, and what were described as "less legitimate substances." Vincent Astor had booked a suite and a new Marion Davies film would be screened twice out on the promenade deck. Paul Whiteman's sixteen-piece band, which had been booked for the Cuban outing, remained aboard for the maiden.

Bugle calls urged visitors ashore and it rained as *Leviathan* left the pier. But out beyond the Narrows black clouds gave way to brilliant July sunshine, ensuring a calm crossing with no seasick passengers. The first day, there was one catering snafu—they were one hundred covers short for lunch in the first class dining room; the chief steward had planned to accommodate one hundred in the Ritz-Carlton but forgot. One mid-ocean ceremony was unveiling Howard Chandler Christy's portrait of President Warren Harding, placed where the destroyed Rupprecht portrait had originally hung. Alcoholic unrest surfaced: a passenger who opened champagne in the dining room was prevented from drinking it by the master.

On arrival morning in Cherbourg, further alcoholic clarification came. The Supreme Court ruled that liquor was permitted in American-flagged cabins and restaurants but not for the crew. No liquor could be sold on board; passengers had to bring their own.

Eight hundred would disembark into tenders bound for France and the overlong French welcome precipitated a four-hour delay, postponing Southampton arrival until after 10 P.M. *Leviathan* tied up at Berth 43/44 in the Ocean Dock. Ironically, *Mauretania* was moored across the way. The next day, guests were invited to a *Leviathan* luncheon in hot Southampton with, predictably, no drink provided. Worse, passengers who had brought liquor over from America could not get it past customs men waiting at bottom of the gangway.

These were minor problems, however. Maiden voyage festivities continued. In addition to the other celebrities, Jascha Heifetz, Mischa Elman, Al Jolson, and Albert Lasker sailed westbound. Returning to Cherbourg, the vessel picked up 155 more passengers. In addition, six French pier workers who had stowed away were found and removed. But ten additional illicit passengers were discovered at sea, having boarded by mingling with a cleaning contingent and hiding on board.

The only disappointment that surfaced on the westbound leg was an aggrieved delegation from second class whose representatives sought an audience with Captain Hartley. They complained that their food was indifferent and their entertainment nonexistent. "Everything for first," they argued vociferously, "and nothing for us." Whatever the vaunted appeal of the glamorous United States Line vessel, it was clear that archetypal passenger vagaries had remained resolutely in place.

Leviathan reached Ambrose at 0455 on Monday, July 23. She had entered service with prestigious splash, realizing a maiden voyage profit of $379,000. The United States Lines' largest and handsomest new liner was in service, booked almost to capacity that entire summer of 1924.

The Gibbs brothers' maiden venture proved equally successful. They had brought off a stunning achievement, entering triumphantly into a demanding profession. Both were established unquestionably as responsible for the United States Lines' huge success.

One wishes that *Leviathan*'s sailing days had continued for the balance of her life. But alas they did not. She became a victim not only of the Depression but also of lack of patronage because of Prohibition's long shadow. After the Twenty-first Amendment's ratification, the long-shuttered bars did open for business, but only for three years; the ensuing Depression offset that advantage. She was removed from Manhattan's west side piers and returned to Hoboken exile. Long, idle stays along New Jersey's waterfront continued, a recurring banishment that had started with her World War I internment.

Leviathan remained tied up there for so long that when, in January 1938, she sailed on her final

eastbound crossing for scrapping she had to take on fuel off Staten Island; so much drifting silt had accumulated beneath the idled hull that barges loaded with fuel were unable to enter the slip alongside *Leviathan*. She was also made lighter by topping both masts and removing ten feet from each funnel to permit passage beneath the Firth of Forth bridge en route to Rosyth.

William and Frederic Gibbs watched her departure from their Manhattan office at 21 West Street. She had on board a skeleton crew of 165 and a British master. Throughout the crossing, *Leviathan* endured a plague of fire, fog, and steam problems. Only twenty-four of her thirty-six boilers were in service by the time she reached Scotland. Fuel oil oozed everywhere and, almost daily, engine room fires broke out. Perhaps most dispiriting for the crew was that either frigid weather contracted the steam whistle's cable or an electrical short circuit caused it to roar into spontaneous life, resulting in prolonged ghostly mid-ocean wails.

Leviathan arrived off the Firth of Forth pilot station at 1:32 P.M. on February 3, 1938, and then had to wait a further ten days for a tide that would permit passage up to Rosyth. There, after a dispirited auction of her furniture, the enormous derelict was rendered profitably into scrap metal.

I must close with a familial *Leviathan* anecdote about my first cousin David Townsend. His father, Greenough Townsend, worked for the United States Lines booking department, rising to become chief of passenger services. In the summer of 1931, when David was two years old, he and his older brother Anton had been put to bed in their cabin. David, confined within a crib, started rattling it, as was his wont. Anton insists that the crib's rattle started *Leviathan*'s engines and she began moving away from the pier.

Opposite: An interior view shows Gibbs's first class Dining Saloon aboard completed *Leviathan*. The surrounding colonnade separates outermost tables that reach windows to either side. (Newport News Shipbuilding Collection)

Left: The pool is complete. Alsation lay architect Charles Mewès's signature columns are in place, interspersed with restored marble benches. The space's divided staircases are behind the camera. (Newport News Shipbuilding Collection)

CHAPTER FIVE

THE JAZZ AGE, TRANSATLANTIC

If you are contemplating passage in Tourist Third Cabin, you will find respectively the same careful thought for your comfort. The fittings, of course, will be somewhat less luxurious, but no less pleasing.

—White Star Line brochure, circa 1922

As you sail away, far beyond the range of amendments and thou-shalt-nots, those dear little iced things begin to appear, sparkling aloft on their slender crystal stems. . . . Utterly French, utterly harmless—and oh so gurglingly good!

—French Line flyer, 1921

Opposite: This upper deck view of *Leviathan*—taken alongside in New York—
shows lifeboat davits extended over the side during lifeboat drill. The absence of canvas covers
indicates inspection of each boat's equipment. (Newport News Shipbuilding Collection)

Long before refurbished Leviathan *embarked her first passengers, an alien infestation was already*

subsuming ocean liners sailing out of New York. A very different clientele—neophytes recruited from the hinterlands—were starting to board in droves. That novel admixture was not the prewar American gentry European owners craved but hordes of the unsophisticated, succumbing to the lure of inexpensive tourist third cabin class. These were the urgently needed replacements for the vanished immigrant tide that Congress had legislated out of existence in 1921.

For that new breed, shipboard could be a minefield, sometimes reducing eagerly awaited adventure into worrisome ordeal. Not only had tourist third cabin occupants never been to sea before, many seemed never to have ventured beyond their hometowns. And their cherished European fling could easily degenerate into a vexing social challenge. In truth, many of those impulsive voyagers found themselves uneasy with the creaking paneled majesty into which they had committed themselves. Adrift in a sometimes baffling wilderness, they did their best to negotiate one daunting maze after another.

Foremost burden was debilitating seasickness, a universal affliction for which few curatives existed save one: instant but, of course, impossible midocean landfall. Whereas one widely sold British product—Mothersill's Seasick Remedy—was essentially useless, a competing nostrum, marketed candidly as Cocaine Lozenges, proved devastatingly efficacious.

Sea motion notwithstanding, social pitfalls remained. Almost all tourist third cabin passengers came to grief in the dining saloon, whether deciphering menus or determining correct usage for a bewilderment of glasses and cutlery. Few had ever dealt with servants and the ritual ministration of stewards was sometimes perceived as threatening. Also awkward was conversing with newfound and equally tongue-tied table companions. Too often, hoping to offset gaucherie, defiant or antagonistic bluster rose unbidden to the surface.

Even within the privacy of their cabins uncertainty reigned. Hovering steward or stewardess often seemed more menacing than helpful. Though a sink occupied every cabin corner, communal tubs and toilets lay along the alleyway. Tourist third cabin clientele found parading to and from those public facilities in bathrobe and slippers,

burdened with towel and soap box, quintessentially embarrassing.

Moreover, once there, the bathing ritual was confusing. Though bath stewards had filled their tubs, drying off sticky saltwater proved difficult. Most never understood the purpose of the basin of hot fresh water that the steward left on a wooden rack spanning the tub; it was to rinse off that salt residue.

Throughout fusty lounges and smoking rooms, similar alienation persisted. When and where to sit, with whom to chat, let alone what to say either to fellow lost souls or to ship's staff, whether purser or officer.

Yet one overriding plus contravened otherwise negative minuses. Save aboard American-flagged vessels obliged to observe Prohibition, well-stocked and tended bars were commonplace in every class. Regardless of social quandaries, European shipboard offered heavensent evasion of the Eighteenth Amendment of 1919. President Wilson had hoped to veto the measure but the Senate had sufficient votes to override him.

Almost at once, Prohibition's regime turned out to have been disastrously ill-advised. Temperance advocates' conviction that outlawing the sale of alcohol nationwide might be a grand specific for countering all of society's ills proved wishful thinking at best. Not surprisingly, it created an unanticipated phenomenon: millions of previously law-abiding Americans turned into casual lawbreakers. Even citizens who had never previously imbibed flocked to illegal speakeasies where bootleg liquor of all kinds was readily and plentifully available.

After fourteen flawed and increasingly violent years, Prohibition was abolished in 1933 when its enforcing Volstead Act was repealed. But throughout the 1920s nowhere was evading Prohibition easier than beyond the twelve-mile limit girdling America's coastline. It would be safe to say that, if it did nothing else, Prohibition bolstered the bottom line of every European shipping company. They welcomed Americans on board with as much drink as possible. Bellboys on French Line vessels were drilled to understand the first words thirsty Americans blurted as they mounted the gangway: "Where is the bar?" "Booze cruise," a term coined by the tabloids, became shorthand for the popularity of ships that advertised and offered unlimited alcohol just beyond Ambrose Channel.

Clad distinctively in red, *Royal Princess*'s talented Ukrainian string quartet plays of an evening in the capacious Piazza during the vessel's maiden westbound crossing in October 2013. (Photographer Mary Maxtone-Graham; Author's Collection)

It was European shipboard's surfeit of drink, alas, that fashioned the 1920s transatlantic stereotype of perennially drunk Americans. Those Yankee "wets" were not the only onboard inebriates but they seemed the most numerous. Masters-at-arms came to know too well the onerous necessity of a repetitive late-night chore, steering or sometimes carrying insensible clients back to their berths. *Aquitania*'s surgeon became dauntingly familiar with the symptoms of delirium tremens.

What became identified as the Jazz Age eroded shipboard's traditional hauteur. Flappers with shorter skirts and daring, corset-free silhouettes precipitated overwhelming behavioral change. Giddy dances such as the Charleston and black bottom became the rage. Abandonment of prewar social mores in general fomented unusual and excessive seagoing misbehavior, and abusive alcoholic consumption only encouraged the mania.

The Jazz Age accelerated every crossing's tempo. Lounges and bars were noisier and more crowded, formerly civilized exchanges tended now to be shouted or slurred, and even casual vulgarity became common shipboard currency.

I neither cherished nor admired that indulgence, which is a source of nostalgia for many. I was too young to have experienced it firsthand but the gulf separating prewar from postwar transatlantic shipboard seemed somehow demeaning. The peace of crossings in the old days was no more, the civilized tenor of string players having been replaced by the invasive racket of snare drum, plucked double bass, and wailing saxophone.

The ships still sailed as before, delivering their passengers to the opposite shore, offering admirable food now accompanied by a deluge of drink. Public rooms seemed to have become de facto speakeasies, echoing with the same stridency as illegal outlets ashore, as though passengers were determined not to relinquish the infectious naughtiness of America's Prohibition drumbeat.

Miraculously, fragments of traditional shipboard are reappearing. Aboard many cruise ships, Polish, Ukrainian, or Russian string quartets play of an evening, signaling a refreshing change from the overamplification characterizing so many performances; haunting chamber music can be heard at sea again.

To my mind, shipboard is a natural haven for stringed instruments. How pleasing to savor Strauss, Bach, Schumann, or Brahms as one's vessel moves imperturbably across the nighttime ocean.

CHAPTER SIX

SS AMERICA AND ANOTHER WAR

We will always build good ships, at a profit if we can,
at a loss if we must—but always good ships.

—motto of Newport News Shipbuilding and Drydock Company

The launch of America "is one of the most important events of the year."

—President Franklin D. Roosevelt

The vessel will replace the old Leviathan.

—New York *Herald Tribune*, August 22, 1938

Opposite: Alongside her Newport News fitting-out pier, SS *America* is nearly ready
for her maiden venture out of New York. An elevated boot topping indicates an absence
of fuel, water, furniture, and passengers. (**Newport News Shipbuilding Collection**)

Over the years, no fewer than a dozen ocean liners have been christened America. *For European*

shipping lines it proved an inescapable temptation: for westbound vessels packed with immigrants, America or New York in particular was the destination of choice surpassing all others.

Among that historic flotilla was Cunard's paddle steamer *America* of 1848; a second Scottish-built *America* was constructed for North German Lloyd in 1863. The Fabre Line's *America* followed in 1881, then National Lines' *America* three years later, and the United States Lines' Harland & Wolff–built *America* of 1905. An *America* was entered into service by the *Navigazione Generale Italiana* in 1908. There were also two later USS *Americas*, naval vessels, the most recent a helicopter vessel.

In 1940 the U.S. Lines' *America* was designed by William Francis Gibbs. I crossed on her westbound from Southampton to New York in mid-March of 1947. It was a momentous journey on many counts, one of my twin Michael's and my watersheds. We were eighteen and our parents were separating. Newly minted Americans rather than dual citizens of the U.S. and UK, Michael and I were leaving Britain with our American mother and returning to Massachusetts; our older brother, Peter, would remain in London with our father.

That postwar voyage lay in marked contrast to our previous eastbound aboard HMS *Patroller*, part of a wartime convoy sailing out of New York in August 1944. On that crossing, we were among two dozen repatriated British evacuees, adolescent children housed in the pilot's ready room. *Patroller* was an American-built escort carrier, manned at the time by the Royal Navy.

After two years of Great Britain's postwar "utility" regime, embarkation aboard *America* signaled not only the trauma of familial dissolution but also the sudden availability of white rather than perennially gray bread, unlimited butter, bananas, oranges, desserts, and, particularly, a plenitude of chocolate.

That much I remember well, but as more than six decades have passed I can recall few shipboard details. Among our fellow passengers were two singers, the popular French cabaret artist Charles Trenet and the Norwegian soprano Kirsten Flagstad. Passenger rather than performer, the Frenchman spent many mornings pacing back and forth across the after sports deck.

The vessel had been restored to peacetime service in 1946 after an impressive wartime career as

troopship *West Point*. In command was Captain Harry Manning, the man who would become first master of *United States*. A Gibbs & Cox ship, the visual genes of her larger and more famous successor were unquestionably present but with several design differences.

First steel had been laid down in August 1938 at Newport News, described by the proud yard as "our hull no. 369." She would cost $17 million and would be the largest passenger vessel ever built in America. Admiral Emory S. Land, head of the United States Maritime Administration, rolled up his sleeves and drove one of the first rivets establishing the 669-foot (204 meters) keel plate on August 22, 1938. Later that day, after a celebratory luncheon at the James River Country Club, Admiral Land was presented with a Newport News check for a few cents, token compensation for his keel-laying effort.

Maritime historians and the press characterized *America* in retrospect as either a replacement for recently scrapped *Leviathan* or a third of the *Manhattan* and *Washington* class of vessel. She was definitely not a sister ship, merely a similarly mid-sized steamship. In Washington's Experimental Model Basin, a miniature *America* prototype underwent fifty-four changes, accumulating an exhaustive track record of more than five thousand test runs. The vessel's hull was subject to continuous experimentation, including a bulbous bow, a fine hull, and, conversely, a full waterline. Films were taken of hull no. 369's reaction to artificial wave conditions reproduced at will. And the final choice, a configuration exhibiting the most "kindly sea behavior," happened to be no. 118, which had produced an "easy sweeping wave formation."

America would emerge as a twin-screw, turbine-driven liner displacing 26,455 tons with an overall length of 723 feet (220 meters) and a draft of 32 feet (9.75 meters); in final form, her original 92-foot (28 meters) beam had been expanded to 93 feet, 3 inches. She would be equipped with some of the largest lifeboats ever made in America, each designed to accommodate 125 people.

Steam was produced by six Babcock & Wilcox boilers, housed three each in two separate engine rooms, one forward, the other aft. Only her number 2 funnel vented boiler uptakes; the forward one was not operational but contained an emergency

Shipyard draftsmen cluster around the scrupulously tested wooden model of *America*, calculating the number of steel plates required to fabricate the hull. (Newport News Shipbuilding Collection)

generator, a safety predilection that Gibbs would repeat for *United States*.

It was the apparition, common to several vessels of the period, of a fake funnel set in a new location, a reversal of the dummy funnel's classic position as apparent afterthought added to the tail end of the queue. Perhaps most famous was the one incorporated into the profile of White Star's *Olympic* class; all of their number 4 funnels were dummies. So, too, was *Normandie*'s number 3 and last funnel.

Conversely, the same company's final two ships—*Britannic* of 1930 and *Georgic* of 1932—were equipped with two stylishly short, motor ship stacks of which only one, the number 2, had any connection with the engine room. Both number 1 funnels were dummies, devoid of any uptake linkage whatsoever. Instead, they housed a variety of ancillary shipboard necessities—the engineers' lounge, the radio room, and some reserve water tanks.

That fortunate provision doubtless accounted for *Georgic*'s miraculous survival when a German bomb was dropped down her number 1 funnel during World War II near Port Tewfik. Thanks to the courageous work of her crew the vessel was saved. And because of that near-death experience, postwar *Georgic* sailed transatlantic with just a single stack, her surviving number 2 funnel serving, as it always had, as her solitary working funnel. Other companies also installed forward dummy funnels: Norwegian America's *Oslofjord* also had a fake number 1.

In fact, the location made sense because the number 2 stacks on most all two-funneled vessels were sited almost directly above the engine room. Aboard *America*, because the two engine rooms were forward and aft of the number 2 stack's location, uptakes from each had to be adapted so that they were routed both fore and aft. Constructing uptakes that would wend their way forward to vent through the number 1 funnel was not only awkward but, in this event, unnecessary.

It is interesting to note that *America*'s number 1 dummy funnel had inside it an emergency generator equipped with both a fuel tank above it and, in addition, batteries that could also start the generator if required. For the first time at Newport News, steam and whistle pipes were housed *inside* the funnel rather than cluttering its exterior, a design refinement that would also be employed on *United States* to come.

America was christened by first lady Eleanor Roosevelt on August 31, 1939. Her matrons of honor were Mrs. Emory S. Land, wife of the man who had driven the keel plate's first rivet, and Mrs. Basil Harris, whose husband was a United States Lines vice president. Hull no. 369 was poised, ready for launching, at the top of inclined shipway 8.

Mrs. Roosevelt would be introduced by shipyard president Homer Ferguson. Among the brass on the launch platform, the only missing principal was the vessel's distinguished naval architect. It turned out later that, bored with every christening's predictable folderol, William Gibbs had climbed to the top of some scaffolding the better to observe how his ship would look when she was afloat. As she slid prettily into the water, the shipyard's Apprentice School Band played "The Star-Spangled Banner."

America's initial trials took place on June 4, 1940. She slipped her cables at 0400 hours and headed out into Hampton Roads en route to the Virginia Capes. By 10:30 A.M., she was producing 34,000 horsepower. There followed a three-hour intense run at speed, including one jolting episode when the rudder was put hard over to starboard then almost immediately hard over to port in a brutal test of her steering gear. In the afternoon, at 2:30 P.M., 30 fathoms of anchor cable were paid out as she anchored off Virginia Beach for the night.

Acceptance trials took place five days later. On June 9, *America* steamed north to Boston, reaching there at 8 P.M. After anchoring overnight, she entered the Boston Navy Yard's dry dock the following morning. Teams of Newport News dockworkers traveling aboard disembarked into yard scows to clean the hull as the water level receded. Later, they would paint the underwater plating.

The keel for *America*, identified as hull no. 369, was laid in the yard's Shipway no. 8 in August 1938. Herewith, an early view of her preliminary construction, the keel complete, some bottom plating added and a scaffolding surround in position. The second view, taken on August 1, 1939, a month before christening, shows the completed vessel surrounded by timber scaffolding. Overhead is an added gantry. (Newport News Shipbuilding Collection)

After leaving Boston, *America*'s destination was a measured mile course off the coast of Rockport, Maine. Once arrived, there were two sets of measured mile runs at three successive speeds, 18, 21, and 21½ knots. During *America*'s return to Newport News she underwent a grueling full power run for eight hours, during which her top speed was clocked at 25.3 knots.

After those trials, it was decided that both of *America*'s funnels had to be raised 15 feet (4.5 meters) to keep stack gas off her after decks. In April of that year, a 15-foot model of the vessel, built to the scale of one-quarter inch to the foot, was unveiled for display, first temporarily at the New York World's Fair and then in United States Lines' head office at 1 Broadway. Curiously, though, lengthened funnels would not be added to that model until long after the war, in 1964.

The vessel was officially delivered to both the United States Maritime Commission and the United States Lines at 3:10 P.M. on July 2, 1940. Weeks after that acceptance, under the command of Captain Giles C. Stedman, the vessel headed north to her home port of New York where she arrived on July 29, 1940, tying up at Pier 59. After more than a week of maiden arrival hoopla, including press receptions and dinners, *America*'s maiden voyage started on August 10, 1940.

Because of European hostilities, it would be a cruise rather than a crossing. Seven hundred and ninety passengers embarked, sailing out of New York for a twelve-day jaunt through the West Indies. They would go ashore successively at Saint Thomas, San Juan, Port-au-Prince, and Havana, a bellwether of typical Caribbean calls of the period. Because she was designed for North Atlantic service, few of *America*'s interiors were air conditioned and searing Virginia temperatures of 106 degrees Fahrenheit in July 1940 caused the death of a crewman on her delivery day.

Thanks to her cosmetic funnel surgery she seemed, from afar, a miniature of the *United States* to come, because two similar tall red, white, and blue funnels dominated the profile. In truth she would be hopelessly outclassed by her prestigious successor a dozen years later. The two vessels were not equivalents at all. *America* was smaller and slower, with a service speed of 22 knots, a modest passenger capacity of 1,202, and, prewar, a crew numbering 618; postwar, that last would rise to 643.

It was unfortunate that Gibbs could not have wangled the same naval subsidy for *America* that he managed for *United States*. In that event, the U.S. Lines might have fielded comparable consorts on the order of Cunard White Star's *Queens*. The French Line suffered the same problem with its last two liners, *Normandie* and *France*. Though each excelled as a large, fast flagship, they remained, as the British say, one-offs: no equivalent consort joined either of them in service. Although *Bretagne*, a proposed *Normandie* sister, was ostensibly on the drawing boards in the late 1930s, the outbreak of World War II effectively scuttled the project.

America's class nomenclature adhered to Atlantic Conference rules wrought at Berlin's Hotel Adlon four years earlier. Because of the imbroglio about conflicting price scales aboard rival newcomers *Normandie* and *Queen Mary*, conference members voted quixotically to have all North Atlantic first class cabins rebranded cabin class. Subject to that confusing edict, *America*'s 1940 cruise brochures offered the following accommodations in three classes: 543 in cabin (really first), 418 in tourist, and 241 in third.

Already, Gibbs was preternaturally fire conscious when selecting and approving *America*'s furnishings. Although his choices fell short of the ruthless regime that would dominate *United States*'s interiors, most of *America*'s public room chairs stood on metal rather than wooden legs and, wherever possible, anti-inflammatory qualifications determined the choice for many curtain, carpet, and upholstery fabrics.

In the light of the war that would engulf the United States after Pearl Harbor, the country's national attitude prior to that attack seems retrospectively naive. The truth was that many Washington insiders were convinced that America's noninvolvement in what they perceived as an exclusively European conflict should and would be sustained.

Of course, they were dead wrong. Even before SS *America*'s debut, the Low Countries were overrun, Denmark and Norway had been invaded, France surrendered, remnants of the British Expeditionary Force were evacuated from Dunkirk, and the Battle of Britain raged over England. A German blitzkrieg was en route to Moscow. Yet regardless of the fact that the conflict had leapfrogged to global dimensions, the same myopic isolationism still enveloped Washington.

America's christening and launch day, August 31, 1939. An overview shows the sheltering gantry, sloping walkways to upper decks, scaffolding dismantled, fore poppet in place, and red, white, and blue bunting garlanding the prow. The bandstand is nearest the camera. At the vessel's stern, the Stars and Stripes flying, rudder and twin screws are in place and some of her riding crew stand on the after mooring deck. The scene below the bow, just after Eleanor Roosevelt had shattered the Champagne bottle and sent America down the ways. A distant figure atop the gantry's aftermost crossover could well be William Francis Gibbs, who had climbed up to watch his vessel's baptism. Here she is afloat, just aft of the launch's Shipway no. 8. (Newport News Shipbuilding Collection)

Though nobody's fault, it was an unhappy co-incidence that America's largest and newest ocean liner should have been commissioned at that inauspicious moment. During her first nine months of service America never crossed what had become an increasingly hostile North Atlantic. U.S. Lines restricted her to home waters, dispatching the vessel either on safe Caribbean itineraries or on two cruises through the Panama Canal. In that artificial wartime role, she was a rare de facto cruise ship that accommodated separate classes.

Wherever she sailed, America's black flanks were overpainted with her name and company in large letters as well as two prominent Stars and Stripes, each bearing forty-eight stars. At night, she remained fully illuminated at a time when North Atlantic and coastal vessels were being stringently blacked out. As a precaution against magnetic mines—which have, alas, no neutrality discrimination—her billboard hull was adorned in January 1941 with a wartime invention called a degaussing cable. Electrical current generated on board and directed through that encircling cable effectively and completely neutralized the vessel's magnetic field.

Despite the vessel's avowed neutrality, two of her crew were later exposed as members of Frederick "Fritz" Duquesne's ring of German spies, established during the late thirties in New York. Duquesne was a South African who had fought for the Boers and remained virulently anti-British. Two of his thirty-one patiently recruited subordinates served as crewmen aboard America: Franz Stigler, who had emigrated from Germany to America in 1931 and become a citizen, was chief baker. A junior confederate, Erwin Siegler, also worked in the galley. They observed and passed on details about Canal Zone defenses during America's two transits. Both would sign off when she became a U.S. Navy troopship. Subsequently, all thirty-one members of Duquesne's organization were arrested and convicted by the FBI, the largest espionage roundup in the bureau's history.

The end of *America*'s placid cruising preamble came on May 28, 1941, some six months before Japan's attack on Pearl Harbor. The vessel was recalled from Saint Thomas and, after offloading passengers in New York, repaired at once to Newport News. By June 1, the navy had taken ownership and a hasty preliminary conversion to *West Point* was undertaken. She was formally commissioned under command of Captain Frank H. Kelley Jr., USN. Remaining with him on the bridge was *America*'s former master Giles Stedman who, because he held a U.S. Naval Reserve commission as commander, would serve as executive officer for several months.

Before she sailed from Portsmouth, Virginia, her crew loaded aboard tons of foodstuffs not only for the vessel's reefers but also to resupply the Coast Guard vessel *Ingham*, managed by the Treasury Department and serving at that time as Lisbon's station ship. In those early days, *West Point*'s dining room fare remained on a par with *America*'s peacetime splendor. Only later, after full troopship conversion, would it be restricted to a more plebeian wartime mode. Covered with a coat of gray paint, the hull's neutrality flags were no longer visible. Her only wartime identification was a white *P23* on either gray bow, short for her naval designation *AP23*.

She returned to New York and tied up for four days at United States Lines' Pier 86 on July 12. From there, *West Point*–ex-*America* would depart on what was identified as the true maiden voyage, her first Atlantic crossing. But the voyage lacked any semblance of traditional gaiety. Her small passenger load did not even embark at Pier 86 but clambered aboard—almost surreptitiously, it seemed—from government lighters off Staten Island's Quarantine Station.

These were not conventional passengers but consignments of repatriated Axis consular officials, 137 of them Italian and 327 German. Once they were aboard, *America* proceeded to sea at 2:55 P.M. on July 16, 1941.

The contrasting moods of that involuntary eastbound passenger load are interesting. Whereas the Italians were pleased and enthusiastic about conditions aboard *West Point*, the Germans, whom the crew instantly branded "the undesirables," were, crewman John Dion recorded in his forbidden diary, "loud, demanding and very obnoxious." They complained repeatedly about everything, from accommodations to food to service. They also insisted vociferously that U.S. Marines passing through the dining room during mealtime were "spying" on them and boasted to all who would listen that *West Point* would be dispatched by U-boats on its return to New York.

After an otherwise uneventful crossing, the vessel tied up in Lisbon at 0935 hours on July 23. A deputation of German consular officials on the pier exchanged Nazi salutes with their returning colleagues who lined *West Point*'s railings.

The vessel's return to New York would involve reverse consular repatriation of 371 Americans and 67 Chinese. Regardless of Washington's putative isolationism, the State Department was closing down American consulates all across the continent. In addition, a variegated group of displaced Americans, British, and continentals was also expected. They ran the gamut from Sweden's Prince Charles Bernadotte, nephew of King Gustav V, to a dozen apparently "stateless" refugees.

One American was the nurse Marian McGill who had survived torpedoed Holland America *Maasdam* south of Iceland in June 1941; rescued by the British, she had made her way to Lisbon. Another American survivor from a sunken ship was Philip Faversham, a civilian ambulance driver en route to the United Kingdom aboard *Zamzam*, an Egyptian freighter that had also been sunk by a U-boat. After a brief spell of internment in occupied France, Faversham escaped to Lisbon, bringing with him two dogs, Millie and Muzzie, entrusted to his care by Jewish Americans, who had leaped from his train's window. A Belgian couple, a professional singer and his wife, had fled to France where, trapped yet again by invading Nazis, they took refuge in a Dunkirk cave for ten days during the port's evacuation. Somehow, they and their pet Pekingese managed to reach Lisbon.

From Berlin came American Richard Hottelet who, as overseas correspondent for the newspaper *PM*, had been arrested early one March morning by the Gestapo and imprisoned. His glasses were confiscated—"to prevent suicide" he was told—and he was never formally charged. Despairing of ever being freed, he was finally released after four months of stubborn U.S. consular efforts. Back in America, Hottelet would establish his journalistic reputation by working with Edward R. Murrow.

Most of the remainder were Americans, embroiled by war in Europe, who were desperate to

SS *America* in her original profile, with squat funnels. At the time normal transatlantic passage was deemed unwise, and U.S. Lines marketed cruises only in home waters. Both sides of her hull were painted with unmistakable symbols of neutrality, twin American flags together with the vessel's name and owning company.
(Newport News Shipbuilding Collection)

get home. By mutual agreement, the Maritime Commission and American Export Lines had established a flat rate for adult passage of $319.60. Children paid half price and infant fare was only $22. Passage for dogs cost more than for infants; for a berth in the ship's kennel owners paid $25 each.

This unique passenger mélange converged from many different directions and so they were slow to arrive. While awaiting them, Captain Kelley did not trust the pro-German consular authorities to share accurate information of their whereabouts. Made uneasy by the relentless arrogance of the "undesirables," the master decreed that not one German would be allowed ashore until all

westbound passengers had reached the pier. Although the Italians were quickly disembarked and crewmen bound for liberty streamed down the gangway, U.S. Marine detachments maintained a strict watch that effectively imprisoned the German consular staffs on board.

For every one of those unhappy detainees, Captain Kelley's dictum served as the perfect penalty. Trunks and suitcases packed, the entire German contingent was forced to remain on board, parked in their cabins, sprawled throughout public rooms or pacing open decks, hanging over railings and staring disconsolately at what was—for them only—forbidden Lisbon.

The standoff continued for four days, until every one of Kelley's westbound passengers had assembled on the pier. Then, and only then, were the Germans permitted to disembark. Undesirable to the bitter end, they stormed ashore without a word of farewell or thanks. At the same time, food supplies, including welcome citrus fruits and crates of American coffee, were transferred for delivery to the *Ingham*.

As *West Point* steamed down the Tagus River, she passed the Coast Guard vessel, glowing prettily at her berth in the late afternoon sun; whistled salutes were exchanged. *Ingham*, incidentally, holds the longest service record in the history of the Coast Guard, having been originally commissioned in 1936. After America entered World War II, when the Coast Guard was formally attached to the U.S. Navy, USS *Ingham* started out hunting Nazi U-boats in the North Atlantic. She sank one before being transferred to the Pacific, where she served as flagship for several amphibious landings. Later, during the Vietnam War, she completed countless gunfire support missions and subsequently rescued at least twenty Cubans escaping their homeland. USS *Ingham*'s decommissioning on May 27, 1988, concluded a record-breaking fifty-two years of continuous service.

The German passengers' predictions notwithstanding, *West Point*'s westbound return was as uneventful as the eastbound. As Ben Robertson, a war correspondent sailing home from London, later wrote for a New York newspaper: "We sailed on, two days of sunshine, two of rain and wind, a final night through fog. Then we arrived in New York—home again and glad of it, and nearer than ever to war."

Her funnels lengthened and her hull emblazoned with the nation's flag, SS *America* enters the port of New York for the first time on July 29, 1940. A week later 790 passengers embarked for the vessel's maiden Caribbean cruise. (Newport News Shipbuilding Collection)

By June 15, 1941, SS *America* had been converted from an ocean liner into gray-painted USS *West Point*, what the navy described as a Convoy Unit Loaded Transport. Behind her, aircraft carrier USS *Hornet* is being fitted out. (Newport News Shipbuilding Collection)

The only frightening incident was a mattress fire in a cabin, obviously set by a careless smoker, which was luckily immediately extinguished.

Early on the foggy morning of August 1, 1941, *West Point* steamed into New York Harbor. By 1 P.M. she had tied up at Pier 61 where more than two thousand relatives and friends were waiting to greet them, among them Richard Hottelet's vastly relieved mother. State Department personnel in the pier shed cautioned disembarking passengers to say nothing about the war to flocks of reporters who were meeting the inbound vessel. But most of them, thrilled to be back in the States, cheerfully ignored the recommendation.

Immediately, *West Point* returned empty to Portsmouth for a trooping conversion that was completed in an amazingly swift fortnight. The vessel was transformed into what was called by the Navy Department a Convoy Unit Loaded Transport. Peacetime furnishings were offloaded and ultimately would be consigned to a New York warehouse; Newport News's warehouses were chockablock with wartime matériel. A small allotment of the vessel's original beds and bureaus was kept aboard in those cabin class quarters destined to accommodate military officers and/or nurses.

An influx of familiar troopship appurtenances transformed the remaining interiors. For enlisted men, hundreds of standee bunks, that infamous U.S. Navy invention from World War I, came aboard and were crammed into every available cabin. Whereas standee bunks on the *Queens* were steel pipe rectangles laced with canvas and no mattress, those aboard *West Point* had regular spring foundations and were stacked five high rather than *Leviathan*'s three. Only narrow access corridors separated them; "quartered like sardines" was the way one GI passenger would describe things.

There were significant external changes. A palisade of life rafts—sufficient capacity for all ship's occupants, soldiers and crew alike—covered every promenade deck window, the glass of which had already been overpainted battleship gray. Four 5-inch guns were mounted on strengthened deck sections, two forward and two aft, and the after docking bridge was removed for the duration. Batteries of antiaircraft ordnance were mounted in circular armored steel tubs, including Bofors, quad fifties, and Oerlikons. All officers and crew were now U.S. Navy personnel. The hull, superstructure, and twin funnels were painted with a camouflage dazzle paint scheme that remained in place throughout the war.

An interesting and unique lookout was carved through the summit of the number 1 dummy funnel, what the crew described as "a steel-lined foxhole." It was the vessel's most prominent and visible lookout point. The funnel top was cut in a rectangular direction fore and aft and a platform welded below. "A very shaky ladder" 30 feet long led up to it. Dubbed the stack watch, it was normally manned by an officer and four men, with a rangefinder for the guns that rose four feet above the funnel top and could rotate through 360 degrees. Additionally, there were two fixed-mount binoculars.

For *Battle Bill, Condition 1*, fourteen men might be involved in what was frequently rough duty. Fully 135 feet (41 meters) above the waterline, the stack watch was posted at the extreme end of an inverted pendulum, swung violently from port to starboard, unshaded in summer and unheated in winter. Those turbulent conditions were amplified by *West Point*'s 23-knot speed. If there was an after wind blowing, those on watch might be cloaked in fumes from the number 2 working stack. Whenever the foghorn was blown they were drenched by a steam assault. Throughout the war, only during the most inclement weather conditions was that brutal stack watch ever canceled.

Capacity rose from *America*'s 1,202 to *West Point*'s 7,687. But that was not the absolute limit: on one voyage, she embarked a record total of 8,531, in addition to her crew of 785. On another, when carrying civilian evacuees from Singapore to Bombay, a boy was born, the only wartime birth recorded; predictably, his given name was Westpoint Leslie Shelldrake.

West Point would sail all over the globe, throughout the Middle East and also to Auckland, Sydney, Singapore, India, and Manila. She traveled either alone or in convoy with other American flagged ships, including *Wakefield* and *Mount Vernon*. In early November 1941, *West Point* called at Halifax to embark 241 officers and 5,202 men of the 55th Brigade, Bedfordshire and Hertfordshire regiments, carrying them in convoy to Bombay.

Later in the war, she took huge numbers of GIs transatlantic to the European theater of operations in preparation for D-day. The U.S. Army's 275th and 276th Infantry regiments filed aboard from Boston on December 6, 1944, for a winter crossing to—where? Either no one knew or no one was telling. From the crowded decks, hundreds of the obligatory condoms that the men carried were inflated and sent aloft like flights of white balloons, the GIs' irreverent farewell salute to Boston as *West Point* steamed otherwise majestically downharbor.

None of that 7,764-strong detachment had ever been to sea. The first days out on the midwinter Atlantic, violent weather claimed hundreds of victims. Soldiers showered and shaved with seawater and were issued black cakes of saltwater soap. It was the only way they could lather up, but the soap's persistently sticky and unpleasant residue never really washed off.

Mass toilets—heads, in navy lingo—had been installed, long steel troughs flushed with seawater that drained overboard. They were covered by rows of outhouse seats cut through long planks. Whenever the vessel rolled badly, seawater sometimes flooded upward, backing up the drainage system, overflowing and soaking the backsides of many unhappy occupants.

Meal service was similarly primitive. Whereas officers and nurses could order traditional meals in Gibbs's cabin class dining room, thousands of noncommissioned subordinates had, according to GI diarist Frank H. Lowery, only "a huge mess hall located down in the hold of the ship." My guess is that the troops were fed in an emptied and institutionalized tourist class dining room, which Lowery incorrectly identified as one of the vessel's holds. Mandatory requirement for a chow hall, whatever its location, is an adjacent galley. There would have been no such convenience within reach of *West Point*'s cargo holds.

Whatever the space, it contained long metal chow tables bolted to the deck at which men ate standing up. As aboard all World War II troopships, lunch was a wartime casualty; only breakfast and dinner were ladled into the men's mess gear. After eating their fill, they washed and rinsed their dishes in consecutive GI cans full of, first, hot soapy and then clear water before departing. In 1942 cabin class's Dining Saloon was remade into a troop mess hall as well.

Though the food was edible, the unadorned steel deck beneath their feet became slippery with water and spilled food. The detachment's first sergeant, a senior noncom called Palacio, was responsible for providing KP as well as deck or latrine-cleaning details on a daily basis. Hundreds of GI passengers learned to elude Palacio, slipping out of sight whenever he approached in order to avoid conscription.

Conversely, recruitment for his special work details sometimes paid dividends. One private assigned to KP duty in the officers' mess found that he could "liberate" an entire canned ham. That night, with the addition of some purloined loaves and a no. 10 can of mustard, he and his buddies feasted on ham sandwiches slapped together out on deck. There are no more resourceful conspirators than a passel of hungry soldiers.

Financially, there were restrictions. Standing wartime regulations ruled that no GI passenger could board with more than five dollars in his possession. Its intended use was buying candy bars and Cokes in the onboard PX or, as the navy called them, Gedunk stations. However, during most of *West Point*'s wartime crossings, the majority of those five-dollar allowances were forfeited during ruinous but almost continuous poker sessions with navy sharks.

When the weather behaved, troops congregated on deck, yarning, singing, and, if the figurative smoking lamp was lit, lighting up cigarettes. Smoking on deck after dark was strictly forbidden. It was also verboten to throw anything over the side. Enemy submarines were always on the lookout for either pinpricks of flaring matches or jetsam that frequently lingered in a troopship's wake.

Everyone speculated about the European port of disembarkation. I have always wondered at the necessity for withholding that information from thousands of men who were patently out of touch with anyone ashore. But the probable truth was that those on the bridge charged with delivering troops to the European theater of operations may still not have received that intelligence from Washington, even by mid-voyage.

Along the gossipy troop decks, persistent odds-on favorites were Liverpool or Le Havre. But when, after a wearisome week of heaving confinement, green slopes finally appeared over the bow on the morning of December 13, it turned out to be not Wales or Normandy but Portugal, then Spain, and finally, unmistakably recognizable, Gibraltar's brooding rock. Escorted by a Royal Navy destroyer screen, *West Point* passed through the straits.

Because the Allies now had almost complete air superiority in the Mediterranean, the vessel was partially illuminated at night and smoking on deck was permitted. Two days later, having traversed neutral Spain's coastline, they arrived off the devastated French port Marseilles, awash with remnants of bombed and scuttled Axis tonnage. No safe anchorage existed within the wreck-littered harbor, so *West Point* dropped the hook outside the breakwater.

Both regimental detachments were ferried ashore in local lighters and landing craft. For those green soldiers struggling down companionways with packs, weapons, and steel helmets, the sight of that devastated European port was sobering, their first exposure to the ravages of total war. On board, *West Point*'s crew immediately busied themselves in preparation for a mixed westbound embarkation of American wounded and Axis prisoners of war.

Newport News personnel traveling aboard *West Point*'s final crossings conducted detailed surveys about the scope of the vessel's reconversion back to civilian life. It would be a monumental task because *West Point* had been the Second World War's most extensively converted troopship. Almost all her cabin bulkheads had been removed to create larger berthing compartments, and now those vanished barriers would have to be rebuilt and reinstalled. Almost every space on board would need work; the cabin class library, for example, had been plumbed as a troop washroom.

The vessel's long and distinguished wartime career ended with formal U.S. Navy decommissioning at the close of February 1946. For more than fifty-six months, she had completed 151 voyages, sailing 436,144 miles and carrying a total of 505,020 passengers. Her fuel capacity of 1,370,000 gallons allowed her to steam to Europe and back with an additional 2,000 miles in reserve. Various messes on board dispensed some twenty tons of food daily.

At least six times throughout the war, a German mouthpiece nicknamed derisively "Axis Sally" broadcast that *West Point* had been sunk. Refuting those claims as baseless propaganda, *West Point* sailed from Le Havre into the port of New York on July 11, 1945, tying up on the north side of the French Line's Pier 88, the same slip in which *Normandie* had burned and capsized more than three years earlier.

Shortly thereafter, when she reached Virginia, the name *West Point* was struck from naval registry

and her navy crew disembarked. Ordnance detachments came aboard to retrieve armaments and ammunition. Standee bunks were disassembled and manhandled ashore. Troop latrines were cut up and scrapped, mess tables detached and removed, and stacks of unused life rafts lofted ashore in shipyard cribs.

A thousand shipyard workers from Newport News toiled on renovating *West Point* back into *America*. Patch plates that had been welded over portholes were burned off and removed. In dry dock, two layers of wartime paint came off: the outer wartime camouflage and, beneath it, an earlier and now almost quaint symbol from the past, neutrality warnings and a faded Stars and Stripes.

Then all 80,000 square feet of the hull were sandblasted, using 400 tons of sand. Immediately, the naked steel was sprayed with phosphoric acid to

West Point under way as a troop transport, her hull painted in its early wartime pattern. The number 1 funnel was not employed as a working stack and its sealed-off uptake permitted conversion into what was described by the crew as "the steel-lined foxhole." Higher than the crow's nest, men stood two-hour watches. Perched atop that often wildly swinging funnel, it remained a routinely unpleasant posting. (Bill Lee Collection, U.S. Navy Photo, National Archives print #80LG-71251)

America under way in early 1946 after her reconversion to a passenger liner. This was taken by shipyard photographer Marcus Ritger as the vessel was resuming peacetime service on the North Atlantic. (Bill Lee Collection)

eliminate rusting before three coats of protective paint were applied—primer, antifouling red below the boot topping, and finally a black, anticorrosive mix that conformed to the company's peacetime livery. One nice touch: *America*'s funnels were repainted in their peacetime red, white, and blue and illuminated at night; those living nearby were delighted to see something other than wartime gray.

The rudder was checked and refurbished and propellers were burnished, their blades ground clean of wartime nicks. Anchors and anchor cables were lowered to the dry dock floor for scaling

and painting. Final cosmetic touch, at the bow and stern, the steel letters for *AMERICA* and, aft, port of registry *NEW YORK* were welded in place and painted white. The only gilded work was applied to recessed letters adorning the vessel's name boards.

Only after all wartime gear had been disembarked would the healing process begin. Abused decks, 10,000 square feet of them, were either covered with an asphalt composition called Levelite or refinished with fresh lengths of Oregon pine. Flexible mastic compound was forced into the interstices between them and the recessed bolts that anchored wooden decking to underlying steel disappeared beneath round pine plugs. Then powerful belt sanders were deployed, smoothing that new decking flawlessly. To my mind, once the sawdust has been cleared away, restored ship's decks offer pristine vistas that surpass with ease Versailles's most elaborate parquetry.

Wooden railing caps along open decks that had been carved and initialed by thousands of bored GIs had to be unbolted and replaced by lengths of sanded and varnished teak. Deckhouse walls were scraped, sanded, and painted, window casements and doorjambs resealed and pointed.

Technical improvements proliferated. Because of a new manning act legislated by Congress, crew quarters would need upgrading as well. On Sports Deck, two crew lounges were created, one for bridge officers and the other for engineers. Shipboard engineers, whose watches are inevitably spent far below deck, were traditionally rewarded with daylight-filled space for their off-duty hours. A pair of additional evaporators increased water production by 40,000 gallons a day. On the bridge, LORAN (long range navigation) had been in place since before the war, a device that determined the vessel's location anywhere in the world, thanks to coordinates of two fixed broadcast signals from known positions.

The decorating firm Smyth, Urquhart & Marckwald, responsible for *America*'s original interiors, was signed up again to re-create replacement furnishings, as well as all rugs and curtains. Dorothy Marckwald designed a Duck Suite aboard *America*. Flights of aluminum ducks were deployed across the cabin walls to pleasing effect; it became the most prized accommodation on board.

Astonishingly, every stick of furniture removed from *America* in August 1941 had, in somewhat evasive parlance, "been disposed of." When some of the original manufacturers were approached for furniture replacements, they refused to accept orders because postwar labor unrest restricted their output. Had those strikes not occurred, *America* could have been readied more than two months sooner.

Existing artworks that had not been "disposed of" were brought out of storage and painstakingly restored. Charles Baskerville created not only an additional colorful circus mural but also a new lacquer surround for entry into what was now called the first class lounge. Postwar *America* accommodated three classes, sensibly renamed as of old: first, cabin, and tourist.

The indoor first class pool was shortened by three feet, a successful attempt to reduce continual flooding. In its original configuration, sea motion precipitated amplifying wave cycles that sent pool water splashing all over the space; miraculously, the shortened dimension corrected the problem.

Hundreds of shipyard cleaners embarked with buckets, mops, scrubbing brushes, and rags. Filth, stains, and detritus that five years' trooping had inflicted on those distressed interiors were, after repeated swabbing and wiping, gradually removed. The most stubborn defilement was graffiti excised

Captain Harry Manning on the bridge of *America* in 1947. The photograph was a widely circulated United States Lines image. One copy reached Bill Lee, signed and dedicated to him by the master. Manning was trim, squared away, and dedicated to his work. (Bill Lee Collection)

Four of *America*'s original interiors. The entry into first class's (called cabin class) Main Lounge, with flowers atop every table. Reflecting the dance floor's shape, a round dome has been set into the deckhead above, not unlike a similar provision in first class's Ballroom aboard *United States* to come. The sitting room of a cabin class suite. Far below, a pristine engine room. In the background, beyond turbines and boilers, a spread of dials and meters indicates the starting platform. (Newport News Shipbuilding Collection)

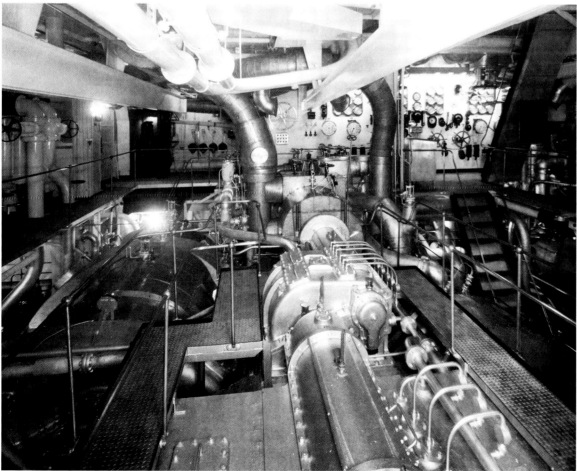

Steve Tacey's photograph of *Australis*, as *America* was renamed after Chandris bought her for Australian immigration service. In fact, Tacey sailed to Australia on board her as a child with his family. (Steve Tacey Collection)

from latrine walls. Daylight once again flooded promenade decks as solvent and razor-blade scrapers patiently restored clarity to acres of gray-painted glass in the window frames.

Underfoot, new linoleum was unrolled and cemented down along every alleyway while cabins and public rooms were freshly carpeted. New furniture was redistributed throughout the vessel in the same configuration as the discarded originals had been in 1940. Fresh curtains were hung. From manufacturers, arriving cartons of mattresses, pillows, blankets, towels, bath mats, and washcloths were stacked in strategically located cabins, awaiting the day when U.S. Lines stewards and stewardesses, together with their housekeeping superiors, would reembark for business.

Peacetime's patina gradually reemerged. Along alleyway bulkheads, lithographs and paintings were rehung. In every main lounge, after dance floors had been sanded and varnished, sofas, armchairs, tables, and lamps were grouped. Pianos and bandstands were also maneuvered into place. In an inevitable ceremonial flourish signaling the return of civilian passengers every ship's piano was tuned.

America resumed sailing transatlantic for United States Lines until 1964, when she was sold to Chandris. The Greek company transformed her into one-class *Australis*, effectively doubling her capacity. She was completely air-conditioned, her hull painted white, a pool installed on her after deck, and her funnels repainted black and blue. She sailed from Newport News for the last time on November 18, 1964.

Chandris put her in service delivering British emigrants to Australia. Once those new Australians had gone ashore in Sydney, duplicating P&O/Orient's two-class continuum, the vessel would embark cruise passengers for Pacific and then Atlantic crossings, completing the vessel's global circumnavigation back to the United Kingdom.

Fourteen years later, *Australis* would be renamed *America* and sent cruising by newly formed Ventura Cruises. She completed two summer cruises out of New York in June and July 1978, but in August she was repurchased by Chandris and renamed *Italis*. She sailed back to Perama in Greece and had her forward (dummy) funnel removed.

On January 18, 1994, *Italis* ran aground during a severe Mediterranean storm on the north end of the island of Fuerteventura in the Canaries. (Ironically, what became the vessel's grave terminated

with the intact corporate name of one of her final owners.) Her forepart pierced and imprisoned atop the rocks, the hull finally broke in half. The stern section did not drift loose for some time and the vessel's surviving forepart could be seen by passing vessels until it, too, finally vanished into the sea in 2007. As Bill Lee tells it, scattered remnants of her bow plating "are only recognizable by those who knew and loved her."

It is fortunate that *America*'s restoration merely followed the example of her first hasty incarnation of August 1940. As such, it required little supervision from Gibbs & Cox personnel, who were preoccupied by the company's massive wartime commitment to the United States Navy.

That extraordinary national effort had been masterminded from the (now) thirteen floors of Gibbs & Cox's expanded offices where a combined force of two thousand draftsmen and engineers had collaborated in establishing and implementing William Francis Gibbs's remarkable standardization of shipbuilding measurements and methods nationwide. Throughout the war, the firm produced twenty-six acres of blueprints each month.

What Gibbs's genius established was veritable mass production of newbuildings throughout a disparity of shipyards across the country. That unique naval architectural revolution would dragoon America's shipbuilders into novel conformity. "Tall, cadaverous Mr. Gibbs is the overall coordinating genius," suggested *Time* magazine's cover story in September 1942, describing the brilliant naval architect as a veritable "technological revolutionist."

What Gibbs achieved was standardization of all plans, specifications, measurements, and even purchase orders throughout every shipyard, large and small alike, around the country. Every vessel built and launched in America during the war, whether Liberty or Victory ship on the West Coast, landing craft in Ohio, escort vessels in Alabama, or warships in Bath, profited from new, universal standards of measurement and assembly, perfected by William Gibbs into a national grid of naval exactitude.

Acceptance and adoption of that mandatory system updated every shipbuilding parameter to a hitherto unknown conformity. Mass production of ships, founded on the bedrock of strict standardization, was made possible on an enormous scale. Miraculous results followed, the pace of construction relentlessly accelerated and production schedules radically reduced. Liberty and Victory merchant ships were churned out in a matter of days rather than months or weeks and the delivery of more complex naval vessels such as destroyers reduced from more than two years to less than one.

Involved were not only smaller vessels; larger ones profited as well. The aircraft carrier USS *Lexington* was launched more than a year ahead of schedule. Moreover, thanks to Gibbs's innovative insistence on both high pressure and high temperature steam aboard his 364-class destroyers, those vital naval workhorses would exhibit superior performance over enemy equivalents. A similar high steam pressure and temperature system would be implemented by Gibbs aboard *United States* to come.

One of Gibbs & Cox's most invaluable wartime achievements was establishment of a peerless model department. Once a vessel's plans had been completed and accepted, a steel model was immediately put into work. These were extraordinary creations, not hobbyists' wooden fabrications to be admired from afar but scrupulously fashioned steel miniatures, their plating, decking, and bulkhead thickness laboriously and perfectly reproduced to scale. Those exacting constructions, by their very nature, immediately exposed any potential inaccuracies or shortcomings in the original plans. Rather than having to change and rebuild faulty finished elements in completed vessels, those incredibly accurate prototypes revealed design shortcomings instantly. Exposing them that early meant the problem could be corrected at a fraction of the cost.

A perfect case in point was formulation of one shipboard compartment's steel prototype that incorporated of necessity a wooden lower deck. Summer humidity marginally expanded that nonsteel element and, inevitably, the height of the completed structure grew, creating potentially fatal inexactitude.

Though Gibbs was happily tied to his own firm, he reluctantly accepted a posting to the nation's capital, dragooned by the War Production Board into supervising the country's cargo ship construction program. He found himself at immediate odds with the entrenched Maritime Commission, which had already formulated ambitious plans for America's postwar merchant marine.

But William Francis Gibbs was less concerned with postwar mandates than the necessity of streamlining wartime newbuilds, employing the same astonishing mandate with which he had already revolutionized the navy's procurement programs. Standardizer Gibbs hurled himself into the fray. He not only achieved miraculous savings, he pruned hundreds of unnecessary duplications. The number of merchant ship classes, for example, was reduced from six to three. On a lesser but equally crucial scale, various types of geared turbines being manufactured were shrunk from twenty-seven to eight, and competing designs of turbogenerators for naval ships were winnowed successfully from seventy-seven to seventeen.

Already rich with astonishing achievements, Gibbs had rung up yet another. He had arrived in Washington with a rather mixed reputation, and when he resigned and returned to New York that reputation shone brighter than ever. He was, after all, the guiding genius of the biggest naval architectural firm in the world. Gibbs & Cox had been responsible for an astonishing 75 percent of all U.S. Navy wartime shipping, both merchant and naval. Gibbs returned to Gibbs & Cox, which he noted gratefully to himself had only two bosses, himself and Frederic—no board of directors and no public relations image makers whatsoever.

Now Gibbs & Cox could turn its full attention to *America*'s successor. It was 1946 when John Franklin of U.S. Lines had summoned William and Frederic to his office to outline his suggestions for *United States*, describing the vessel he wanted as follows:

We must have an outstanding ship the public can get behind, like a Cup defender.... I want berths for two thousand passengers, accommodations of the same quality as *America*'s—not super, but very good—and the ability to make a round trip across the Atlantic every two weeks, like the *Queens*. It must gain the blessing of the Navy and the Maritime Administration by being quickly convertible to a transport. Efficiency and fuel consumption must be well in advance of anything known today.

After two years of planning and dreaming, William Gibbs completed the plans. One of his earliest collaborations involved working briefly with another naval architect outside the firm. His name was Theodore Ferris, and his New Yorker granddaughter Susan has one of his earliest drawings for *United States* framed on her living room wall.

Although that *United States* was nearly in train, another and historically neglected *United States* would momentarily intervene, as we shall see.

Australis was renamed *America* briefly, then became *Italis*. In early 1994 she ran aground on the Canary Island Fuerteventura and finally broke in half. Tacey managed to get aboard for a final visit to his favorite vessel. (Steve Tacey Collection)

ALUMINUM OF
52-S 53-S
ONLY

CHAPTER SEVEN

BUILDING UNITED STATES

It is in simple terms to combine the maximum driving power you can achieve with the lightest displacement compatible with the work the ship must do, and with the longest, finest, cleanest lines that will serve to make a good wholesome seakeeping ship.

—John R. Kane, Vice President, Newport News Shipbuilding

To the Big Ship and everything you've always wanted, doubled!

—William Francis Gibbs's favorite toast

Opposite: The day shift's end. Hundreds of workers descend from the huge vessel taking shape in the no. 10 Shipway at Newport News. The vessel grows at a phenomenal pace, being built and fitted out at the same time, with many hull elements prefabricated elsewhere. (**Newport News Shipbuilding Collection**)

craft, and cargo vessels understandably predominated. After VE Day and long before the Korean invasion of 1950, that particular newbuilding drought persisted, forcing the Navy Department to face up to a nagging reality: the country had no fast liner that, in case of wartime need, could be adapted as a hospital or troopship for immediate deployment.

To correct that lamentable omission, the department decided to subsidize construction of a trio of merchant vessels. For all three, quid pro quo of their federal funding would be instantaneous call to the colors should the need arise. *Constitution* and *Independence* would be built for American Export Line and the third, *United States*, would operate under the aegis of United States Lines.

There was to have been a preliminary *United States*, however, not the ocean liner SS (Steam Ship) *United States* indicated above but the USS *United States*. That additional letter preceding SS is crucial, betraying its role as a combat vessel, a United States Ship destined for the navy.

This particular newbuild was to be a "super-carrier," the largest ever conceived, with an island command center that could be retracted down into the hull. Her keel was laid in Newport News Shipway no. 11, the yard's largest, on Easter Monday 1949, April 18. Two numerals identified the vessel, NNS (Newport News Shipbuilding) hull no. 486 as well as her formal naval designation CVA-58.

One thousand and ninety feet (332 meters) overall—a hundred feet longer than her namesake ocean liner to come—and displacing 65,000 tons, her dimensions were mind-boggling. The hull would have a beam of 130 feet (40 meters) while her overhanging flight deck, extending farther over each side, would be 190 feet (58 meters) overall. Her draught was 37 feet (11 meters) and she would be able to steam at a brisk 33 knots, thanks to eight boilers driving a quartet of steam turbines, each capable of delivering 70,000 horsepower.

For ordnance, the vessel would boast eight 5-inch naval guns, a pair of them mounted defiantly on the bow, as well as formidable antiaircraft clout. From her capacious deck, USS *United States* would be able to launch up to eighteen two-engine B-29 bombers, each with a 110-foot wingspan and capable of delivering atomic bombs to targets up to

two thousand miles away. Nuclear missiles of the period weighed five tons apiece. In addition, the vessel was equipped with fifty-four conventional jet fighters.

The manpower required to operate that seagoing naval station would include a crew numbering just over three thousand, plus 2,480 air wing personnel. The behemoth's price tag would be $189 million. Of that sum, $152 million paid for construction while the balance of $37 million covered armaments and equipment. The yard's Shipway no. 11 had been equipped with triple rows of keel blocks and an accumulation of highest grade steel described as "forty load plate"; in other words, 40 pounds was the approximate weight of a 1-foot square slab. As the *New York Times* would report, her keel was laid with "a minimum of ceremony but a good deal of secrecy." In fact, the keynote descriptive seemed less secrecy than uncertainty.

The following Friday, only five days after the keel had been laid, a devastating bombshell erupted. On April 24, Secretary of Defense Louis Johnson, with whom President Truman had replaced departing James Forrestal, ordered construction to stop "at once and at the least possible cost to the government." (James Vincent Forrestal was both the last cabinet-level secretary of the navy and the first secretary of defense. Dismissed by President Truman on March 28, 1949, he suffered a nervous breakdown and was hospitalized on the sixteenth floor of Bethesda Naval Hospital. On May 22, the day of his scheduled discharge, his body was found on the roof of a first-floor covered walkway. The belt of a bathrobe was tied tightly around his neck. Apparently, after failing to hang himself, he had jumped to his death.)

In fact, when construction ceased, the navy's cost for its supercarrier would be about $5 million. Shipyard accountants suggested that the navy would have to pay $3 million plus 5 percent or 6 percent interest. Bowing to the inevitable, yard president J. B. Woodward temporized by telephone to the reporters: "Naturally, to have a job that we had started and felt well qualified to do but of course, the national interest must come first."

What triggered that abrupt turnabout was the U.S. Air Force's insistence that it was the most propitious deliverer of atomic bombs. B-36 bombers could drop their payloads well beyond the range of planes launched from a carrier. By way of immediate and indignant response, the navy insisted that smaller B-29s flying from supercarrier USS *United States*, laden with atomic weapons, could take off, fly to specified targets, and then return to their floating home base.

Perhaps part of the navy's inspiration arose from the epic wartime achievement of Colonel James Doolittle, who headed the first task force of twin-engined bombers ever launched from an aircraft carrier. That bold air strike on the Japanese mainland took place on April 18, 1942, only four months after Japan's attack on Pearl Harbor.

It is worth detailing briefly if only because its planning had been the result of seamless collaboration between the navy's Admiral Ernest J. King and Army Air Force chief General Henry "Hap" Arnold. In Pearl Harbor, sixteen B-25b twin-engined army bombers were loaded and lashed down onto USS *Hornet*'s flight deck. Then, in company with Admiral William F. Halsey's USS *Enterprise* and escorted by destroyers, the task force set sail for the enemy's homeland. There would be no return and retrieval of the aircraft once they had dropped their bombs; instead, Doolittle's crews were instructed to continue flying eastward and touch down at Chinese airfields.

Hornet had planned to approach within 400 miles of the Japanese mainland before launching the bombers. But when the American armada was 600 miles offshore, Japanese picket boats spotted it. Although most of those hostile craft were destroyed, Doolittle's element of surprise had been compromised, forcing his B-25s to take off earlier than anticipated.

The damage they managed to inflict on Tokyo and Nagasaki was minimal, but the psychological blow to Japan's high command was decisive. None of Doolittle's bomber squadron reached their Chinese objectives and several of their captured crews were summarily executed by the Japanese.

Postwar, the interservice gloves were off, that navy/air forces cooperation of 1942 forgotten. After VJ Day, the United States Army Air Forces decided arbitrarily that aircraft launched from carriers were outmoded; its giant B-36s, it was maintained, could drop atomic bombs from greater altitude and with superior accuracy compared with carrier-originated aircraft. The atomic bomb, the army authorities concluded publicly, rendered aircraft carriers obsolete.

Some idea of Johnson's strategic savvy can be gleaned from a shoot-from-the-hip declaration he made as newly appointed secretary of defense shortly after assuming office: "The Navy is on its way out. There's no reason for having a Navy and a Marine Corps. We'll never have any more amphibious operations. That does away with the Marine Corps. The Air Force can do anything the Navy can, so that does away with the Navy."

Thus spake the obtuse public servant who pulled the plug on USS *United States*. The moment construction of CVA-58 was halted, Johnson diverted the money that would have built her to fund additional fleets of B-36 bombers for the air force. Conversely, Forrestal had proclaimed in 1945 that successfully raising the Stars and Stripes atop Iwo Jima's Mount Suribachi ensured "a Marine Corps for the next 500 years."

Time and the early shortcomings of Korean strategy would deliver a coup de grâce to Secretary of Defense Johnson. His consistent downsizing of the country's naval capabilities made it clear that U.S. forces in Korea were being catastrophically shortchanged. In September 1950, following a nationwide political furor, he resigned from office. At the same time, mothballed carriers from World War II were rushed into service.

Even sweeter naval revenge occurred shortly thereafter. On July 12, 1951, only slightly more than two years after newbuilding CVA-58 had been summarily canceled, an order for CVA-59 was placed with Newport News Shipbuilding. Laid down in the same berth, Shipway no. 11, it became hull NNS no. 506 and would emerge from the yard as supercarrier USS *Forrestal*. Since then, fourteen more have entered service.

As a marine, I found it hard to absorb the banality of Secretary Johnson's sweeping dismissal of both the Corps as well as the entire United States Navy. A short time later, marines storming ashore at Inchon would help break open the Korean stalemate. Similarly, the present-day pivotal roles of aircraft carriers around the globe serve as heartening refutation of his hastily ill-conceived prediction. Battleships have disappeared but the carrier strike force remain the backbone of the navy's essential post–9/11 surveillance.

Although William Francis Gibbs had not been involved with the doomed supercarrier's design, we should remember that on the eve of World War II he had been asked by the Soviet Union to submit

A Newport News riveter driving home *United States*'s unique semi-steel/semi-aluminum rivets. He is assembling a composite wall. Next to him, ready for use, is the power wrench with which he will remove the nuts and bolts his chilled rivets must displace.
(The Mariners Museum, Newport News, VA)

plans for a Russian battleship. Significantly, he designed instead a huge aircraft carrier that, displacing 85,000 tons, could launch both bombers and fighters. Though the Russian navy rejected his submission, one must assume that he had to have first-hand awareness of CVA-58, the carrier that was never built.

And once the project had been canceled, what happened to all that steel? My surmise is that the refined steel plate assembled for USS *United States* might well have been reallocated by Newport News Shipbuilding for construction of SS *United States*. No hard evidence confirms this and the Newport News house organ, the *Shipyard Bulletin*, studiously avoids any reference to the matter. But I think it probable; at least Secretary Johnson could not co-opt those tons of forty-load plate to build B-36s.

So planning for both predecessor *America* and subsequent *United States* had to coincide with

Gibbs & Cox's epic wartime expansion. As already documented, the majority of the American navy's wartime armada had been designed by Gibbs & Cox. At the same time, drawings and specifications for both *America* and *United States* were also put into work. We have discussed the debut of the first; now comes the time to lay the keel for the second.

At 10 A.M. sharp on the chilly morning of February 8, 1950, a crane began lowering a 55-ton prefabricated keel section from high above down toward the floor of Shipway no. 10. Only inches above the surface it paused, and five minutes were allowed for shipyard photographers to record its hovering appearance before they were requested by loudspeaker to leave the dock. One hundred and eight feet (33 meters) long, the section was, in fact, an inverted T-shape, incorporating the keel's vertical member as well as its length of horizontal bottom plates. Like substantial steel knuckles, strengtheners would ensure retention of its right-angled shape.

That first section would then be joined by two others. Also lowered by crane, one extended forward, the other aft. Locking that trio of keel sections into perfect alignment was a demanding and pivotal procedure. Similar to the scrupulous positioning of outdated keel plates, they served as the hull's seminal elements. Had their direction departed from the keel's proposed vector by even a fraction of a millimeter, *United States*'s amplified hull would have been skewed fatally off course.

Already in place, delineated in broad stripes of bright yellow paint extended toward Shipway no. 10's fore and aft extremities, was an outline of Gibbs's 990-foot (302 meters) hull that, over the next sixteen and a half months, would rise above. When completed, *United States* would be categorized as what is described as Panamax, able to fit within the 1,000-foot-long locks of that strategic waterway. Exceeding a thousand feet overall by a fractional but crucial margin, neither of Cunard White Star's two *Queens* nor forthcoming *France* could pass through the canal, their ineligibility labeling

At 10 A.M. on the chilly morning of February 8, 1950, the first of three sections of keel plates was lowered by crane onto the bottom of Newport News Shipway no. 10. It was 108 feet (33 meters) overall with stout knuckles holding it rigidly upright. Two identical extensions, one aft and one forward, were later conjoined to complete the entire keel. (The Mariners Museum, Newport News, VA)

The keel already laid, hull plating first gathers amidships; the line of supportive steel flanking the hull plating is rigged to receive additional timber supports. Following the keel's forward thrust, timber scaffolding accumulates relentlessly. As the plating accumulates, the addition of a prefabricated section near the bow shows the vessel's profile emerging. (Newport News Shipbuilding Collection)

them post-Panamax. Crowding Shipway no. 10's margins were cords of wooden framing components that ultimately would surround and support the growing hull.

Despite its size and engineering complexity, *United States* would take shape relatively quickly, profiting from the improved pace of construction resulting from the assembly of prefabricated blocks. Significantly, Shipway no. 10's floor was perfectly flat. Once completed and christened, *United States* would neither slide nor plunge into the waters of Jamestown Bay; rather, they would be brought to her, flooding the dock and floating the hull off its keel blocks for the first time very early on the morning of her christening.

Perhaps the oddest thing about that keel laying, historically and traditionally a festive event, was that so few spectators were on hand. Quite simply, no invitations had been sent. Of course, both Gibbs brothers were present, so too John B. Woodward—always addressed familiarly as "J.B."—and William E. Blewett Jr., president and executive vice president of the shipyard, respectively. But there were no representatives of the Maritime Commission from Washington and not a soul from United States Lines' New York office. Inevitably, some photographers and newsreel cameramen were in evidence; in the manner of enterprising adherents of the fourth estate, they showed up uninvited.

In addition to her unprecedented speed, *United States* would involve a series of shipbuilding firsts, unique not only to American newbuilds but to newbuilds throughout the world. She would be the first totally air-conditioned ocean liner, her hull would be largely but not exclusively welded, she would have furnishings and fittings that were nonflammable, and she would have large parts of her superstructure and deck fittings fabricated of aluminum; moreover, additional aluminum elements would be employed all over the vessel.

As the first ocean liner to embrace aluminum in such quantity, completed *United States* would profit handsomely from an extraordinarily efficient power-to-weight ratio. In fact, construction of *United States* in the early 1950s involved the employment of some 2,000 tons of aluminum, more than in any other structure—maritime or municipal—in the world. Gibbs had specified the lightweight steel substitute not only for his towering funnels but also for davits, railings, lifeboats and

their oars, deck chairs, picture frames, and passenger cabin keys.

Every one of these keys was attached to an aluminum tag, tapering to a ring at the narrow end. At the broad end was imprinted *US Lines*, *New York* and, along the center, *SS United States*. Numbers mounted on every cabin door were aluminum as well, welded to a rectangular horizontal plaque. So, too, many of the rivets that attached shell plating to frames were partially fabricated of aluminum.

Long after *United States* was withdrawn from service, metallurgists devised for today's shipbuilders a means of successfully marrying steel to aluminum in one bruising procedure that fuses the two metals into a single compatible block. Nothing of the kind existed in the 1950s. Aboard *United States*, at every point where steel met aluminum, a protective insulation made of magnesia block was inserted to prevent electrolytic corrosion between the two metals.

There would be a vogue, among many cruise industry newbuilds of the 1980s, for extensive use of aluminum along upper decks. But over the years the practice has disappeared as shipyards renounced aluminum for a variety of reasons, foremost among them its expense, but also that it tended not to retain its shape and strength.

Despite *United States*'s largely welded hull, in addition to a quarter of a million steel rivets, it also required 1,200,000 rivets fabricated of a contemporary steel/aluminum alloy. Like their steel counterparts, they had to be heated to high temperatures so that the steel and aluminum would be effectively melded. Then these same rivets would have to be chilled just before being driven to retain maximum strength. Because those aluminum alloy rivets had to be kept cold up to the very last moment, they were delivered to riveting teams stacked inside wheeled refrigerated carts with four round lidded access holes atop them, exactly like flavor choices on Good Humor wagons. Sixty-five thousand of those composite rivets would stitch together each funnel.

Ocean liners are, paradoxically, very public yet very private in the same instance; *United States* served as a prime example of that inherent duality. To impress journalists, critics, passengers, and spectators, her broadside view had to compel. Ranged along the length of her various deck levels were seven arresting verticals, listed here in descending order of prominence.

Inescapably first were two towering, red, white, and blue aluminum funnels, the number 1, at 60 feet (18.3 meters), a little taller than number 2. They were adorned with the definitive livery of the United States Lines, made up of the primary and instantly identifiable colors of both a lighthouse and the Stars and Stripes. They were, in both design and arresting intensity, similar to the color scheme that had enriched *Leviathan*'s funnels, first painted in Shipway no. 1 of the same yard more than two decades earlier. Atop the brilliant red shafts, a broad white band separated lower rubrication from the dark blue of the funnel tops.

But there the similarity to *Leviathan*'s funnel trio ended. The number 1 funnel had a small post atop its forward end while surrounding the after

ends of both funnels were projecting sampans, sloping flat fins designed to loft stack gases above and away from the after decks. Since the funnels' shafts were tear-shaped—round forward and pointed aft—those sampans extended behind the funnels as horizontal caps. Glimpsed from below, either on board or from the pier, their prominent, right-angled after corners conveyed a pleasing rectangular finish.

The funnels themselves were touted by Newport News officials as the tallest ever to appear on a liner. The only competitor would have to have been Hamburg America Lines' *Imperator* of 1913, the company's precursor to *Vaterland*. Her three funnels as originally installed were each nearly 70 feet (21 meters) tall, slightly higher than Gibbs's pair on *United*

A view along the starboard side of a promenade deck. The welter of cables and hoses is significantly lower than usual because of the vessel's prefabrication. A shower of sparks to the left indicates that a worker with a grinding wheel is smoothing the edge of some jagged steel. (The Mariners Museum, Newport News, VA)

States. The effect was not only lofty but, because they were so thin, essentially fragile looking.

Fragile or no, it became clear on completion of her maiden voyage that *Imperator* was alarmingly top-heavy. In November 1913 she had returned to the shipyard and all three stacks were shortened by 3 meters, less than a year after she had entered service. So for the bulk of *Imperator/Berengaria*'s career, her stacks were no longer record breakers, leaving Gibbs's *United States* funnels legitimately the tallest ever.

They never seemed skinny because of their bulk, boasting a footprint far exceeding *Imperator*'s originals. *Imperator*'s fore and aft stack dimension was 25½ feet (8 meters) long and 18 feet (5.5 meters) wide. Gibbs's paired stacks had a fore and aft configuration of 60 feet (18.3 meters) and a 55-foot (16.8 meters) beam, creating a substantial presence crowding the Boat Deck.

There is an interesting and revealing footnote about a pivotal design change that remedied the final and successful configuration of both of *United States*'s funnel sampans. The story was related to me by Bill Lee, younger brother of the man responsible, Howard E. Lee Jr.

An apprentice when he first joined the NNS workforce, Howard had already started as an apprentice at the yard in the early 1940s before he and most of his contemporaries resigned to join the armed forces. After returning to civilian life, the GI Bill enabled Howard Lee to obtain a bachelor of science degree in electrical engineering at Clemson College in South Carolina. He had served as a radar man so he decided to transfer to engineering. He also became an amateur pilot, flying small aircraft from the airstrip formerly adjacent to Newport News' Kecoughtan Avenue. In the words of his younger sibling Bill: "Howard applied the concept of 'lift' associated with airfoils to shipbuilding."

In 1950, back on the Newport News payroll, Lee was assigned to the Engine Technical Department. Thus it was that he found himself involved with tests being performed, using the same wind tunnel in which a scale model of *America* had been placed to improve her after-deck smoke clearance. Those test results had instigated the abrupt lengthening of her funnels.

Now the same facility was being employed to test hull no. 488. The seldom-used facility stood no more than a yard away from the shipyard's main office building and, whenever tests were under way, quantities of smoke poured from the housing's after end. No chimney had ever been rigged but, as every shipyard building was clad with sheet metal, the walls were not damaged. Moreover, smoke of various kinds emerging from a variety of shipyard infrastructures was commonplace.

The required stack gases were generated inside a vertical 4-inch pipe immersed in a water-filled cooling jacket situated beneath the model. After they had been filled with chips of white pine and ignited, smoke poured out of both funnels in satisfactorily dense white plumes.

Lee's job was subjecting a ⅛-inch-to-the-foot scale model of *United States* to varying wind strengths as both funnels emitted streams of smoke. For the purpose of filming those tests, hull no. 488 had had its flanks striped with diagonal yellow/black hash marks, slightly suggestive of dazzle paint adorning the sides of World War I liners. It served as a yardstick to record and measure the length of smoke streams trailing aft. Crucial was keeping those streams aloft for as long as possible.

After screening the filmed footage repeatedly, Howard Lee discovered a means of extending those smoke lengths to prevent them from dropping prematurely and fouling the vessel's after decks. He found that they could be made to stay aloft much longer simply by adjusting the slope of the sampans.

All of William Gibbs's sampan configurations, including *America* and the quartet of *Santa* ships for Grace Lines, had been designed to slope downward, conforming to the modernistic look of their funnels. But Lee discovered that when he leveled those sampan slopes on the *United States* model, keeping them parallel to the horizontal plane of the keel, the smoke flew aft for a longer distance.

Gibbs was invited into that wind tunnel facility to see how admirably Lee's modified sampans behaved but only acknowledged the improvement with a grunt, one of his famously monosyllabic expressions signaling approval. He incorporated that new sampan shape into both funnels' design schema. It became one of the few correctional changes devised by a subordinate for one of the sometimes prickly naval architect's design mandates. Gibbs never acknowledged Lee's invaluable contribution, a surprising deviation from his instinctive politesse.

Shipyard workers painting *United States*'s rudder. Hanging a rudder is one of every shipyard's worst chores because the stern's overhang prevents cranes from delivering the rudder into position. Sky hooks—U-shapes welded onto the exterior stern plating for the vessel's life—are used in conjunction with chain hoists and brute force.
(The Mariners Museum, Newport News, VA)

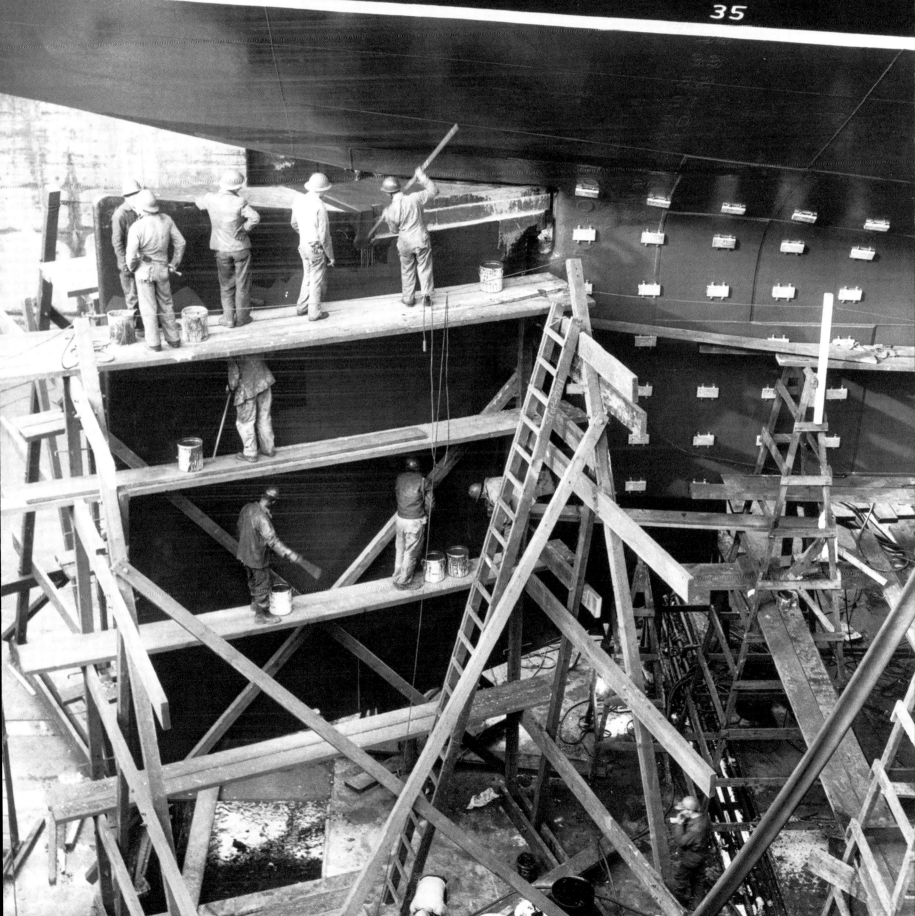

The dashing rake and radiance of the twin stacks were heroic and jaunty. As both passengers and publicists would learn, they cried out to be photographed from every direction, rising atop what seemed a veritable javelin of a liner.

The second most prominent vertical was a sculpted silver-gray foremast rising directly above the bridge. It was the vessel's only one; there was no after mast as there had been aboard *America*. The revolving radar scanner at its summit matched the height of the stacks. Clearly, despite the length of his soaring paired funnels, for subsidiary verticals Gibbs opted for lower. Whereas both *America*'s masts and her king post quartet towered high above the decks, *United States*'s single mast and king posts were shorter, almost chunky. Height abbreviation was a popular design trick that naval architects sometimes employed not only to enhance the profile but also to convey a subtle message about performance. The unmistakable visual effect suggested that *United States*

was somehow hunkered down, ready to spring forward at speed on the instant.

Four, also silver gray, freestanding king posts—two forward, two aft—served as central crane elements for handling cargo and mail. Once again, they were far shorter than those aboard *America*. All those verticals rose from gleaming superstructure boasting the repetitious intricacy of steel dental molding. Its topmost garlanding included a serial lifeboat row; beneath that were the vertical hash marks of public room fenestration. Very long terraced and railed after decks extended toward the stern. Forward, the white-banded foc's'le head was supported by a powerfully raked stem, the profile component that most hinted at the vessel's astonishing mechanical prowess to come.

Those were the exterior structural elements that created the vessel's bravura public spectacle. Below was the unseen, within what is often described as "the belly of the beast." Concealed well below the white superstructure, hidden inside

One of Elaine Kaplan's exquisitely engineered five-bladed propellers traveling by crane into position. Two of them, mounted on the vessel's outboard shafts, would contribute to her remarkable speed. So, too, those projecting blades mandated *United States*'s oddly shaped underwater stern profile on both sides. (The Mariners Museum, Newport News, VA)

yards of anonymous black hull plating, were elements of Gibbs's incredible maritime power train, linked by copper cabling and lagged piping, an intricate assemblage of boilers, turbines, gears, bearings, shafts, and propellers that, in deafening concert, would produce and deliver *United States*'s unbelievable rate of speed. As far as Gibbs was concerned, aspects of this ultimate "big ship" featured in his favorite toast would remain shrouded in mystery long after he was gone, a purposely concealed manifest of awe-inspiring power.

In truth, the secret of her phenomenal performance was the vessel's imbalanced corollary of displacement to horsepower. Like a successful runner or hurdler, *United States* boasted extraordinary musculature within a lightweight, well-toned body. Installed inside her radiant public profile was an innovative powerhouse producing on demand a quarter of a million horsepower. Boilers delivering a raging cauldron of steam at a pressure of over 925 pounds per square inch drove four incredible turbines destined for transatlantic immortality. And beneath the after hull, Gibbs had two additional secret weapons, about which more to come.

Capitalizing on strict naval security, Gibbs had managed to keep details of his design top secret. Construction photographs remained strictly classified and a builder's model he grudgingly displayed in U.S. Lines' Manhattan headquarters had its underwater strakes fully concealed inside a plywood shield, transforming it from a full hull to a waterline model.

The startling innovations that plywood hid were twofold, both contributing to the vessel's extraordinary turn of speed. First, the hull's bottom plating beneath the extended stern was completely flat. As sufficient propeller thrust was delivered, *United States* would actually levitate in the ocean, planing up toward the surface like a giant surfboard, reducing drag phenomenally and permitting faster passage.

A second innovation would also help. The two inboard propellers were fashioned with four blades while the outer pair bore five. In fact, the necessity to expand the confines of the vessel's after hull to accommodate that propeller quartet created what one mystified newspaper reporter described as the "weird" outward bulge of her after plating. But that, too, disappeared behind the plywood with which Gibbs concealed his hull's underwater configuration from the public. All four of those propellers—

which Newport News old-timers always describe as "wheels"—had been designed and fashioned by a crack engineer on Gibbs & Cox's staff, an incredibly competent woman named Elaine Kaplan. She was, Gibbs once pointed out, "the equal of any technical person I've ever known."

Another distinct construction advantage from which Gibbs profited was that fitting out proceeded in tandem with construction of the hull. Customarily, the two procedures are consecutive. Only after the completed hull has been launched does fitting out usually begin, as anonymous echoing steel interiors are clad with interior finish, plastered, painted, carpeted, curtained, and furnished. But because of *United States*'s modular construction at the bottom of a dry dock, she would be 70 percent fitted out by the time of her christening, complete with superstructure, funnels, masts, and (though still inactive) propellers. Another invaluable plus of dry dock construction is that because the hull takes shape below ground level, shipyard cranes need not be so tall.

One cannot describe *United States*'s interiors without dwelling on Gibbs's safety-conscious naval architectural design, buttressed by his stringent rules regarding flammability. We should start with *United States*'s public rooms, not their fitted-out finish delivered by interior designers but their physical dimensions and arrangements. Most of them departed determinedly from the transatlantic norm.

Two separate and very different marketing opportunities were pursued aboard most passenger vessels, whether dispatched between old world and new or out to the Far East. The first, the essential mundanity of the cabin, was the very antithesis of the second, the decorative dynamics of public rooms and decks.

Cabins are not only bedrooms; they often serve as passenger retreats. Most are ingeniously but seldom elaborately wrought. They must meet the demanding requirements of bedrooms within a moving structure that is afloat, in which occupancy is never restricted to one night but an extended tenancy of at least a week. Repetitious jolting and swaying is commonplace. Hence, sensibly designed cabins have heavy furniture, often bolted to the deck. But the visual appeal of those bedsits without kitchens makes for negligible marketing fodder.

Offsetting those limitations were the promotional possibilities of every vessel's shared spaces. Whatever the company's nationality, public room spreads always offered lavish perspectives. Drop-dead impact and decorative overkill became, faute de mieux, an intrinsic part of every company's marketing strategy. Brochures and advertisements alike portrayed lounges, dining rooms, and corridors larded with ever more compelling extravagance.

Aboard post–World War I vessels, consider the encrusted elegance of Italian liners such as *Saturnia* or *Giulio Cesare*, also *Bremen* and *Europa*'s ultramodern ballrooms of 1929 or the interiors those great 1930s rivals *Normandie* and original *Queen Mary*. First class passengers aboard *Normandie*, the French Line's art deco masterpiece, occupied an incomparable assemblage of public rooms, staircases, and hallways like nothing ever seen before (or since). They remain utterly unique: heroic, soaring vistas encompassed remarkable dimensions and unparalleled ostentation. All of those largely double-height spaces conveyed incomparable grandeur and elegance. Tomas Tilberg, a Floridian naval architect whose Swedish father, Robert, designed *Queen Mary 2*, told me once that, to the present, *Normandie* vibes can still be detected throughout many contemporary interiors.

All those predictable design clichés were studiously avoided aboard *United States*. This was primarily a naval auxiliary: drama was out, dependability was in. To start with, only one public room boasted a double-height ceiling. First class's Dining Saloon incorporated a musician's gallery overlooking its tall central section. And a modest round dome was incorporated into the deckhead above the Ballroom's dance floor. But apart from those singular exceptions every other interior space topped out at a relentlessly conservative height.

Even the most cursory inspection of the vessel betrayed serious, naval sinews. Long corridors were frequently interrupted by purposely arranged jogs for additional structural strength. Every doorway was equipped with a cutaway panel in the lowest corner across from the hinges to allow for deployment of a working fire hose through the closed door, if necessary. Staircases for passengers and crew alike tended to steepness and corridors were essentially narrow. The very texture of the vessel's interior walls and public rooms seemed metallic and clean swept, almost antiseptic. This was not only Marckwald's but Gibbs's preference as well.

My friend David Pike is a dedicated *United States* aficionado. He never sailed on her but collects every photograph he can and fabricates elaborate scale models. But even this Gibbs disciple once wrote me, "I like her lines, her story and her speed but hate her interiors! I soooo love the art deco interiors of *QM*, *QE*, *Caronia*, *Normandie*, and *Ile De France* etc. but the *Big U* reminds me of a doctor's waiting room when I was growing up."

Fitting-out components were either preassembled elsewhere or arrived at Shipway no. 10 for transfer by crane onto or into the hull. Although shower stalls arrived as prefabricated units, Marinite wall sections were loaded on board for installation. No less than half a million square feet of asbestos were installed between every cabin partition, fire-safety enrichment that would prove a daunting disadvantage during the vessel's later years.

In the extensive galley servicing all three classes of passengers, prefabrication was impossible because cauldrons, urns, fryers, grills, mixers, and peelers had to be positioned arbitrarily within the appropriate sections adjacent to the correct rotating circular doorways through which stewards carried laden trays to reach first, cabin, or tourist class dining rooms.

Gibbs's fire phobia was perfectly understandable. He had watched *Normandie* burn on the north side of Pier 88 in February 1942. And once the gutted vessel had capsized it was he who mandated the means of her incredible salvage: removal of masts, funnels, and superstructure down to the strength deck as well as recompartmenting the hull.

Gibbs was determined that there should be nothing in the decor of his new U.S. Lines vessel that could possibly burn. To that end, he tried to get Theodore Steinway to build him aluminum pianos but was turned down. So he publicized the fact that the only wood anywhere aboard *United States* was found in every piano casing and in the galley's chopping blocks. In fact, those pianos and chopping blocks became one of the vessel's most tiresome public relations mantras. But wooden handles on galley knives and wooden scrubbing brushes were apparently overlooked; so, too, bakers' rolling pins were made of wood. Balsa wood was packed inside the vessel's bilge keels and lignum vitae bearings were housed in her propeller bossings, but Gibbs dismissed these latter exceptions as not being located within passenger spaces.

Elsewhere, he was ruthless. Instead of teak, the ship's decks were covered with a bright green, nonflammable material called Neotex. When Commodore Manning was presented with a reclining

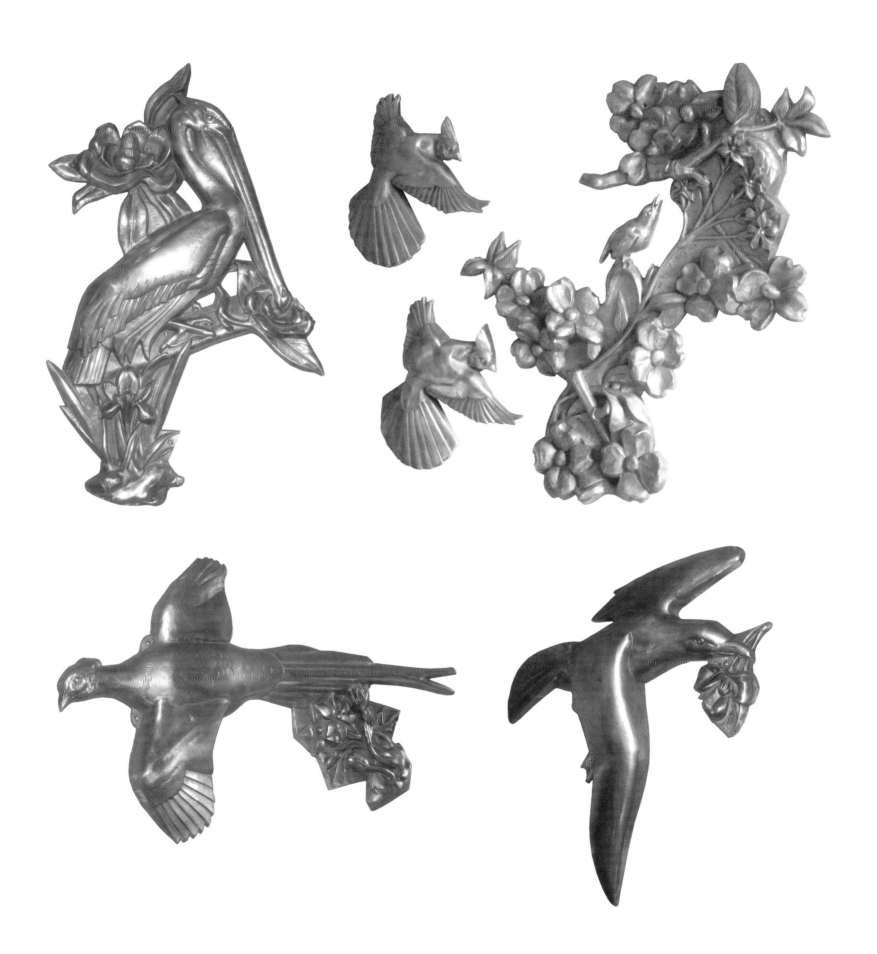

chair for his day cabin, Gibbs ordered it removed because of its interior wooden framing. So, too, free Philco radios presented to all the officers were returned because of their mahogany cabinets. Occasionally, violations of the no-wood rule were dealt with more indulgently. One of the vessel's bakers had constructed a little supplementary wooden shelf in his bakery. Gibbs removed it without comment. The next time the vessel tied up, he brought on board an identical but nonflammable replacement made entirely of aluminum, fabricated in Gibbs & Cox's model shop.

Truth be told, Gibbs violated his own rule every time he embarked aboard *United States*. Because of his inveterate superstition, he always carried surreptitiously in an inside pocket a six-inch wooden ruler to knock on in case he uttered something that he felt might tempt fate.

The U.S. Lines president John Franklin wanted the designers who had masterminded *America*'s interiors to do the same for his newest flagship, thus the firm Smyth, Urquhart & Marckwald was signed on again as overall decorator of *United States*.

Dorothy Marckwald had been involved in ocean liner interior design for years, responsible for twenty-two vessels, the two most famous Grace Line's *Santa Rosa* and *Santa Paula*, both designed by Gibbs & Cox. Marckwald's design imprimatur was brightly colored fabrics and stylishly upholstered furniture. One of her famous decorative bywords was never to use greenish yellow anywhere because it might well remind people of the state of their stomachs during rough crossings. Aboard *America*, Marckwald had instigated the famous Duck Suite, which Mrs. Constance Smith would reproduce aboard *United States*.

The designation of the Duck Suite was U (Upper Deck) 89, one of fourteen of the most spacious suites on board. Six of them were grouped amidships in the center of the vessel. The Duck Suite was aftermost on the starboard side, composed, when needed, of three adjoining cabins: U87, U89, and U91 could be deployed together as a lavish suite. Smith had executed many murals on canvas and paper aboard *America* but on *United States*, adhering to the fireproof mandate, she painted on aluminum leaf instead, portraying the ducks in question afloat on a tranquil pond. It was the suite invariably occupied by the Windsors when they sailed. Across the alleyway was a row of

inside singles, three of which housed the couple's maid, valet, and an iron and ironing board. The duchess insisted that her bed linen be ironed afresh after each night's sleep.

There was a second ornithological display in another suite on board, the work of a young Polish enamelist named Mira Jedwabnik. She had created the round plaques atop the tables in the smoking room, prettily reflecting stars in the night sky overhead. Her twenty-four individual round plaques adhering to the walls of another suite were not ducks but varieties of native North American birds.

Although I touch on the vessel's famous suites in this chapter, I trust readers will understand that, for the most part, I prefer withholding further decorative comment about *United States*'s public rooms, cabins, corridors, and decks until after she has entered service. To my mind, comprehension no less than appreciation of a ship's decor demands the presence of the vessel's occupants—passengers and crew alike—surrounded by and functioning within a conventional mid-Atlantic venue. Describing the colors and configuration of the smoking room, for instance, will make infinitely more sense when the song of the shaker can be heard as well as the riffle of shuffled cards and the rattle of backgammon dice, every one of those evocative sounds buttressed by shipboard's inescapable lift and creak.

Similarly, the most convincing evaluation of a dining room demands that provisions have been dispatched onto elevators from reefers below, that ranges, grills, and urns are fully operational, that one can smell shipboard meals being prepared, plated, and delivered from galley to table by deft stewards. Similarly, dancing couples twirling around the Ballroom should be moving in responsive synchronicity to live music produced by musicians seated and playing on the bandstand.

In sum, however new and technically advanced a vessel, rest assured that life at sea aboard *United States* will duplicate every ocean liners' atmosphere of yore. I trust readers will be comfortable with this hypothesis. Only after archetypal passenger/crew symbioses have been established and meshed into place will the vessel's 'tween deck components make the most decorative sense.

There was one fitting-out hiccup that sent shock waves around the yard and also up in New York at both Gibbs & Cox and United States Lines headquarters. On September 16, 1950, the day immediately after the Inchon, Korea, landings, the Joint

Chiefs of Staff ordered the Maritime Administration to alert Newport News: abandon hull no. 488's peacetime fitting out as an ocean liner and proceed immediately to troopship design instead. Apparently, the ultimately positive results of General MacArthur's bold end run had not yet emerged; Congress and the navy alike felt that America's largest and fastest vessel should be readied for wartime contingency. Reflecting identical ominous urgency, at the same time, twenty-five mothballed Victory ships were activated and ordered ready for service. That jarring Washington edict would not create design difficulties for Gibbs & Cox because planning for the vessel's combat mode had long been in readiness. It was peacetime suppliers all over the country who would be most discommoded.

One and a half months later, however, that potential call to the colors was just as abruptly rescinded. On November 2, Secretary of Defense George C. Marshall advised Secretary of Commerce Charles Sawyer that the Joint Chiefs had reevaluated their September 16 decision and decided that work inside hull no. 488 should proceed as before. U.S. Lines President Franklin was as vastly relieved as everyone else. "We are delighted," he announced jubilantly, "to have our ship back!"

There were no further strategic interruptions. The following spring, in late June 1951, hull no. 488, nearly fitted out as an ocean liner, would be ready for christening and launching.

An aerial view at Newport News shows both *America* nearest the camera and, separated by an aircraft carrier fitting out, from NNS hull no. 488, not yet officially *United States*, with her number 1 funnel still unclad. (Charles Anderson Collection)

CHAPTER EIGHT

CHRISTENING, TRIALS, AND MAIDEN

We wanted to build it, the Navy wants it and it is absolutely necessary for the merchant marine, for national defense and the country's prestige on the seas.

—Vice Admiral William W. Smith, Chairman, Maritime Commission

We wanted to break away from the old nip-and-tuck, half-a-knot seesaw the liners before us had played. We wanted a record as modern and clean as the lines of the vessel herself.

—Chief Engineer William Kaiser

The meek shall inherit the earth—if they're nimble.

—William Francis Gibbs

Opposite: With its cover in place, crews suspended on bosun's chairs put a second coat of paint around the number 1 funnel's white band. (Newport News Shipbuilding Collection)

The first seminal event of every ship's life is laying the keel. For the Big U, *three consecutive keel*

sections had been deposited by crane onto the floor of Newport News' Shipway no. 10 at ten o'clock on the morning of February 8, 1950. She had grown from that modest beginning at a spectacular rate, crowding the confines of her berth; once final hull sections were attached, 15 feet (4.5 meters) of bow and stern overhung each end of the dock.

Christening, the next significant milestone after keel laying, would take place just over sixteen and a half months later, on June 23, 1951. A veritable forest of staging had been disassembled and removed from the dock, lumber in sufficient quantity, the *Shipyard Bulletin* calculated, to build a 2,000-ton wooden vessel 235 feet (71.5 meters) long. On June 22, the day previous, the dock had been partially flooded to a depth of 21 feet for the first time. Only then could the watertight integrity of all hull no. 488's underwater compartments be rigorously confirmed.

The next morning, at 0430 hours on christening day, more water was admitted. Half an hour later, the third largest ocean liner in the world was afloat. At once, the after gate beneath the stern was withdrawn and the vessel was dragged by cable sufficiently far out of its berth for inclination tests. Not until 10 A.M. was she winched back inside and positioned carefully, her cutwater snugged up to what had become a spectator arena. Like a red, white, and blue spinnaker, a billowing cascade of bunting adorned the bow.

That Shipway no. 10 had been fully flooded early that morning delighted William Francis Gibbs. As a result, not one of thousands of assembling spectators or reporters would be able to decipher anything about his vessel's secret underwater configuration.

As opposed to keel laying's February chill, June 23 was sunny and humid. The 46th and 50th

Right: The top of one of *United States*'s funnels is still on the ground before being hoisted atop the shaft. Once there, it will serve as a perfect bird's-eye view. (William Miller Collection)

Opposite: Under construction, the number 1 funnel reveals its interior plumbing. (Newport News Shipbuilding Collection)

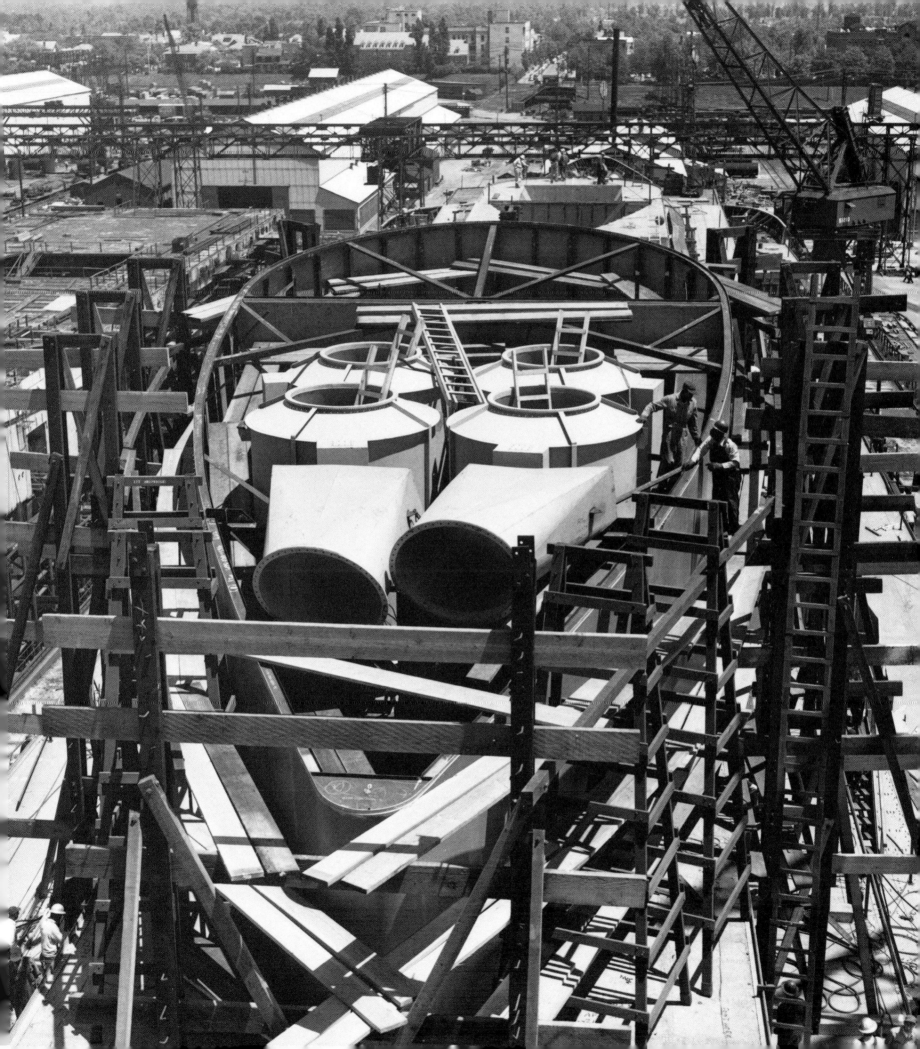

Street gates were opened at 11 A.M. sharp and the public started crowding into the dock's dry area. Although an attendance of around thirty thousand had been anticipated, only a third that number showed up; the overriding humidity inevitably reduced attendance. What visitors described as the formidable "knife edge" of hull no. 488's bow remained the compelling and undisputed centerpiece; in truth, it was not a knife edge at all but comfortably graspable by a single hand.

Spectators discovered they enjoyed novel and gratifying proximity to the hull. Crowds witnessing a plunging launch must stand or sit relatively far from the ways. But those inside Shipway no. 10 that hot June morning jostled to within feet of the vessel.

The ceremony's most crucial prop, a Champagne bottle, vintage unknown, was suspended on a beflagged line attached to the forepeak high above. Several large platforms, also bunting bedecked, had been erected. Center stage was the speaker's platform, already sprouting its microphone cluster. A railed rectangle with staircase ascents, the platform had been positioned directly beneath and within easy reach of the prow. Just to its right, taller but of surprisingly modest area, was a camera and press platform, achievable by ladder only. As christening time approached, it became jammed with the ungainly tripodded newsreel cameras of the day.

The 50th Army band from nearby Fort Munroe was accommodated on yet a third bunting-clad platform a short distance to starboard. As always, the musicians had a capital view and their music filled those sometimes endless waiting moments that every christening audience knows too well. Playing out beneath that merciless sun, they suffered cruelly from the heat, kitted out in woolen uniforms, caps, and Sam Browne belts.

They were not alone in their discomfort. As the sun ascended over the increasingly airless dock, heat and humidity became oppressive. By day's end more than twenty spectators would require treatment for heat prostration. As though underscoring the vessel's naval resonance, visible in neighboring Shipway no. 9 rose the gray-painted island of dry-docked carrier *Lake Champlain*. More naval resonance: prominent among the spectator

crowd were dozens of uniformed men, not only officers in whites with black/gold shoulder boards but enlisted swabbies, also clad in whites. Though they mingled with hundreds of shirtsleeved civilians, that christening remained indubitably and overwhelmingly a navy show.

Hull no. 488 was the first ocean liner in the world built in a dry dock. Like so many of Gibbs's inspirations, it set an example for every other shipyard. Passenger hulls these days profit from what might be described as stealth launches. Once the dry dock in which they have taken shape is flooded, today's newbuilds float almost imperceptibly off keel blocks rather than plunge spectacularly down sloping ways into the water.

The launch master wanted the vessel pulled out of the dock at precisely low slack water. She would have to move from the berth immediately after being christened, requiring the godmother to be as tightly cued and deft as though dealing with a plunging launch. Once named, the vessel would recede at once, impelled, in this event, not by gravity but by winches, moving her bow out of reach with the same irreversible finality. A half dozen tugs lined up outside were in place, ready to maneuver SS *United States* south to her fitting-out pier the moment she emerged. Just prior to that exit the Champagne bottle *had to shatter*.

Although the special excursion trains that brought government contingents from Washington arrived later than expected, nothing was delayed. The railways' predictable tardiness had been factored into the yard's scheduling. Visitors were bused for early and hasty luncheons at local hotels, then to the yard and Shipway no. 10.

Awarded the honor of christening hull no. 488 was Lucile Connally, second wife of the Texas senator Tom Connally. Mrs. Connally's two matrons of honor were her daughters, Mrs. Arthur E. Keyes and Mrs. Edward L. Cochrane. The three of them, clutching wilting bouquets, stood center stage on the platform beneath the bow as speakers and VIPs alike thronged the ascending staircases.

An orgy of speechifying would open the proceedings, some seemingly interminable and long-winded, branded succinctly in the nation's capital as stemwinders. It seemed counterproductive programming for a christening preliminary. One of that ceremony's delights, no less than the excitement of seeing an enormous mass about to move for the first time, is its brevity and simplicity. The

Opposite and left: A specially printed booklet documenting details of the christening. Inside was a studio portrait of Lucile Connally, wife of the retiring Texas senator and godmother of *United States*. (Michael G. Jedd Collection)

thousands assembling had come to see a ship named and set afloat; burdening them with a dose of political posturing beforehand tended to vitiate things.

The launch master had explicitly cued Fort Munroe's bandmaster. At exactly fifteen minutes past noon, having just completed a Sousa march with a flourish, he struck up the national anthem. Those in the crowd either saluted or clamped damp palm to sweating shirt. Then the crowd quieted as loudspeakers crackled and hummed into life.

First at the microphone was J. B. Woodward, Newport News' president. After quoting Mansfield's poem describing *Queen Mary* as "that rampart of a ship," he reported that hull no. 488 would not "glide in thunder from the slip" but would be launched like no other. After further remarks, he introduced John Franklin, president of the United States Lines, who spoke at emotional length about his father, General Philip Franklin, who had headed the company before him.

Then Senator Connally, husband of the vessel's godmother, who would be retiring from the Senate shortly after thirty-one years' service, spoke at effusive length. Like most senators, perhaps especially those from the South, mellifluous oratory was almost second nature; if his speech could not

Beneath the bunting-clad bow, the launch platform complete with waiting godmother and her attendants. To the right, an extremely crowded camera platform has been erected. Newport News' hull no. 488 is about to become officially *United States*. On the speaker's platform, speeches have already begun and, shortly thereafter, Lucile Connally will christen the vessel. Denied inclusion as a speaker (or did he reject it?), William Francis Gibbs stands instead anonymously among the spectators. (The Mariners Museum, Newport News, VA)

quite be construed as a filibuster, it occasionally seemed so. At long last, the senator introduced his wife Lucile, the godmother.

Before we deal with her stellar performance, it has always struck me that, once again, there was a glaring absence on the speaker's platform: no turn at the microphone had been scheduled for the man whose genius had conceived and designed the vessel. But by the same token William Francis Gibbs was seldom at ease in pivotal social gatherings. The accompanying photograph says it all, revealing Gibbs in shirtsleeves, looking curiously detached and confused, standing on the dock floor just below and, incidentally, well away from the speaker's platform.

Finally, the time had arrived for Lucile Connally's moment in the spotlight. She performed with competence and brio. Before grasping the bottle, Mrs. Connally recited the traditional benediction clearly into the microphone: "I christen this vessel *United States*. May God bless her and all who sail in her." The next *Shipyard Bulletin* reported that she seized the Champagne bottle and gave it "a lusty swing." Thrusting it against the steel bow only inches away, she shattered it with one punishing blow.

One of the best of dozens of christening photographs was taken by Alfred Eisenstaedt shooting for *Life* magazine. He had waited patiently (and uncomfortably) perched on a precariously narrow wooden stringer right below the launch platform, only inches above the water. Balanced thus on one foot for a full hour, he waited and snapped his shutter just as the bottle broke, capturing a dramatic and perfect exposure.

The unease triggered among the maritime fraternity by a stubbornly unbreaking Champagne bottle is legendary. There had been a recent embarrassment at Newport News during a warship christening when the bottle had resisted every effort to break it, not only by the godmother after several tries in vain, but also by a helpful flag officer who after a dozen more brutal attempts did no better. The secret, of course, was heavily scoring the bottle beforehand with a file, which, in that event, had apparently not been done.

Once christened, no longer hull no. 488 but veritably *United States*, multiple winches on either side of the pier were activated. Cued by the christening, shipyard workers started the vessel into motion as though she were sliding down conventional

ways, drawing just-named *United States* firmly away from the launch platform and out toward the James River and her gauntlet of waiting tugs. Although under tow, *United States* afloat seemed a veritable red, white, and blue javelin of an ocean liner.

Already selected as her master was equally colorful Commodore Harry Manning, a former navy man. He had begun his maritime training as a seaman on New York's nautical school ship *Newport* back in 1914; next, he became a crewman aboard the sailing barque *Dirigio*. Then Manning was posted, as already noted, aboard *Leviathan* while undergoing final conversion from troopship to ocean liner, also at Newport News. There followed a brief assignment aboard *President Roosevelt* and, shortly thereafter, he would be appointed first officer of *America* and subsequently its master.

Harry Manning's wanderlust was not confined to ships. In 1930 he'd qualified as an aeroplane pilot as well. Manning loved publicity, sometimes flying above his former ships to double-check their performance.

During that aeronautical phase, he had two close calls with death, one theoretical, the other actual. He had volunteered to serve as navigator for pilot Amelia Earhart's 1937 attempt to circumnavigate the globe by air. By good fortune, when they landed at Hawaii's Hickam Field that July, it turned out that Manning's U.S. Lines leave was about to expire; prevented from continuing, he was replaced by a man named Fred Noonan. Had Manning remained as Earhart's navigator, he would have vanished as completely and mystifyingly over the Pacific as she and Noonan did; or, perhaps, he might have navigated her safely to her next landing. We shall never know.

His piloting days ended abruptly the following year when he suffered a catastrophic crash at Roosevelt Field. He was so badly injured that for several days he was not expected to live. That put paid to Manning's flying career.

In 1940, while serving as master of U.S. Lines' *Washington*, Manning played a crucial role in World War II's first American/German confrontation. A U-boat surfaced and its captain ordered the vessel to disembark her passengers into lifeboats before he torpedoed her. Manning refused to do so, insisting on his rights as master of a neutral ship. After successfully defying the U-boat's commanding officer, Captain Manning continued his crossing.

In 1944 he was posted shoreside briefly, assigned to the U.S. Maritime Service's radio training station on New York's Hoffman Island. But in 1947 he was reappointed master of the *Washington* after it had been released from U.S. Navy war service. Subsequently, after serving briefly as master of *America* until 1948, he was relieved and transferred to Newport News, where he helped oversee construction of

United States. Finally, with William Gibbs's and the Department of the Navy's approval, the pinnacle of his seagoing career was officially conferred, elevation to the rank of commodore, United States Lines. Aged fifty-five, Harry Manning was given the prestigious command of the company's latest flagship. A dandy-looking man, Manning was short and, according to one of his

The moment Lucile Connally breaks the bottle, attached winches take up the slack and move *United States* briskly out of Shipway no. 10. Tugs take control of the vessel and move her safely to the nearby fitting-out pier.
(Newport News Shipbuilding Collection)

Trials
1952

UNITED STATES

S. S. UNITED STATES

NEWPORT NEWS SHIPBUILDING AND DRY DOCK COMPANY

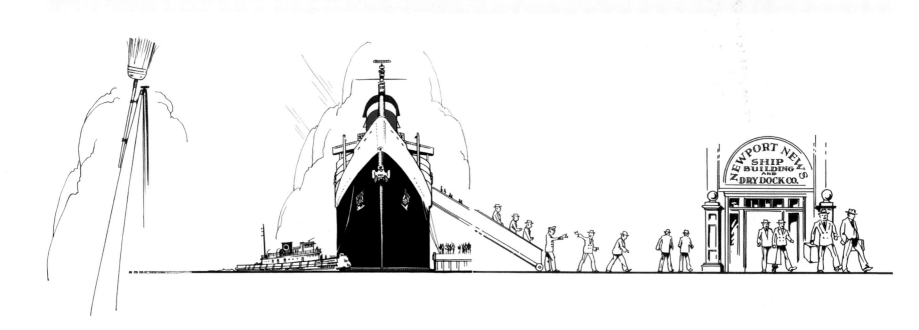

NEWPORT NEWS SHIP BUILDING AND DRY DOCK CO.

pursers, always immaculately dressed, wearing service ribbons at all times.

It was he who climbed atop the vessel's bridge early on the morning of May 16, 1952, in company with U.S. Lines' president John Franklin and the Gibbs brothers. Master for the trials was Captain E. D. Edwards of the Virginia Pilots Association; his executive officer was Fred Fender. They would remain in command until such time as the ship was officially handed over.

Cables were singled up, then slipped, and she was undocked and started moving slowly away from the pier. There is no more intoxicating moment in any passenger vessel's life. For sixteen months, hull no. 448 had been an inert prisoner, either in Shipway no. 10 or as christened *United States* but still shackled alongside her fitting-out berth for a year. Although propellers were in place, they were not yet operable; she had been moved from one imprisonment to another, towed by half a dozen cautious tugs.

Departure for trials was different, however. Suddenly and miraculously, *United States* was proceeding under her own power for the first time, like a child's achieving its first halting steps across a nursery threshold. Self-generated engined motion creates a distinctive and compelling sensation, an almost palpable shipboard perception that electrifies every crewman on board. Months had been spent toiling in anticipation of this long-awaited moment.

For the men and women who would work her, first movement under power was cherished wherever they served on board. Whether officer or quartermaster on the bridge, engineer on the starting platform, steward making up stateroom berths, sous-chef preparing lunch, bartender slicing lemons for cocktails, even the lowliest hand mopping down an anonymous steel alleyway far below—all were captivated the moment *United States*'s great heart began to beat. That steel beehive was, after all, their home away from home and now, remarkably and gratifyingly, it had sprung to life.

That crew response, incidentally, was not shared by most of the six hundred visitors on board from New York and Washington. Those guests were outsiders, for whom the liner's departure from her berth was no more than a routine preliminary for the trials to come, rather like undocking a ferry about to cross the Hudson or Potomac.

For every one of her trials, Gibbs ordered ruthless confidentiality down on the engine room's starting platform. At his direction, William Kaiser's engineers cloaked every pressure gauge beneath concealing canvas covers so that no reporters—who were prohibited access to the engine rooms anyway—could derive even the faintest hint of the vessel's operational performance. Gibbs's mania for secrecy was familiar to every crewman on board.

With increasing revolutions of her four shafts, the excitement as the vessel gathered speed would never again be equaled. Vibrant expectancy consumed every one of the crew as *United States* headed majestically out into Jamestown Bay for her trials. The weather that May 16 morning was bright and cheerful as the company's new flagship steamed for the Virginia Capes. The deep waters offshore there would negate any possibility of retardation during trials because of what is described as bottom interference, one of the disadvantages that plague customarily used measured miles off Maine and Cuba.

Two hours later, when Kaiser was instructed to ramp up his incredible power plant, speed—incredible speed—was achieved, an astounding 30 knots and climbing. Rewarding phenomena emerged, one immediately, the other to be confirmed back at the yard: a complete absence of vibration and, despite traveling at a never before experienced speed, extraordinarily low fuel consumption.

The response throughout the vessel was ecstatic. Even the most uninformed visitors, essentially landlubbers, grasped immediately that they were aboard an incredible vessel proving her extraordinary worth. One of those invited guests, Jorge Sanchez, told a reporter, "I have never had such a wonderful time." Vice Admiral Edward L. Cochrane, administrative chairman of the Maritime Commission, was quoted that first day: "I'll be disappointed if it is not better than any liner afloat, or of any large naval vessel, larger than the destroyers. We will do better."

That first day's stunning achievement would be offset in the afternoon by a mechanical glitch. Alarms were triggered on temperature monitors mounted atop two of the four main turbine bearings' reduction gears; they were overheating, a not unusual response for new machinery subjected to demanding performance. Those signals were early warnings only; no damage was done but continuation of the trials was inadvisable until automated lubricant delivery to those bearings had been restored.

Opposite: In 1952, United States Lines published multiple brochures documenting its latest vessel, including the forthcoming trials. Inside the handsome cover was a charming two-page spread celebrating the ship's debut. The infamous masthead broom makes its first appearance in print. (Michael G. Jedd Collection)

It was the moment to introduce some interior views of *United States* as well. Inside the colorful cover that appears on page 130 were photographs of private and public rooms. The most famous of the vessel's fourteen suites was undoubtedly the Duck Suite. The Promenade Deck restaurant would ultimately be renamed the Special Restaurant. First class's Dining Saloon shows table close-ups, including each one's aluminum lamp. (Michael G. Jedd Collection)

Champagne

Bin No.		Bottle	Half Bottle
	BOLLINGER		
3	Extra Quality Brut, Vintage..	$ 6.50	—
4	Extra Quality Brut, Special Cuvee	6.00	$3.50
	VEUVE CLICQUOT PONSARDIN		
6	Brut, Vintage	8.75	4.50
	CHARLES HEIDSIECK		
8	Brut Rosé, Vintage	7.75	—
10	Brut, Vintage	6.75	4.00
	HEIDSIECK & CO.		
9	Dry Monopole, Vintage	7.50	—
	PIPER-HEIDSIECK		
11	Brut, Vintage	8.50	—
	KRUG & CO.		
13	Brut, Vintage	10.75	—
14	Brut réserve	8.25	—
	LANSON Pere & Fils		
15	Brut, Vintage	7.00	4.00
36	Black Label, Brut	6.00	—
	MERCIER		
16	Brut, Vintage	6.25	—
17	Extra Dry	5.25	—

When ordering wine it is only necessary to quote the Bin number.
Kindly consult your wine steward for the finest vintage available.

Champagne

Bin No.		Magnum	Bottle	Half Bottle
	MOËT & CHANDON			
18	Dom Pérignon, Vintage	—	$13.00	—
19	Dry Impérial, Vintage	$12.25	6.75	$3.75
	MONTEBELLO			
21	Brut, Vintage	—	5.75	—
	G. H. MUMM & CO.			
22	Cordon Rouge, Brut, Vintage	—	7.75	—
23	Cordon Rouge, Brut	13.50	6.50	—
24	Extra Dry	—	7.00	4.25
	PERRIER-JOUËT			
25	English Cuvée, Brut, Vintage	—	7.00	—
37	English Cuvée, Brut	—	6.25	—
	POMMERY & GRENO			
26	Brut, Vintage	—	8.25	—
	LOUIS ROEDERER			
27	Cristal Brut, Vintage	—	11.50	—
28	Brut, Vintage	—	7.50	—
	POL ROGER			
29	Brut Special, Vintage	—	7.00	—
	VEUVE LAURENT-PERRIER & CO.			
31	Brut, Vintage	—	7.25	—
34	Cuvée Grand Siècle, Non Vintage	—	10.50	—
	TAITTINGER			
32	Comtes de Champagne Blanc de Blancs, Brut, Vintage	—	13.00	—
33	Rosé, Brut, Vintage	—	8.75	—
39	Brut, Vintage	—	7.00	—

When ordering wine it is only necessary to quote the Bin number.
Kindly consult your wine steward for the finest vintage available.

Champagne

Champagne
Sparkling
Rosé and
Miscellaneous

Wines of
Bordeaux

Wines of
Burgundy

Alsatian
Moselle
Rhine

Sherry
Madeira
Port
Scotch Whisky

Irish
Bourbon
Rye
Canadian } Whiskies

Gin
Rum

Cocktails
Aperitifs
Mixed Drinks

Liqueurs
Cognac
Brandies

Beers
Ales
Minerals

The minute word came up from Chief Kaiser, bridge telegraphs were rung down and speed throttled back. *United States* returned at slowed revolutions alongside the pier to have the problem investigated. In fact, things would not be put right for a month. But at the same time as the ship's and yard's engineers investigated those overheated bearings, fitting out continued apace.

Dating from those first incomplete but widely publicized trials on May 16, SS *United States* achieved an instant, mythic reputation nationwide. Kudos flowed from every direction, the kind of product hyperbole for which press agents, public relations hucksters, and Madison Avenue regulars would happily kill. The ship and its reputation surpassed the solid gold allure of showbizzy excellence conferred upon the era's cultural benchmarks—long-running Broadway hits, Radio City Music Hall blockbusters, hypnotic weekly radio fare, or must-have Brentano's best sellers.

That unstoppable word of mouth compelled even the uninformed to take note. Not surprisingly, the most meaningful ships for Americans of the 1950s were warships, an understandable legacy of recent hostilities. Cherished foremost was America's first fighting ship, USS *Constitution*, or "Old Ironsides." Similarly, Americans agreed with John Paul Jones about not giving up the ship, were devoted to the ironclads *Monitor* and *Merrimack*, dutifully remembered the *Maine*, savored Admiral Dewey's "You may fire when ready, Gridley," and remained outraged by December 1941's battleship carnage at Pearl Harbor.

At the same time, they apparently cared little for historic vessels that were *not* warships, scarcely cognizant of merchant fleets. The only exceptions are *Titanic*, of course, as well as Cunard White Star's *Queens*, largely because of their indispensable wartime role in preparing for D-day's buildup and, postwar, delivering hundreds of GI brides to New York aboard *Queen Mary*.

Few were familiar with the name Gibbs or had even the faintest idea what a naval architect did. Then, too, transatlantic travel by sea was an option unavailable to most. The privilege of booking a stateroom that would race them to Europe was confined to a relatively small percentile of the population. Don't forget, the 1950s preceded the flowering of popular Caribbean cruising for the masses that would be inaugurated a decade later.

Yet offsetting that almost universal merchant ship disinterest were ubiquitous raves about merchant vessel *United States*. I sense it boiled down to love of country, pure and simple, the same heartfelt national chord that always, inevitably, moved William Francis Gibbs. Something about the liner's

Opposite and below: A deluge of essential ephemera for all *United States*'s passengers came off the presses. A handsomely bound *Wine List*, revealing a seductive selection inside. A festive menu cover. Passenger lists were printed for each class on every crossing; herewith, the cover and first page of a westbound cabin class passenger list from July 1957. Final document is an individual entry form, offering options for a bewilderment of shipboard tournaments, from canasta to Ping-Pong. Curiously, it requests *room* rather than *cabin* number. (Michael G. Jedd Collection)

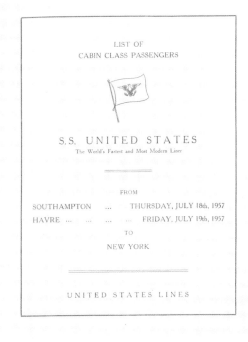

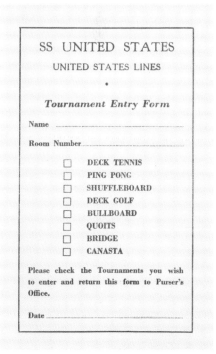

undeniably patriotic name, its red, white, and blue funnels, no less than its record-breaking performance turned the country on. One is reminded of Franklin's instructions to the Gibbs brothers back in 1946: ". . . an outstanding ship the public can get behind, like a Cup defender."

United States crossed a remarkable maritime Rubicon. She became a recognized and remembered ocean liner, on a par with familiar warships cherished in the country's national conscience.

Indeed, the vessel's overt Americanism was one of its strongest suits. A future passenger, sixteen-year-old Vickie French, announced to her family as they boarded in Southampton for return to New York that the ship "made them so welcome; so not Europe, so American." Another passenger suggested: "We're back in America already."

On the European continent, however, U.S. Lines seduced potential Gallic clientele differently. In magazine advertisements issued from the company's Paris headquarters at 10 Rue Auber (six doors away from the French Line's office), the first line of copy describing *United States* interiors conjured up Charles Baudelaire's evocative panegyric from his (what else?) *"L'invitation au Voyage"*:

> *Là, tout n'est qu'ordre et beauté*
> *Luxe, calme, et volupté.*
>
> (There, all is only order and beauty,
> luxury, calm, and sensuality.)

Obviously, *United States*'s appeal was peddled according to readers' specific nationality.

I have found that American fellow passengers who speak with me after my shipboard lectures inevitably inquire, some almost reverentially, about *United States*. Robert Lloyd's jacket cover painting for this volume reproduces in glorious color a famous U.S. Lines aerial photograph of *United States* galloping across the Atlantic; its wide circulation just after the maiden voyage doubtless spread the *Big U* word as well.

Regardless of the May 16 trial's mechanical failure, word of mouth about her speed spawned mesmerizing interest across the nation. *United States* would not depart the yard again until June 21. Additional numbers had embarked for that occasion. Now there were 1,704 on board, including an expanded national press contingent, senior United States Lines executives from New York, a bevy of officials from Washington's Maritime Administration, and the usual assignment of shipyard personnel.

This time, when *United States* steamed out into Jamestown Bay, she headed into the teeth of a force eight gale. There were no excessive bearing temperatures this time but, as anticipated, remarkably different excesses instead. The vessel tore across the surface, producing a fine haze of seawater the length of her boot topping. Despite punishing headwinds, speed of over 40 knots was achieved. Gibbs's flat stern plating as well as the additional blade count of his inboard propellers paid incredible dividends. At speed, *United States*'s entire stern planed up toward the surface to such an extent that drag was reduced to near nonexistence.

It was an unprecedented performance. In a very real sense, the vessel took the Blue Riband in those turbulent waters off the coast of Virginia. Returning triumphantly to the yard, an upended broom, secreted on board, could be seen lashed permanently to the summit of the vessel's only mast, blatant and time-honored symbol of a clean oceanic sweep.

Those second trials produced yet more crowing headlines. Though out-of-town reporters went home, New York's journalists remained on board to participate in (and, it was hoped, write about) the vessel's celebrated maiden entry into New York, her port of registry.

Reverberations from the trials prompted members of the House Committee on Merchant Marine and Fisheries who had been aboard to suggest that a companion vessel for *United States* be put immediately into work, creating a "balance like the two *Queens*."

On June 9, preceding those official Jamestown trials, were miniature trials of a 50-inch *United States* in Central Park's model boat pond. It was the work of amateur model builder Frank Cronican, an unemployed salesman and theatrical scenic designer who had already completed large models of *Normandie*, *Queen Mary*, and *Independence*. Fabricating *United States* in miniature was problematical because no plans had been released to the public. But working doggedly from whatever photographs he could scrounge, Cronican not only completed a creditable likeness, he managed to obtain an enviable imprimatur: signed approval from William Francis Gibbs himself.

On the scheduled afternoon of June 9, New York City was deluged with a cataclysmic hailstorm that set back Cronican's model trials for a full day. But on the afternoon of the tenth, he brought miniature

United States on an elongated wheelbarrow from his studio to Central Park. After donning waders, he set his hull down by hand in the boat pond's shallow waters. He had arranged somehow for smoke to pour from both funnels (he never revealed how he did it) and she was driven successfully three times around the pond by four electrically driven propellers. Cronican went on to become a highly successful professional model maker.

It was a gray, murky summer day, on June 23, 1952, exactly a year after her christening, that incoming *United States* rendezvoused off Ambrose Lightship with a quartet of U.S. Navy destroyers, USS *Warrington*, *Perry*, *Goodrich*, and *William Wood*. That official detachment was buttressed by a huge turnout of unofficial craft as well, recruited effortlessly by some adroit publicity. Back on Sunday, June 15, the United States Lines had placed an advertisement in the *New York Times* weekend magazine documenting the day's specifics.

Many small boat owners have asked when the great superliner, the new *United States*, would arrive in New York Harbor. This is her schedule: Ambrose at 0900, Battery at 1215 and docking at 1300 hours.

Those small boat owners ensured that New York would extend a zealous, almost hysterical welcome that would last for six tumultuous hours. Coast Guard cutter *Tuckahoe*, carrying Mayor Vincent Impellitteri together with a host of state and municipal dignitaries, embarked aboard the vessel as she anchored at Quarantine off Staten Island. Then *United States*, garlanded with signal flags, her mast still topped by that clean sweeping broom, paraded majestically upharbor.

It was indeed a parade. Two destroyer escorts steamed in the van while the remaining pair followed astern. Accompanying outriders included spouting fireboats, tugs, packed ferries, and countless yachts and small craft. Overhead droned television and newsreel camera planes while helicopters *whup-whupped* from stationary vantage points throughout intermittent summer showers.

The disappointing weather could not dampen New York's municipal fervor. Third officer John Tucker leaned almost full-time on *Big U*'s whistle, responding with deafening blasts to innumerable salutes from both her accompanying flotilla and other vessels moored alongside flanking Manhattan and New Jersey piers. Cacophonous blasts and whistled shrieks alike reverberated among the skyscraper canyons. Rather than the tickertape blizzard that would be unleashed by the vessel's triumphant return to her home port after the maiden voyage, wastebaskets full of confetti were emptied from some office windows, fluttering down to streets below.

Five Moran tugs waited in readiness to bring their charge bowfirst alongside Pier 59. Clambering up the traditional ladder from one tug were not one but two docking pilots, Chester A. Evans assisted by Fred Snyder. After entering through one of the vessel's open port doors, they were lofted to the bridge by elevator and stood in the drizzle on the starboard bridge wing.

Their final command, after only twenty-five minutes, was "Make fast as she is." Visibly impressed with *United States*'s remarkable maneuverability, both pilots assured Commodore Manning, "She sure handles easily." Then they handed him their Sandy Hook pilot chits for signature, shook hands with the Gibbs brothers, and descended grinning to the pier.

Over the next week and a half hospitality was the order of the day. Chef, galley staff, stewards, and maître d'hôtels were put through their paces as *United States* was inundated, day and night. Thousands of privileged guests crowded aboard, either for lunch or, *amis de maison* in black tie and long dresses, for cocktails, dinner, and, inevitably, speeches.

The length of one stifling day, the vessel was thrown open to the public, forerunners of the same compulsive admirers who would descend en masse on sailing day. Later that inaugural week, *United States* tied up farther upstream, on the south side of Pier 86, nowadays permanently co-opted by carrier USS *Intrepid*'s Sea, Air and Space Museum.

Then the long awaited day of departure arrived on the bright morning of July 3, 1952. Though there were accommodations on board in three classes for over two thousand, only 1,660 would be embarked for the maiden voyage. U.S. Lines was keeping a cautious reserve of vacant cabins available for passengers housed nearest the propellers; in the event their racket made sleep impossible, empty alternatives would be needed to house them. About fifty of those discommoded by that unhappy-making limitation clutched at straws, waiting with passports, tickets, and stacked suitcases in one corner of Pier 86's shed, hoping that

Opposite: On an overcast summer day, *United States* steams triumphantly into the port of New York for the first time on June 23, 1952. (Newport News Shipbuilding Collection)

room might miraculously materialize. But it never did; without exception, the proscribed passenger ceiling of 1,660 berths was ruthlessly maintained.

Right next to them, as though rubbing salt in their wounds, New York's Department of Sanitation band thumped out a nonstop medley of patriotic airs, from "Dixie" to "Columbia, the Gem of the Ocean," and "Anchors Aweigh," indiscriminately serenading everyone in hearing—deprived nonpassengers, embarking passengers, and hordes of visitors who were crowding aboard to see them off. The pier shed was jammed, so, too, both passenger and visitor gangways and, almost immediately, every open deck, public room, and alleyway.

Through that crush of chattering humanity, first lady Bess Truman escorted her daughter across the gangway at 10:30 A.M. Aged twenty-eight, Margaret Truman had been invited as the maiden voyage's guest of honor. Despite soaring summer temperatures, she wore a blue knitted dress and matching blue shoes with a pink hat and gloves. A Secret Service detachment did its best to segregate the presidential party from inquisitive crowds and cameras. The "first daughter," as the press dubbed her, boarded with close Washington chums Dulcie Horton and her husband, John, she the daughter of Treasury Secretary John Snyder. They would share a Main Deck suite.

In fact, they would remain aboard only for the eastbound leg; the Hortons were to accompany Margaret on a six-week tour of Europe after the Cherbourg arrival. The Truman and Horton luggage was adorned with red-rimmed tags, identifying them from a distance as first class passengers. Cabin class luggage tags were dark blue while tourist were encircled with pale blue only. General John Franklin, head of the U.S. Lines, and his wife boarded, accommodated for the maiden voyage in the Duck Suite.

In those days, visitors overran departing ocean liners berthed along Manhattan's west side, new ones especially. Their price of admission was negligible, a 50-cent contribution to a seamen's charity. There were no restrictions and certainly nary a whisper of today's post–9/11 bugbear, that familiar dread buzzword SECURITY. Sailing day's visitor tally said it all: eight thousand boarded United States to see off her 1,660 passengers, a more than four-to-one ratio. Another five thousand, according to police estimates, gathered along Twelfth Avenue to watch her sail.

Most of those onboard visitors knew not one departing passenger. They were merely part of a symptomatic breed, endemic to New York and its suburbs, who were determined to inspect glittering United States firsthand. What doubtlessly attracted them in such plenitude had to have been the vessel's remarkable Jamestown performance no less than her well-publicized arrival ten days earlier. If they could not sail on the maiden voyage, even if they might never embark again in any capacity, at least they could tell their children and grandchildren that they had been aboard legendary Big U on the day of her maiden departure.

Chief purser John Lock later reported that those visitors accompanied delivery of five thousand parcels, five thousand pieces of mail, and a veritable blizzard of twelve thousand telegrams. In the 1950s, long predating today's preoccupation with cell phones, e-mail, and Twitter, the closest simulacra of instant messaging were telegrams—tan, rectangular flimsies folded and sealed inside windowed envelopes. The messages they contained bore the additional gravitas of uppercase type only, spooling from rattling teletypes onto paper strips that were automatically cut to length and pasted in place one above the other. Telegrams intended for ships' passengers were delivered on specially printed Bon Voyage blanks and envelopes, in those days routinely available in every Western Union office nationwide.

Perhaps not surprisingly, those evocative missives have vanished today, as has the army of young men and occasionally women who hand-carried them to their recipients. Every one of those congratulatory telegrams not only would adorn cabin mirrors in many United States cabins for the next few days, they would also be preserved, stuffed into suitcase lids' pockets, and brought home. Together with a passenger list and the earliest United States postcards, they remain forever precious memorabilia evoking participation in that historic voyage.

Margaret Truman notwithstanding, the most significant passengers on board were the Gibbs brothers, sailing on the only voyage either would ever make on their dream ship. That first round-trip to the continent and back had already been entered formally into the ship's blue, leather-bound logbook as United States Voyage #1. She would sail eastbound to Cherbourg and Southampton, followed by a westbound return to New York.

United States's reporter/passengers crowd the starboard side's Promenade Deck to watch the accompanying tug flotilla. (Newport News Shipbuilding Collection)

Though never a repeat passenger, William Gibbs would famously telephone the vessel every day she was at sea, eastbound and westbound alike, conferring in technical depth with both commodore and chief engineer. It must never be forgotten how gratified he felt to have designed the largest vessel ever built in the United States, which would shortly become—*and remain forever*—the world's fastest. Yet despite that justifiable pride, Gibbs apparently felt no valid compunction to reembark; quite honestly, I expect he was just too busy. But never too busy to ensure that his entire staff responded each time *United States* boomed a greeting on its way past the West Street office en route to sea. Gibbs & Cox staff were encouraged and expected to observe the moment by standing briefly to attention beside their desks.

Now, at midmorning on July 3, 1952, *United States* was about to enter formal transatlantic service, sailing from New York for the first time. Two crucial departures were involved, ultimately the ship's but, before that, those visiting hordes. Well before eleven o'clock, announcements and gongs began echoing continually throughout public

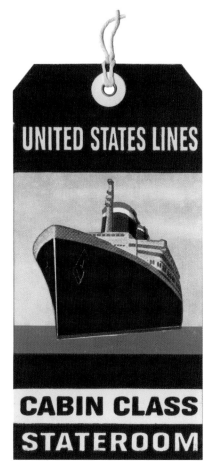

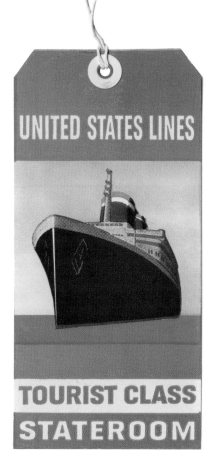

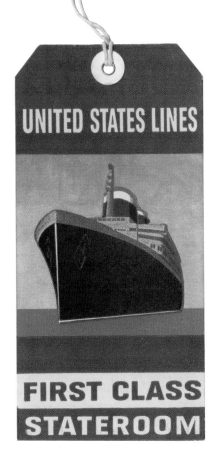

Color coded by class—red for first, dark blue for cabin, pale blue for tourist—baggage tags and stickers were printed and posted in advance to booking passengers. Similarly color coded baggage tags were used for hold luggage. (Michael G. Jedd Collection)

rooms and alleyways, urging visitors to leave with that cautionary summons as old as the sea: "All ashore that's going ashore!"

As they always did, hundreds routinely ignored these earliest warnings. Only after several repetitions did they begin moving reluctantly toward gangways, many calling out extended farewells to their passenger hosts. Officers and crew, increasingly impatient, hastened those chronic, Champagne-infused dawdlers down both passenger and visitor gangways, off the ship and onto the pier. The words "Good riddance!," though never spoken aloud, were doubtless muttered.

By noon doubled watches, always de rigueur for pilotage waters, had been mustered. Out on the starboard bridge wing were the Gibbs brothers, General and Mrs. Franklin, guest of honor Margaret Truman, and the Hortons. Commodore Manning and the pilot stood apart, ready to usher the vessel out into the channel. In Southampton, it was common practice for special sailing days, if a showy or speedy departure was required, to position ocean liners bow out, pointing into the stream. But no such provision had been made for *United States*; she would exit the berth traditionally, backing sternfirst into what most New Yorkers refer to as the Hudson but which nautical professionals describe stubbornly as the North River.

Cables had been singled up as the vessel awaited clearance. Final release would be signaled by the color change of a standard Manhattan traffic light mounted atop the shed roof at the seaward end of her finger pier. This was a common fail-safe against the possibility of collision with North River traffic masked by flanking docks. When the company's marine superintendent, the only professional on the apron, was satisfied that the channel was unobstructed, he telephoned the all clear. At seven minutes past noon, Pier 86's traffic light turned from red to green.

Only then, all cables slipped, would *United States* undock and begin moving, incremental start of voyage number 1. With right rudder hard over and the jangle of slow astern rung on the engine room telegraph, the liner inched away from and along the dock, an almost imperceptible first stirring. Yet for those who had been awaiting that irresistible curtain raiser—first engine tremor and actual motion—it triggered contagious excitement. It was not so much their vessel's movement but the persuasive sense of the apparently moving pier, spied from open deck, porthole, or promenade deck window, that infused passengers, as it always does, with the thrill of voyage's beginning. As two Moran tugs pushed beneath her port bow, *United States* moved majestically astern, gliding past the

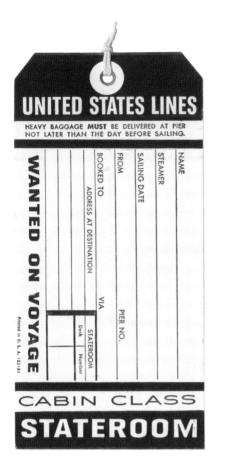

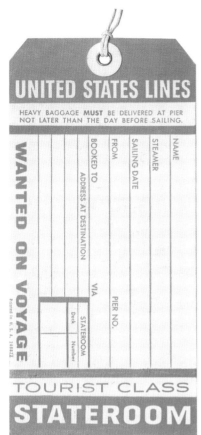

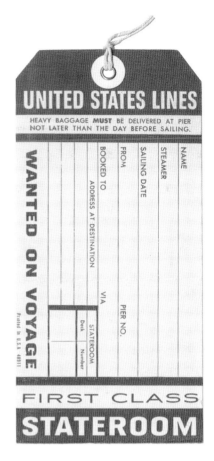

apron at Pier 86's end and out into the stream to near calamity.

Clearly, when the marine superintendent had surveyed North River before implementing the traffic light's color change, he had checked only to the north. Enriching New York's harbor that maiden voyage day was the start of Fleet Week, an annual occasion during which several U.S. naval vessels descended on the port. A few gray ships of the line were already moored at empty finger piers along Manhattan's west side. But amphibious assault ship USS *Alshain*, AKP 55, having been assigned an anchorage just south of the George Washington Bridge, was still proceeding upriver.

As she approached Pier 86 from the south, the giant liner suddenly exited sternfirst across her path. The navy captain thought for an awful moment that Gibbs's great ship was about to become their "hood ornament," as his marine radio man Frank Faulhefer recalls. *Alshain* went full astern on the instant and, by a whisker, collision with outbound *United States* was mercifully avoided.

Pier 86's apron was packed with cheering, waving crowds, those recently offloaded visitors implementing their final but, perforce, anonymous farewells to friends on board. Detached from shore and its cares, *United States* turned and started purposefully downstream, setting off some of the same salutes that had welcomed her arrival ten days earlier. She steamed south, past Manhattan and Brooklyn, not pausing until she reached the outermost end of Ambrose Channel.

Down in passenger country, that preliminary two-hour passage initiated, as always, shipboard's guaranteed continuum of reward. With passage through the Narrows into the Lower Bay, crossing's mood coalesced: embarkation was complete and visitors had gone. Nobody ever said it better than Richard Hughes; from his novel *In Hazard*: "... land newly forgotten—that time when everyone in a ship is at his happiest."

Truth be told, entertaining family or friends seeing one off for more than a few minutes becomes increasingly onerous. Cabins are designed for two occupants only and additions to that body count engender cloying superfluity. In every crowded cabin, the hospitality quotient plummets and a curiously paralytic torpor descends. Canapés and hors d'oeuvres have dried out, opened Champagne has warmed and flattened, conversation flags, and reiterated jokes and japes cease to amuse.

However initially deft and welcoming, cabin stewards are by now otherwise preoccupied. Alleyways' brochure gloss must be restored as all traces of Manhattan litter and smudges are vacuumed or scrubbed from glistening linoleum. Celebratory cabin detritus—empty bottles, trays, platters, and glasses—must be corralled into nearby pantries. Then, and only then, can suitcase and trunk be unlocked and opened, their contents disgorged into drawers and closets, that inescapable shipboard chore impossible while chattering visitors perch atop every bed and chair. It is only at that moment that shipboard cabins make perfect sense.

For that privileged clientele came the happy realization that everyone encountered from then on—fellow passenger and crew alike—was also bound for the opposite shore. That paradoxically fragile yet fulsome shipboard community was being established for the first time aboard this brand-new vessel, as it has been on every liner that had preceded her to sea.

Doubled watches would shortly stand down, bars would open, the gentle lift and fall of the bows would be felt, and table reservations would be nailed down in all three dining saloons and deck chairs reserved along the Promenade, Bridge, or Sports decks. (Their undisputed ownership for the crossing would be identified by name-bearing cards slipped into every chair's aluminum-framed receptacle.)

By the time the pilot had clambered down the Jacob's ladder into Ambrose Light's pilot boat A, it was already 2:36 P.M. The weather was clear and prime sailing conditions were anticipated. Manning was headed along the nineteenth-century oceanographer Matthew Maury's long-established track C, the northernmost great circle route across the Atlantic, employed only when Arctic ice has receded for the summer.

Ambrose Light was and still is the gateway into and out of the port of New York. No longer atop the mast of a lightship, Ambrose Light is now located on a fixed platform legged up from the sea bottom at Ambrose Channel's outer end, figurative first and final sea station for vessels reaching or quitting the northeastern United States. The original lightship is now one of several historic vessels moored at South Street Seaport Museum hard by Manhattan's Brooklyn Bridge.

It was the increasing displacement and dimensions of turn-of-the-century ocean liners that overwhelmed New York's original entry, the Gedney Channel. Earliest vessels used that tortuous waterway to achieve the port's Lower Bay, starting just north of a landmark New Jersey peninsula called Sandy Hook. Although use of that channel was discontinued just after the turn of the twentieth century, its name is forever preserved: all of today's New York pilots are and must be members of the Sandy Hook Pilots Association.

Gedney Channel and its serpentine curves had long served—too long—as the port's sole entry. It was through its challenging sequence of reversing turns that Captain Edward J. Smith, later master of doomed *Titanic*, used to maneuver *Adriatic* in the 1890s with such reckless showmanship. Moreover, it was from New Jersey's oceanfront town Spring Lake that young William Francis Gibbs would sit with binoculars on the front porch of his family's summer mansion, evaluating and often disparaging tonnage steaming past Sandy Hook into New York Harbor.

The Gedney Channel had become dangerously out of date. What larger and longer liners of the day required was an unencumbered straightaway leading directly into the Lower Bay. Just such a replacement channel was excavated starting in March 1899 by the U.S. Army Corps of Engineers. It was completed by the end of June 1906 at a cost of just over $3 million, named after John Wolfe Ambrose. He was himself an immigrant who had become a successful Brooklyn contractor with a rare ecological conscience: Ambrose did his best to discourage the irresponsible habit of dumping unwanted waste that was polluting harbor waters.

As arrival and departure point for the port of New York, Ambrose Channel would continue to serve as finishing post of the North Atlantic's traditional racetrack. Along it, the world's fastest steamships hoped to capture the Blue Ribband, cherished prize for speed across the world's most unpredictable, roughest, and yet busiest ocean. For just over a century, first Sandy Hook and then Ambrose Channel had remained exclusively a finishing post but *never* a starting post for American contestants. That was the lamentable omission that the Gibbs brothers were determined to correct with their extraordinary vessel.

At the racetrack's easternmost end lay *United States*'s objective, the North Atlantic's habitual starting post, a tall lighthouse erected atop Bishop Rock. Within a few days, over that revolutionary summer of 1952, Bishop Rock could and would serve for the first time as finishing rather than starting post.

Bishop Rock was the name of a 114-foot (34 meters) lighthouse rising above a minuscule, otherwise uninhabited rock four miles west of the Isles

of Scilly off Land's End, Great Britain's southwestern tip. At the time of its construction, it was the second tallest in Britain. The record was held by the 160-foot (48 meters) Eddystone Lighthouse, located thirteen miles southwest of Plymouth, the world's first offshore lighthouse.

Today, Bishop Rock is popularly described throughout Britain as "king of the lighthouses." With a low-tide area restricted to 150 × 50 feet (46 × 15 meters), that storm-battered eminence was the world's smallest island with a building on it—in fact, three successive buildings.

The first of Bishop Rock's lighthouse trio was made up of a 130-foot (39.6 meters) -high, iron-legged tripod, its base purposely left open so that fractious waves could, it was hoped, pass harmlessly through it rather than impact upon and destroy solid masonry. But its light would never be lit because, in February 1850, the entire structure was demolished by a raging winter storm.

Within twelve months, a shorter but heftier granite replacement would be put into work. Because

of storms and deplorable working conditions, stone cutters and masons had to be housed on one of the larger Isles of Scilly nearby. Seven years passed before completion. That lighthouse operated until 1889 when it became obvious that even its substantial structure needed strengthening.

Five more years of toil saw Bishop Rock's second lighthouse morph into a third, with its lowest course encased within a surrounding palisade of supplementary granite and cement. Interstices between every granite block were buttressed with quantities of molten lead. Although the lighthouse was still manned at the time of *United States*'s maiden voyage, Bishop Rock has been automated since 1992, topped these days by a helicopter platform. Its light, radiating two white group flashes every fifteen seconds, can be seen for up to twenty-five miles.

But that coveted destination lay far ahead on the afternoon of July 3, 1952. No sooner was his vessel committed to track C, a brief but momentous call came down from the bridge. Commodore Manning

telephoned his chief engineer, Bill Kaiser, on the engine room's starting platform a dozen decks below, uttering only three terse words: "Wind her up."

Kaiser and his 138-man engineering staff did so with a vengeance. Oil-burning nozzles beneath the boilers roared into fullest operation, ramping up a deluge of high-pressure steam at 925 pounds per square inch that racketed into turbine casings. Shaft revolutions increased smoothly and relentlessly toward rates unseen since Jamestown. Three hours later, *United States*'s speed had reached 30 knots and climbing.

When I crossed with her years later aboard *QE2*, Margaret Truman Daniel told me that first thing the next morning, July 4, she and Dulcie Horton prevailed on their cabin steward to open one of their suite's portholes fully. By design, they were normally restricted to two-inch openings to preserve the cabin's air-conditioning. But Margaret wanted to be able to lean her face out through the porthole's rim into the noisy slipstream buffeting the hull. Both women, Margaret and the similarly windblown Dulcie, agreed it was "like being struck in the face with a brick."

Indeed, that eastbound maiden voyage lasted only three and a half days, in an era when crossings aboard every other fast ship consumed five days. It was so fast that *United States*'s shipboard clocks had to be advanced ninety minutes daily instead of the customary sixty.

The first day's run was 696 nautical miles at an average speed of 34½ knots, the equivalent of just under 40 miles an hour. As is commonplace among all shipboard officers and company brass sailing on a new liner, zero public conjecture was circulated about establishment of a record. "Just cruising along," was Commodore Manning's jocular pronouncement to the press at noon on Independence Day. When a reporter visiting the bridge asked William Gibbs how he felt, Gibbs replied with trademark laconicism: "My expectations are rather high, and the ship is running them hard." Asked about the morrow, the commodore brushed off another reporter's query with a cursory "Tomorrow's another day."

It also became another day and night for the more than one hundred passengers who reported that their cabins near Gibbs's rumbling propeller quartet were indeed too noisy. As promised, they were moved forward, away from the stern but not necessarily into superior accommodations. Privately,

purser's assistants believed that many of those requesting cabin reassignment ostensibly away from sleep-depriving racket might well have been prompted by hopes of an upgrade. But not so: malcontents were moved from cabin class aft to empty cabin class accommodations amidships or near the bow, the only improvement aural rather than luxe. It was a rare mid-ocean sight to see fleets of stewards' trolleys, laden with hanging clothes and repacked suitcases, being manhandled along alleyways, transferring so many to different cabins.

The weather was still good with a slight southwesterly breeze and the forecast remained clear. At noon on the sixth, Manning announced that *United States* had completed 801 miles. As jokey afterthought, he confessed: "She is using all four propellers." He had slept for only three of the previous twenty-four hours because much of his night had been passed persevering at speed through summertime fog inevitably encountered while crossing the Grand Banks.

With two confirmed mileage figures at their disposal, the math was easy. Of track C's total length—2,942 sea miles between Ambrose Light and Bishop Rock—1,497 had already been achieved. Incredibly, *United States* was already halfway there. Douglas Willis, a BBC commentator on board, filed a dispatch to London that made perfect sense: "This ship has got it. She'll win the blue ribbon by ten hours."

Later that day, Margaret Truman was invited to the bridge to take over the wheel from the quartermaster for a brief ceremonial moment.

Also on July 6, at five in the afternoon, the vessel passed oncoming *Queen Mary* headed for New York. Advance notice of the encounter was broadcast over loudspeakers throughout the Cunarder, about to be decisively displaced as holder of the Blue Riband since 1938. Public rooms, cabins, and even the cinema emptied as passengers thronged the open decks to watch the American challenger race past. Both vessels dipped their colors en passant. Among spectators out on the Cunarder's deck could be heard an excited American woman cry, "What a thrill! If we couldn't be aboard her on her first crossing, at least we passed her on the high seas!"

Another rival, the French Line flagship *Liberté*, diverted from her passage to New York for a glimpse of *United States*. One effusive cable for Manning was received that same day from the

Right and opposite: Off-duty first class waiters enjoy some sun and an ocean view from one of *United States*'s promenades. Summoned to the Dining Saloon too early, waiters manage a quick catnap before their first sitting passengers arrive for dinner. (The Mariners Museum, Newport News, VA)

school ship *Arosa Kulm*, somewhere over the horizon. Her master, De Marzo, had been in command of the Italian freighter *Florida* twenty-three years earlier. Captain Manning had rescued him and all his crew from their burning and sinking vessel. When he returned to New York, he had been rewarded with a tickertape parade up Broadway for that lifesaving feat.

Bishop Rock's light was spotted for the first time from *United States*'s bridge at 0516 hours on the morning of July 6 as the vessel swept past that coveted goal. The good weather that had smiled on the eastbound's debut had deteriorated into a contrary 60-knot, rain-filled gale. High winds had already

hurled an on-deck Ping-Pong table over the side and visibility was restricted.

Few passengers had slept over that historic night and the bridge was jammed with visitors. Commodore Manning blew a long triumphal blast on the ship's whistle, crowing excitedly that he "felt like a pitcher who has completed a no-hit ball game." *United States* had achieved a new and extraordinary record, completing the eastbound leg of her maiden voyage in an astonishing and unprecedented 3 days, 10 hours, and 40 minutes. *Queen Mary*'s record time had been bested, just as the BBC's Douglas Willis had deduced it would be, by an incredible ten hours.

Both Gibbs brothers shared in the jubilation. Indeed, everyone on board did. Meyer Davis started things off by immediately moving his players from the Ballroom out onto the enclosed first class promenade. There, they struck up "The Star-Spangled Banner." Passengers shouted the words to the anthem, then whooped as the music segued into a conga. A delirious conga line materialized, weaving back and forth along the decks. Over the sound of the music, a fusillade of Champagne corks popped all over the vessel.

Record achieved, the vessel retarded speed for her concluding up-Channel run; she would be too early in Cherbourg. It was 2:30 P.M. on the afternoon of July 6 when she anchored in the port roads. Crewmen were out on deck stringing signal flags aloft, from bow to mast and from mast to stern.

Two pilots, Albert Guerrier and Georges Dubois, boarded to bring her alongside the pier. Many of the forward black strakes along *United States*'s waterline had been scoured clear of paint by her bruising passage, inescapable cosmetic damage inflicted on a new hull traveling at speed: paint that had not yet had time to solidify properly is invariably peeled off. The moment she docked, the bosun ordered paint tenders over the side so that crews could touch up the bow for the morrow's port. Although Cherbourg was *United States*'s first landfall, it would be Southampton where the most poignant celebrations would be observed. For entry into Britain's premier North Atlantic port, the upended broom was tactfully removed from atop *United States*'s mast. Just as the British were magnanimous in defeat, so the Americans decided to be magnanimous following their remarkable victory.

A popular U.S. Lines frontal profile, possibly adapted from *America* of 1940, applicable to both that vessel and her larger fleetmate to follow.
(Michael G. Jedd Collection)

The vessel's reception was exemplary. The weather was perfect and an armada of small boats and pleasure craft escorted *United States* triumphantly up Southampton Water to where waiting tugs ushered her alongside in the Ocean Dock. When a crowded excursion steamer sailed past the moored American challenger, one voice was heard shouting defiantly up toward her bridge, "It won't be long!"

Officially, Cunard White Star would not credit any intention of recapturing the record. The company's major preoccupation, publicly proclaimed, was "preserving schedule." To make their coveted weekly mail service work, the *Queens* had to maintain an average speed of 28/29 knots, a figure well below *United States*'s acknowledged 35 knots. One spokesman issued a peremptory cold shower: "We are not racing. We have schedules and keep to them. We'll certainly do nothing to cause discomfort to our passengers or endanger either their safety or that of our ships."

Regardless, persistent if sometimes contradictory rumors had long encouraged the hopeful. *Queen Elizabeth*, it was said, had "revved up" her speed on a June 1952 eastbound crossing to 34 knots. Even more encouraging, wartime personnel on the *Elizabeth* claimed that, during one memorable westbound passage from Gourock to New York, 39 knots had been sustained in what was described as a "speed test."

But those in the know faced facts. A congratulatory cable dispatched by Captain Harry Grattidge aboard *Queen Mary* to Manning in mid-ocean avoided the speed issue altogether, extending instead the glad hand of good fellowship: "Welcome to the family of big liners on the North Atlantic." Commodore George E. Cove, master of putative challenger *Queen Elizabeth*, said unequivocally at a Southampton press conference: "You can take it for granted that there will be no attempt to beat the *United States*."

Yet, privately, Cove spoke with another voice. Those on the bridge once heard him confide to one of his officers that it would not be a bad idea if a "memorable fast crossing" might occur before his shortly scheduled retirement. The inescapable truth was that flagship *Queen Elizabeth*, more modern and supposedly freighted with dormant speed capability, could not possibly recapture the Blue Riband. Great Britain's favorite dark horse, she was the only rival liner that might have had

A pleasing stern view of the vessel with, inevitably, an incorrectly flown national flag on the after jack staff while under way. (Michael G. Jedd Collection)

sufficient moxie to bring it off. But *Queen Elizabeth* could never approach Gibbs's daunting edge of horsepower over displacement. That was the crucial, missing ingredient and no amount of nostalgic or wishful thinking would ever change it.

United States's Southampton stay was in marked contrast to the post eastbound maiden call of newly restored *Leviathan* back in 1924, the last Gibbs brothers' entry into the port aboard an ocean liner they had designed. At the time, Prohibition had cast its blight on all American tonnage and the luncheon hosted by United States Lines aboard *Leviathan* could not be accompanied by a drop of alcohol.

Yet the lavish midday spread offered aboard the newly arrived champion that glorious July day of

THE NEW
S.S. UNITED STATES

World's Fastest and Most Modern Liner

A year of the vessel's forthcoming voyages—crossings as well as projected cruises—were listed in their own separate brochure. (Michael G. Jedd Collection)

1952 knew no such stricture: a generous dispensation of cocktails in the Ballroom served as preliminary for a wine-rich banquet to follow down in first class's Dining Saloon. As inevitable conclusion to all celebratory in-port luncheons aboard new tonnage, a microphone-topped podium was maneuvered into position at the head table after stewards had cleared away dessert plates and salt and pepper cellars, leaving only coffee cups, liqueur glasses, and ashtrays.

Addressing that shipboard crowd, Viscount Runciman, chairman of the General Council of British Shipping, temporized smoothly: "Competition need

not be inconsistent with cooperation." When Southampton's mayor Edwin Burrow stepped up to the podium, he congratulated the United States Lines' extraordinary vessel "with no reservations whatsoever." Walter Gifford, United States ambassador to the Court of St. James's, never even mentioned *United States* but, instead, recalled with deep feeling *West Point*'s wartime service. Yet again, though seated at the head table, neither Gibbs brother shared that microphone.

The westbound sequel to *United States*'s triumphant eastbound was predictable but equally exciting. The weather behaved and Grand Banks fog, a North Atlantic summer typicality, was not sufficiently impenetrable for Manning to retard speed. The vessel's westbound performance, bound in the opposite direction from Bishop Rock to Ambrose Light, remained consistent with eastbound's, comfortably in the heady mid-thirties.

Manning brought his ship into the port of New York on the morning of July 15. She was accompanied, as she had been on her first entry into the port after her trials, by a flotilla of tugs, ferries, and small boats. As the London *Times* reported, New York was preparing to give "the most colorful and elaborate harbor demonstration in the history of the city."

Once the vessel was alongside, a press conference took place in the Ballroom. William Francis Gibbs thanked New York for the tribute but suggested that not him alone but "many thousands of others had created *United States.*"

Most loquacious of all those interviewed was William Kaiser, the chief engineer. He praised the 138 men of his engine room staff, forty of them

officers. But for the fog, he explained, the westbound crossing might have improved on the eastbound. He went on to say, "I believe the new record will stand for good but I hope someone breaks it." Unspoken but implicit was that he would enjoy the challenge of taking it back. Then he continued, "This ship has so much power she can almost dock herself. She can turn on a dime. She's got it!"

The infamous masthead broom, removed for Southampton entry, was never resurrected. There was a tickertape parade up Broadway to City Hall the following day as Manhattanites pulled out all the stops for the remarkable new champion.

A momentous and jarring aftermath to the maiden voyage, however, put an abrupt end to Commodore Manning's bridge tenancy. General John Franklin, company president, and William Francis Gibbs, two men high in U.S. Lines' hierarchy, had been more concerned with passenger safety than breaking records. Both felt strongly that attempting the Blue Riband should have been approached cautiously, that maiden voyage speed

Distributed to every passenger were details of the incredible maiden voyage. (Michael G. Jedd Collection)

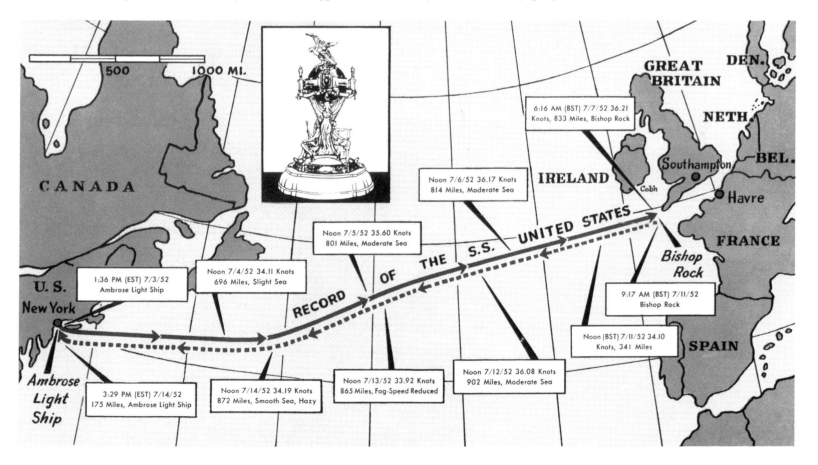

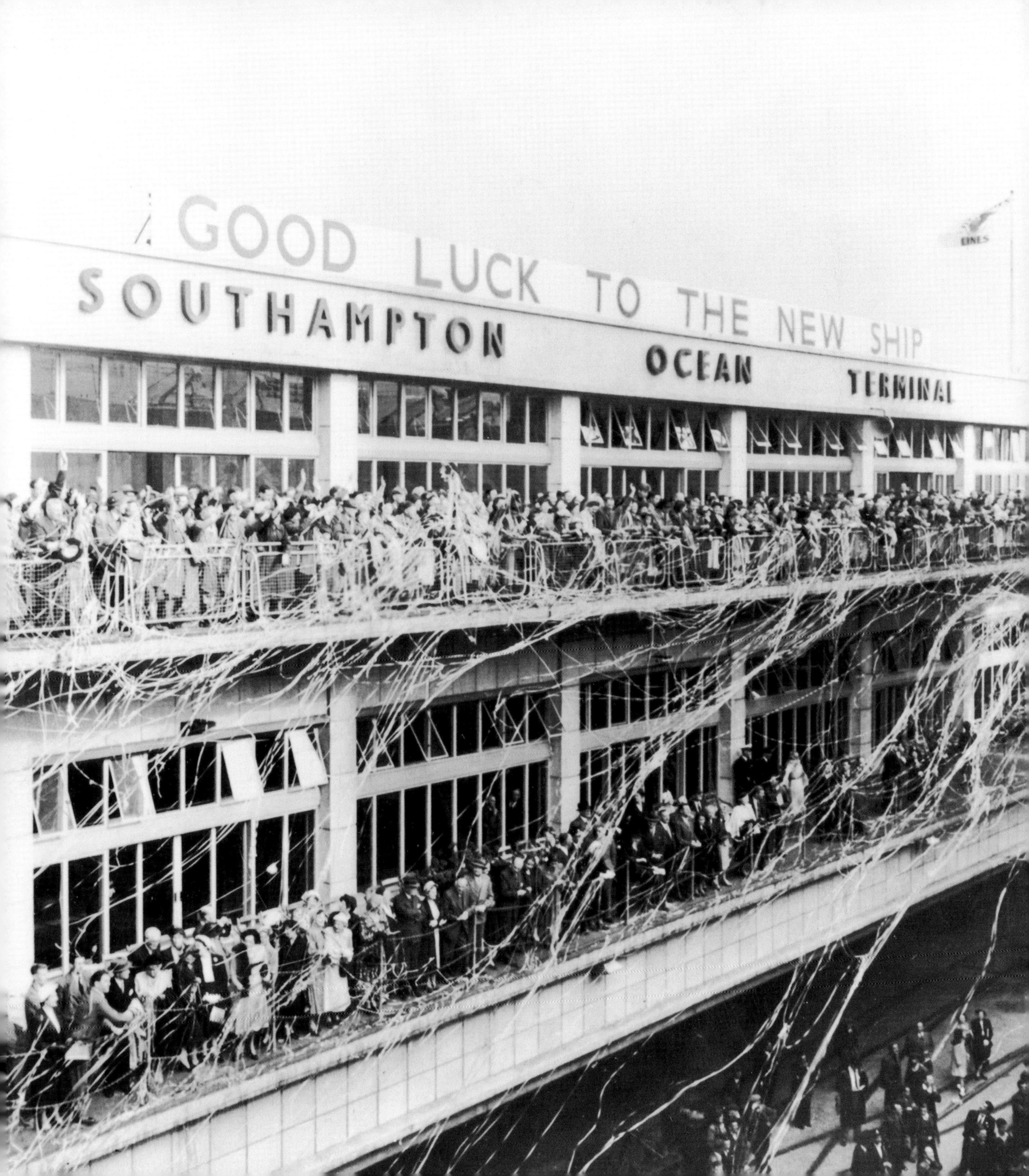
GOOD LUCK TO THE NEW SHIP
SOUTHAMPTON
OCEAN
TERMINAL

should have been retarded until every potential engineering kink had been worked out.

Her crew were relatively untried, as was the complex interlock between boilers, turbines, and shafts and their response to the demands of sustained high speed. Moreover, all the crew, including engineers, deck gang, and stewards, were exhausted long before maiden voyage's end. Far better, Gibbs and Franklin had agreed, that the vessel's engineering elements be nursed and worked up slowly over a period of time, withholding any record attempt until a subsequent crossing.

Apparently, they did not put their case strongly enough to the master. And, if they had, would he have listened? In two words, Harry Manning was a hard charger, a man who predictably—nay, *desperately*—wanted to seize the moment, capitalizing on his vessel's extraordinary possibilities during its first public outing. It is not hard to either comprehend or appreciate the temptation to which he succumbed. In command of a remarkable powerhouse, Manning was more than anxious to prove its worth to everybody—fellow officers and crew, the company, the Maritime Administration, the American public, and perhaps most especially rival merchant navies of the world. It all suited the lyrics of a corny musical tribute played incessantly during both July crossings by Meyer Davis's musicians: "I Love Harry and Harry Loves Knots."

There was also a tempting, self-aggrandizing factor that follows every master's successful maritime achievement, branding the vessel inextricably with his persona. There was no shortage of predecessors. The names of captains of fashionable or fast liners resonated on both sides of the Atlantic: Pritchard of *Mauretania*, Rostron of *Carpathia* and *Berengaria*, Pugnet of *Normandie*, Grattidge of *Queen Mary*, and even Manning himself in earlier command of *America*. And whatever risks, real or imagined, he took during *United States*'s maiden voyage were as nothing to that electrifying aura of success that accrued worldwide, of incalculable import to the company, the country, and its people.

Despite Franklin and Gibbs's disapproval about the maiden voyage, it was on the vessel's second westbound that the die was cast, all because Manning swept arrogantly past *Queen Elizabeth* when leaving the western approaches, without either slowing or saluting. For Franklin and Gibbs, that was the last straw: Manning's contract was terminated immediately upon the vessel reaching New York.

One *United States* junior purser named Ted Fitzgerald surmised that Manning seemed either a sick or an unhappy man, though he had no personal knowledge about illness that might have prompted his precipitous retirement so soon after the triumphant maiden voyage. And it was Manning's daughter who confided to fellow maritime historian Steven Ujifusa that her father was plagued by incurable seasickness whenever he stood on any bridge.

As it was, Manning's dereliction and departure was the only blot besmirching *United States*'s otherwise peerless debut.

Opposite: Warm greetings from the British as *United States* ties up alongside in Southampton. Festooned with tangles of serpentines, the Ocean Terminal's spectator galleries were packed. Atop the building, a special greeting had been erected. (United States Lines; John Anderson Collection)

Left: Back in New York, every officer was presented with a medallion designed by Gibbs, complete with name and rank. On the bottom of the obverse, the Latin motto *Annuit coeptis* (undertaking approved) originates from the Great Seal of the United States. The reverse shows a profile of the vessel at sea in the upper portion, with a map indicating the maiden voyage tracks below. A surrounding border documents the time, speed, and details of both eastbound and westbound legs of the vessel's record-breaking debut. (Michael G. Jedd Collection)

CHAPTER NINE

THE GLORY YEARS

The ship has weathered every rack,
The prize we sought is won

—Walt Whitman, "O Captain! My Captain!"

A superliner is the equivalent of a large cantilever bridge covered
with steel plates, containing a power plant that could light
any of our larger cities, with a first class hotel on top.

—William Francis Gibbs

Joe Stalin would love to know.

—William Francis Gibbs, when asked about *United States*'s rate of travel

Opposite: Though *United States*'s profile is accurate, the same cannot be said
of Manhattan's skyline as of July 1952. (Author's Needlepoint Collection)

or continental owners; regardless which of them won, it inevitably remained an exclusively European achievement.

Now, suddenly, remarkably, stunningly, Gibbs's incredible ship had turned the transatlantic world on its ear. *United States* was the first American liner to win the Blue Ribband in more than a century.

Back in 1851 *Pacific*, a fast and capacious sailing steamer of America's Collins Line, completed a record-breaking eastbound maiden voyage of 9 days, 19 hours, 25 minutes. Edward Knight Collins was a New York shipping tycoon who had amassed a fortune from the coastal vessels of his Dramatic Line. Now, he was intent on usurping steamship pioneer Samuel Cunard's North Atlantic dominance. Until the early 1850s, Cunarders had offered twin advantages of speed and, equally appealing, reliability. At a time when crossing the winter North Atlantic entailed considerable risk, Cunard boasted the enviable imprimatur: "The line that never lost a life."

However, it must be acknowledged that Cunard's earliest shipboard tended to parsimony. Tables laid in the company's dining saloons, for example, were devoid of napkins, catering niceties one would have thought mandatory. Far from accidental, their absence was company policy. David MacIver, one of Cunard's Scottish owners in charge of provisioning and outfitting in Liverpool, once announced dourly, "Going to sea is a hardship … If people want to wipe their mouths at a ship's table, they can use their pocket handkerchieves."

Collins was determined to provide ships that were faster, more elegantly decorated, and with upgraded catering. *Atlantic*, the first Collins liner, entered service in 1850; *Pacific*, *Baltic*, and *Arctic* joined her a year later. For nearly a decade, Cunarders were superceded as the Atlantic's speediest. Awarded a mail contract by Congress, Collins Line vessels steamed at a brisk 12 knots. Not only faster than Cunarders, they were also larger, better ventilated, and more elegantly decorated, and provision of linen napkins in every dining saloon was a given.

Although the American may have trumped his British rivals with superior speed and refinement, his crews' standards of seamanship were no match for Cunard's. The inevitable test came on September 27, 1854. In almost impenetrable fog

sixty-five miles southeast of Cape Race, *Arctic* was rammed by the French steamer *Vesta*, her wooden hull fatally pierced by *Vesta*'s formidable iron prow.

Arctic foundered immediately. Though a few tried saving the vessel and hundreds of its terrified human cargo, most seamen and stokers ignored them, swarming into lifeboats instead. Only a single *Arctic* boatload was rescued, picked up several days later by the barque *Huron*. Its ratio of occupants revealed a horrific imbalance: fourteen passengers were outnumbered by thirty-four crew. *Arctic*'s ultimate death toll was a tragic 322 souls, including Edward Collins's wife and two children.

The line's troubles proliferated. In January 1856 *Pacific* was posted missing with all hands; the wreck has recently been located in Britain's western approaches. With half its fleet on the bottom, the public lost confidence. Even larger, two-funneled *Adriatic* of 1857 failed to attract passengers and Edward Collins's ambitious venture ended in ignominy. Cunard immediately rebounded. Knighted because he had provided troopships for Crimea "without gouging," Sir Samuel's company resumed transatlantic preeminence.

During that incomparable Yankee summer of 1952, there were more than a few in the United Kingdom who wondered if Cunard White Star might seek revenge. The company's marketing slogan promoting the *Queens* remained unchanged: "The biggest and fastest passenger ships in operation." Launched seven years apart, the companion *Queens* were markedly different. Whereas *Queen Mary* was 1,020 feet (311 meters) feet overall, *Queen Elizabeth*, displacing 81,327 tons, had an overall length of 1,031 feet (314 meters), making her the world's longest liner.

Additionally, younger *Elizabeth* boasted a more modern design with her clipper stem, no forward well deck, and two instead of three freestanding funnels. The thinking went, whereas the *Mary* had been bested, perhaps more advanced *Elizabeth* had sufficient power reserves to abrogate Gibbs's feat. In July 1952 speculation about a Blue Ribband challenge was fed by the installation of extra fuel tanks aboard *Queen Elizabeth*. But the truth emerged that their purpose was unrelated to speed. Larger bunkering capacity was being added so that *Queen Elizabeth* could be fueled totally in

Edward Collins, the American shipping man who was determined to replace Samuel Cunard as transatlantic leader.
(Author's Collection, Legacy of Walter Lord)

Opposite, top: *Atlantic*, the first Collins liner to enter service in 1850. Apart from faster crossings and more luxurious interiors, the item that the press most admired on both sides of the Atlantic was her barber's chair.
(Author's Collection, Legacy of Walter Lord)

Opposite, bottom: Detail from a Collins Line certificate, showing various ships of the line. (Author's Collection, Legacy of Walter Lord)

Whereas It is proper that the Common Council of this Commercial Metropolis should express in behalf of its Citizens the gratification so generally felt in the successful establishment of said line, and in the unparalleled voyages which the Steamers composing the same have made. Therefore, be it

Resolved That in the establishment and successful operation of the New York and Liverpool United States Mail Line of Steamers between this port and Liverpool, the citizens of New York, as well as our whole country have cause to entertain a feeling of deep gratification towards the Company through whose capital and perseverance we are indebted for this additional exhibition of American Skill and enterprise; and further

Resolved That the thanks of the Common Council are eminently due, and the same are hereby tendered to

EDWARD K. COLLINS ESQ.

and other public spirited Individuals associated with him, in projecting and carrying out said enterprise; and that we earnestly commend the Steamers composing said line to the support and confidence of the American People as well as to the liberal encouragement of the General Government.

ADOPTED BY THE BOARD OF ALDERMEN, August 5th 1851   *Morgan Morgan* President

CONCURRED IN BY THE BOARD OF ASSIST. ALDERMEN, August 12th 1851   *A. A. Alvord* President

APPROVED, August 14th 1851   *A. C. Kingsland* Mayor

D. T. Valentine Clerk C.C.

ATLANTIC.   PACIFIC.

ARCTIC.   BALTIC.

Southampton, carrying sufficient oil for a round-trip to avoid New York's higher price per ton.

The same surge of popularity that had greeted Collins's initial crossings recurred for *United States*. She sailed at a heartening 96 percent capacity throughout her first five years of service. This is a symptomatic public response to record breakers, especially an American one that had co-opted the Blue Riband so decisively. In those days, Americans outnumbered every other nationality listed in transatlantic passenger lists and now, for the first time in a century, a fast liner flying the Stars and Stripes was available to embark them. Her top-rated performance indisputably confirmed, *United States* morphed instantly into the seagoing Concorde of her day.

Her 35-knot crossings never recurred. Once the maiden voyage was over, *United States*'s service speed was retarded to achieve conventional five-day spans instead of July's extraordinary three-and-half-day triumphs. Regardless, she still attracted enviable patronage and, until *France*'s arrival on the scene in mid-winter 1962, radiated the most glamorous appeal of any North Atlantic carrier. Her social panache easily eclipsed Cunard White Star's venerable *Queens*, exhibiting the same brio with which William Francis Gibbs's superb engineering achievement had swept the seas forever.

She and *America* sailed in comfortable if unequal tandem. Though forsaking its initial pace, *Big U* retained her maiden itinerary: a preliminary call at Cherbourg before crossing the Channel to Southampton and then racing home to New York. For the record, minimum fares for first class cabins were $350, cabin $220, and tourist $165.

America's itinerary was the more ambitious. She incorporated two additional European ports, steaming first to Ireland's Cobh, then up-Channel to Cherbourg and Southampton before pressing on for a final call at Bremerhaven. Adopting that latter convenience, she replaced U.S. Lines stalwarts *Washington* and, transferred from the Pacific, *La Guardia*. Immediately postwar, the two vessels had initiated the profitable business of shuttling service personnel to and from Germany. That Teutonic linkage would later be implemented into *United States*'s itinerary as well, catering to increasing numbers of personnel either joining America's army of occupation or returning home on leave. Although *United States* was never called to the colors as a full-blown troopship, because her

cabin fares remained so far below the cost of airline tickets she embarked increasing numbers of servicemen as well as federal employees bound to or from Germany, starting in the late fifties.

I have always found curious the mixed bag of inducements that shipping lines dangle to attract the public. In a full-page advertisement in the first Sunday magazine of the *New York Times* after the maiden voyage, U.S. Lines solemnly enumerated shipboard statistics with which they hoped to woo prospective passengers. Some of their choices did admittedly convey useful information: "Twelve decks high, air conditioning throughout, three fine American orchestras, two theatres and a swimming pool." But one wonders about others: "Twenty-four Public Rooms, Nineteen elevators, Telephones in every stateroom," and sleeping quarters, it was hinted, "larger than you'd think."

I have never been convinced that potential passengers ever book cabins because of a vessel's elevator count, nor that husbands and wives agreed that an accumulation of two dozen public rooms makes embarkation irresistible. That same strange predisposition exists to the present: mind-boggling hyperbole, particularly touting the number of bars on board, is almost religiously circulated by every cruise line.

Perhaps the most intriguing items included among *United States*'s food perquisites were "Electronic Radaranges [that] cook delicious food in seconds." Of course, U.S. Lines was touting the earliest prototype of microwave ovens to come. My cousin David Townsend, who first crossed westbound on *United States* in November 1953, recalls his African-American Dining Saloon steward Clifford suggesting excitedly that he knew a way to "cook a hamburger in a paper bag in six minutes."

David also remembered one particularly rough morning when he was one of the few who showed up for breakfast in cabin class's Dining Saloon. He asked Clifford for poached eggs and was astonished when he appeared, just moments later, delivering two poached eggs on toast with a flourish.

After eating them, he queried Clifford before leaving: "I know a bit about poached eggs. How on earth did you get them so quickly?"

Clifford replied with a grin that he had seen a friend of his carrying poached eggs from the galley toward first class. He reached over, pinched them from the man's tray, and diverted them to David in cabin class. My cousin could not resist a second

UNITED STATES

NEW YORK

SHIPWAY No 10

question: "Tell me, what is the difference between poached eggs for first class and poached eggs for cabin class?"

Clifford responded with only two words: "Parsley, sir."

Conditioned as we are these days to computers and printers, it should come as somewhat of a surprise that shoehorned down into *United States*'s print shop was a full-size Mergenthaler Linotype, of the size and complexity that had been churning out American newsprint since 1884. The inventor was a German immigrant, watchmaker Ottmar Mergenthaler, who lived in Baltimore. Prior to his invention, no newspaper in the world boasted more than eight pages. Now, aboard *United States*, his Linotype produced the ship's newspaper, invitations, announcements, notices, and a welter of schedules but never menus or passenger lists; their color covers were delivered from shoreside lithographers.

Before we stroll through some of those twenty-four public rooms, a word about what breed of passenger was booking *United States* cabins so enthusiastically in the early fifties. That Yankee cognoscenti exhibited the three immutable C's typifying the company's most desirable clients: curious, classy, and corporate. It has always been a transatlantic given that habitual crossers inevitably book on a new liner, ensuring that they will be among the first of their family, company, or social set to experience it first-hand. What better choice than a glittering American record breaker sailing fortnightly from Manhattan's west side? Some had already sailed aboard *America* as well, either as civilians or as GIs crowded aboard *West Point* during the war.

Below and opposite: Two views of the Duke and Duchess of Windsor arriving in New York aboard *Queen Mary*, one winter, the other summer.
(Cunard White Star Collection)

Added inducement for many of them was the appeal of two VIP fellow passengers who might (or might not) be sailing with them. One cannot over-exaggerate the unfailing snob appeal generated by the Duke and Duchess of Windsor throughout the United States in the 1950s. To have the abdicated King Edward VIII and the Baltimore divorcée on whose behalf he had renounced his throne as social arbiters of Manhattan and Palm Beach encouraged—nay, *bewitched*—adherents of a burgeoning American cult.

The darlings of both public and press, neither Windsor was shy about manipulating their social clout to advantage. Shortly after the war, they started crossing regularly between Cherbourg and New York aboard *Queen Mary*. And it became increasingly annoying to Cunard White Star's booking department that the celebrated pair insisted on what was described as "minimum bed rate," though accommodated in one of the vessel's roomiest suites. Routinely, they embarked with not only forty-seven numbered pieces of luggage and a yapping of indulged pug dogs but also two servants, for whom minimum bed rate was similarly expected.

Cunard White Star's increasing disaffection with what was identified discreetly in house as "the Windsor shakedown" was not lost on U.S. Lines' management. If the British carrier were unhappy losing revenue from a couple occupying a suite for minimum bed rate, the Americans suspected that having His Royal Highness and the woman he loved adorning their passenger lists instead might well impact profitably on subsidiary sales.

That is exactly what happened. When the Duke and Duchess transferred their allegiance from the Cunard White Star to U.S. Lines in 1953, a reactionary sales spike immediately appeared in all three classes. Although the number of Americans who might meet or mingle with the Windsors on board was virtually nonexistent, merely embarking with them aboard the same ship for the same crossing imparted gratifying one-upmanship. For weeks or months to follow, post-voyage reference to "our fellow passengers the Duke and Duchess" permitted name-drops of devastating effect, impressing every one of their hometown stay-at-homes.

Truth be told, the royal couple were not easily encountered, moving as they did around a selective shipboard circuit. To begin with, they never attended boat drill. They breakfasted in their suite—U89, the Duck Suite—and His Royal Highness's

consistent public room was the bridge, to which he was invited daily. There, he sat in a specially installed armchair for hours, reading or chatting with the master and officer of the watch.

In truth, the view from a bridge in mid-ocean has little to recommend it, save for the odd passing vessel or vicissitudes of the weather. Withal, it remains a passenger destination of incomparable esteem. The courtesy of bridge privileges, as they are called, is one seldom deployed save for the most recherché clientele.

The Duchess was once famously quoted as suggesting tartly that she had "married for better or for

worse but not for lunch." Regardless with whom lunch or dinner was taken, however, neither was consumed in first class's Dining Saloon but in an utterly exclusive aerie several decks higher called the Special Restaurant.

It was located on the port side of Promenade Deck between the Ballroom, as the vessel's first class Main Lounge was called, and the Smoking Room. Across the way, to starboard of a midships service pantry, lay a similarly sized cocktail lounge.

Openings fore and aft permitted passenger entrance from either Ballroom or Smoking Room, assuming, of course, their names appeared on the list of reservations.

Decorated by Charles Lin Tissot, the Special Restaurant was floored with dark blue tile segmented by chic white linear accents. Comfortable chairs were upholstered with gray and white fabric shot through with red accents. Transverse walls at either end of the restaurant were dark blue, highlighted

SS UNITED STATES

with decorative crystal inserts in the shape of light rays emanating as though from distant stars and planets. Portside windows looked out onto the Promenade Deck and the sea. After dark, Dynel curtains (one of Gibbs's fireproof fabrics) were always drawn, to both shut out nighttime's invisible ocean while at the same time concealing the clientele from gawkers prowling Promenade Deck. In 2011, one of Tissot's works of art from a Special Restaurant wall was offered for sale on eBay with a starting price of $225,000.

Unlike most extra-tariff eateries aboard ship, the Special Restaurant did *not* have its own galley but was connected via efficient and radiantly heated dumbwaiters with the main galley on A Deck. However delicious, food on the plates ascending *sous cloches* was no more than standard first class fare. Clearly, the Special Restaurant's appeal emerged as less gastronomic than social, its most special aspect its size: diminutive.

Its original deck plan showed that it could accommodate thirty-six passengers. The majority were seated at duos (tables for two), another held five, and two slightly smaller seated four. A hasty revamp immediately after the maiden voyage could not enlarge the space's footprint but a pair of additional two seaters were squeezed in, increasing capacity by four covers to a total of forty, a pittance considering its potential catchment, the 913 who could book in first class.

What that ludicrously limited capacity spawned was arrant exclusivity. In fact, reservations for a Special Restaurant table had to be made when booking a cabin weeks, if not months, in advance. So the famous couple were yet again insulated from staring, fawning, or, God forbid, camera-clicking fellow diners, floating serenely above the fray. They invariably occupied the Special Restaurant's only five-seater table, leaving room for a favored passenger couple as well as, occasionally, the commodore.

A Windsor postscript worth repeating was told me by a recent fellow passenger. The Duke and Duchess had never attended the running of the Kentucky Derby and so, one springtime, a Lexington hostess made her house available to the royal couple. At the same time, she saw to it that dinner invitations and a box at Churchill Downs were provided as well. Shortly thereafter, an invoice for $1,000 arrived from the Duke of Windsor's Palm

Opposite: Donald Campbell, son of the late Sir Malcolm Campbell, the British speed champion on both land and water, sails to America aboard *United States*, on his way to test-drive the latest *Bluebird* on the Bonneville Flats. His vehicle traveled on deck, lashed down on a special cradle to port of the forward cargo hatch. Commodore Anderson and chief engineer William Kaiser pose with the British driver in mid-ocean. (Charles Anderson Collection)

Left: Commodore Anderson poses in his quarters with his "tiger," as the captain's personal steward is always called. His name was Pete Thermopoulis and he sailed with Anderson throughout his time aboard *United States*. (Charles Anderson Collection)

Right: The second and longest-serving master of *United States* was Commodore John W. Anderson, who was appointed in 1952 after Commodore Manning's departure. With a Norwegian heritage and possessed of impeccable seagoing credentials, it was remarked by one of his officers, "He's friendly—but don't cross his bow."
(Charles Anderson Collection)

Opposite: As master of the vessel during the long period when the Duke and Duchess of Windsor were frequent passengers, Commodore Anderson sometimes joined them for dinner in the Special Restaurant: with a group of passengers whose names are unknown (*top*) and before another meal to entertain the American institution Elsa Maxwell in early 1963 (*bottom left*). It proved Maxwell's last crossing; later that year, she died of heart failure. Channel of much royal palaver, the Duck Suite's telephone (*bottom right*).
(Charles Anderson Collection; David Pike Collection)

Above and opposite: A young cocker spaniel was presented to Commodore Anderson during the war when he was in command of freighter *John Ericsson*. The puppy's name was Chota Peg, Hindustani for "small drink." By the time the photograph above was taken, Chota Peg had sailed more than 2 million sea miles and was fourteen years old. Every day, he used to bring his master's newspaper to the cabin and was often seen perched on the bridge railing. (This was taken before his master's promotion to commodore.) When Chota Peg died in 1956, a brief obituary appeared in the *New York Times*. (Charles Anderson Collection)

Beach office, payment requested for the hostess's recent generosity.

Before plunging into the vessel's 'tween decks, we should examine Gibbs's geographical assignments from top to bottom, to find out how different parts of his hull were apportioned among her class trio. As aboard every liner, first class occupied the choicest areas, high up and centered amidships. Cabin class lived aft and tourist class made do with a fragmented domain near the bow.

First class was the largest and grandest, starting at the ship's very summit on Sports Deck. There was a large open deck area and Children's Playroom aft, with a dog kennel just forward and eleven small first class cabins. Below, in descending order, came Sun, Promenade, Upper, Main, A, B, and C decks.

Sun Deck boasted a spread of first class cabins forward lining the starboard side. Port side cabins were for bridge officers. The entire deckhouse was surrounded by an encircling open-air promenade.

Just below, Promenade Deck was devoid of cabins, dedicated instead to first class's major public rooms. From aft to forward appeared a 352-seat cinema, the Smoking Room, Special Restaurant and its companion bar, Ballroom, Main Foyer, and Observation Lounge. To either side, enclosed promenades contained rows of deck chairs facing the sea. At the after end, what were described on deck plans as "lockers" were actually deck pantries from which bouillon and tea were dispensed. The Observation Lounge boasted no forward-facing windows because a cluster of tourist class public rooms obscured the view; first class "observed" only to port or starboard.

Upper Deck was packed with cabins, the largest accumulation of first class cabins on any deck, including the vessel's six highest suites, three per side amidships. Along the center keel line were thirty-three insides, including a block of fourteen separating the outboard suites, servants' quarters for their most affluent occupants.

HARRY S. TRUMAN
FEDERAL RESERVE BANK BUILDING
KANSAS CITY 6, MISSOURI

July 11, 1956

My dear Captain Anderson:

    Mrs. Truman and I hardly wanted to leave the
S. S. United States when we docked at New York. Both
the eastbound and westbound trips were perfect voyages,
and we enjoyed every minute.

    We can hardly thank you enough for all the cour-
tesies extended to us by you personally and by the
United States Lines. The considerate treatment afforded
us was most highly appreciated, and we are both looking
forward to sailing with you again, if fortune favors
us.

    Every good wish.

                  Sincerely yours,

                  Harry Truman

Captain John W. Anderson
Commodore, S. S. United States
United States Lines
1 Broadway
New York, N. Y.

Opposite: The view aft of *United States*'s port side under way, seen from the bridge. It is a midwinter day in 1954 and the vessel's open decks are largely deserted. (Charles Anderson Collection)

Left: Retired President Harry S. Truman sent this letter of thanks to the commodore following a summer round-trip. Bess Truman had last set foot on the vessel when she accompanied their daughter Margaret aboard as guest of honor for the maiden voyage four years earlier. (Charles Anderson Collection)

One deck down on Main Deck were the eight remaining suites. There were only eleven inside cabins on Main Deck, including some stewardess and assistant purser cabins. Approaching the forward end of Main Deck was the Main Foyer containing first class's Purser's Desk, the Travel Office, and the offices of the chief purser, chief steward, and baggage master, this last historic functionary no longer extant, alas, on board any cruise ship. Forward of that foyer, the tapering hull steadily diminished the width of successive first class cabins.

First class's Dining Saloon was located on A Deck. One of its most civilized perquisites was an elevated musicians' gallery that Gibbs had incorporated just aft of the room's tall central section. Below that, bypassing B Deck save for a gymnasium visit, one could descend to C Deck for a dip in the pool, bracketed by changing rooms and showers to port and treatment rooms to starboard.

Cabin class, positioned aft, shared three facilities with first: cinema, gymnasium, and pool. Immediately aft of the cinema was cabin class's raised

games deck, surrounded by open promenade. It also incorporated at its tail end a vital maritime installation, *United States*'s after steering station. Projecting beyond the superstructure to both port and starboard were after docking bridges.

Directly below on Upper Deck was cabin class's Main Lounge, surrounded by a covered promenade on three sides furnished with deck chairs. Aft, an open promenade occupied the stern's round contour. Just forward of the Main Lounge were the library and Writing Room to port and the

Children's Playroom to starboard. Forward of them on the port side only were some cabin class cabins, the highest in the vessel. All cabin class bathrooms, incidentally, contained showers only.

Below on Main Deck was the Smoking Room, surrounded by another covered promenade with deck chairs. Forward, there were more cabins, mostly to port, leading on that side of the vessel to the chief surgeon's office and his assistant surgeons' consulting rooms, dispensary, and waiting rooms. This medical spread was the only public area

aboard *United States* open simultaneously to all three classes: first, cabin, and tourist were granted equal access.

Down another level in cabin class was A Deck, packed with cabins on both sides, together with a barbershop and beauty parlor. Just forward of those fixtures was their Main Foyer, complete with a smaller purser's desk and travel, chief steward's, and baggage master's offices. Across that foyer lay port and starboard entrances into cabin class's shipwide

Dining Saloon. One level lower on B Deck was the gymnasium and a final allotment of cabin class cabins, situated mainly along the starboard side.

Tourist class's domain began near the bow, its highest facility at the forward end of Sports Deck, a sheltered lookout spanning the vessel with benches at each outboard end. There also was a crescent of open deck facing forward two levels below the bridge, a source of fresh air as well as a distinctive forward lookout for the vessel's humblest passengers.

Opposite, below, and overleaf: A variety of port calls—*United States* being secured inside Bayonne's naval annex dry dock. A view of the vessel departing Bremerhaven sometime in the late 1960s. A color view of *United States* alongside at Pier 86 as inbound *Queen Mary* passes en route to Pier 90. (Charles Anderson Collection)

Down two levels on Promenade Deck were tourist class's major public rooms, the ones blocking the first class Observation Lounge's view forward. Amidships was a two-hundred-seat cinema (the class's only carpeted public room), flanked by the Writing Room to port and a library to starboard. The round forward arc of the Main Lounge looked out over an open promenade.

The inescapably fragmented verticality of tourist class continued down to Upper Deck, incorporating in its center a barbershop and beauty parlor and, just forward, the Children's Playroom. At its forward end were the first tourist class cabins occupying both sides of the hull.

Below on Main Deck was the shipwide Smoking Room, butted up to more cabins on both sides of the vessel. Then down another level to A Deck, on which was located tourist class's Dining Saloon, with more cabins just forward. Down again to B Deck, along the starboard side of which an additional stretch of tourist class cabins appeared. These continued yet again down on C and D decks.

Although every tourist class cabin was plumbed with two sinks, the communal baths, showers, and toilets were available only down the alleyway. One cannot but wonder about the reality of that "availability." Along the starboard side of B Deck, for instance, lay a section of thirty-six cabins, inside and

Below: Painter Salvador Dalí is photographed by a host of welcoming Girl Guides and one professional. He was traveling apparently without either his wife, Gala, or his pet ocelot.
(Bill Miller Collection)

Opposite: Commodore Anderson chats with John Wayne on deck.
(Charles Anderson Collection)

Opposite and above: A selection
of Hollywood or television stars who
were often photographed aboard
United States. Commodore Anderson
poses with Gary Cooper outside

the Dining Saloon. Jackie Gleason
and a friend meet the commodore
in the Navajo Grill and Jane Wyman
joins the master for dinner. The
woman on the right is incorporating

United States Lines table flags
into her hairdo. A Russian Cossack
chorus is greeted by Commodore
Anderson in the Ballroom. **(Charles
Anderson Collection)**

A senior trio pose in summer whites
out on deck. From right to left:
Commodore John Anderson, executive
officer John Alexanderson, who would
succeed Anderson as commodore
in 1963, and William Riddington, chief
officer. (Charles Anderson Collection)

Back in winter dress, Anderson and Riddington were photographed on the bridge. (Charles Anderson Collection)

out, which on a crowded sailing accommodated over a hundred. For all those passengers, there existed a single tub for men, another for women, and three showers for either. No mention was made of a bath steward.

Promenade Deck's Ballroom was located just forward of the Special Restaurant. Decorated by the Texan Charles Gilbert, its most stunning feature was a curving athwartship wall made up of vertical glass panels. Each was illuminated by concealed lighting troughs top and bottom and sand blasted with a diversity of underwater imagery—kelp, fish, shells, and assorted marine life. Those sand-blasted portions were additionally highlighted with applications of gold leaf.

One panel had near the bottom a small buxom mermaid, the only such creature on board. She was one of those appealing gewgaws often factored into an ocean liner's decor with an ulterior motive—heaven-sent amusement for bored children at sea. Hard-pressed pursers or their parents could send them on a shipwide hunt for that elusive underwater creature. Since those panels have long been auctioned off, I always wonder where that singular mermaid ended up.

A similar attraction has been cunningly worked into one of *Queen Mary 2*'s nationally oriented murals lining 2 Deck approaching the Britannia Restaurant. The American mural contains a tiny but instantly recognizable image of Homer Simpson seated in front of his television set, found at child's head height very near the fringe of the Statue of Liberty's robe.

At the opposite end of the Ballroom, just aft of the Special Restaurant, was first class's Smoking Room, decorated by the famed sculptor William King whose work graced the collections of the Museum of Modern Art in New York and the Philadelphia Museum. The room's primary focus was a curved central wall greeting inbound arrivals through the forward entry, made up of a Mercator projection showing the world's continents. The artist had banded them with heroic bronze lines of latitude and longitude, including varying time zones as well. Furniture was clubby, bright red barrel chairs grouped invitingly around tables along either side of the vessel and bracketing the entrance. There was an additional way aft to either side of that mural, port and starboard entries into the back rows of the cinema. Each ascended a flight of six steps to achieve the highest level of the gently sloped auditorium floor.

A large first class public room just forward of Promenade Deck's Main Foyer was the Observation Lounge, its decoration the work of Raymond Wendell. He had begun painting at New York's Art Students League and later at Yale, following wartime service in the Pacific with the navy. Small wonder that ocean winds and currents preoccupied him.

He created two complementary 9 × 12–foot murals on curving inboard walls bracketing the center of the Observation Lounge. On the port side, he duplicated a Mercator projection of the North Atlantic, overlaid with bronze arrows, not dissimilar to whimsical flying fish, indicating the direction of prevailing winds. On the starboard side he dealt with ocean currents, also employing a similar overlay of bronze arrows. The effect of both panels was captivating.

Lewis York straddled design choices for two different classes, one for cabin class's Smoking Room, the other the pool. In the Smoking Room, he strove for unabashed Yankee dynamism, decor tapped into popular Americana—rum and whiskey barrels, corncob pipes, banjos, and the down-home imagery of red-and-white checked tablecloths. His pool design trod the same street, its only decorative theme some pole-mounted, apparently fluttering aluminum signal flags erected across the wall at the deep end. They spelled out jovially "Come on in, the water's fine."

When Commodore Manning left the vessel only three crossings after the maiden, he was replaced by Commodore John Anderson, transferred from *America*, who would remain on board until 1964. He would be succeeded in turn by Commodore John Alexanderson, the vessel's third and final master. Of the three, Anderson served longest, nine years in command.

One of his earliest ordeals in command of the vessel was during a monstrous storm that assaulted the British Isles on December 17, 1952. One-hundred-mile-an-hour hurricane winds disrupted power lines all across the country and tore two firemen from the top of their fire engine's ladder. One woman was killed and many more people were injured as buildings collapsed. Roofs were peeled off new buildings and in Liverpool a sailor was blown off his ship. Three fishermen drowned when their dory was swept over a dam and capsized. Although Great Britain's ship and air operations were largely suspended, in late afternoon *United States* prepared to leave Southampton's Ocean Dock. But winds were of such appalling strength that, the moment her cables were slipped, they blew the ship aft along the dock coping.

Passengers braving the open decks for departure ran inside for fear that wind-driven *United States* might topple cranes lining the quay. At the same time, spectators crowding Ocean Terminal's gallery also dashed for cover as the vessel was dragged aft several hundred yards, scraping paint noisily off her starboard side. Seven hastily summoned tugs battled to keep the ship under control. As a last resort, every tug in Southampton was mustered to resecure *United States*'s scarred hull alongside.

His vessel finally berthed securely with doubled hawsers, Commodore Anderson reported to his passengers that, although there was no serious hull damage, he was postponing departure. "A decision will be made when the wind drops," he announced over the ship's loudspeakers. As it happened, *United States* was forced for the first and only time in its career to remain in Southampton overnight.

Gibbs's daily radio/telephone call the next morning dealt with more information than usual. He was very proud of the fact that *United States* had such superb handling qualities. He once screened footage filmed from the bridge as the vessel battled a ferocious winter storm. "Look at that!" he marveled to a friend. "The only thing coming over the bow is spray—not a bit of green water!" Moreover, the vessel neither boasted nor apparently needed stabilizers. Those indispensable antirolling devices had come into use in the early 1950s yet Gibbs eschewed them for *United States*.

As far as the vessel's hotel department was concerned, what splashed over the bow was of less significance than what strode up the gangway. From the very beginning, ocean liners have been inundated with passengers of every size, outlook, and attitude. Occasionally, senior shipboard administrators have been known to interact with them bizarrely. I once met a Caribbean purser who confided in utter seriousness that all passengers repelled him. He had even rearranged his office furniture so that he sat with his back to the door, preventing even a single passenger glimpse. His staff manning the purser's desk dealt with the public their chief abhorred. Patently, the man was in the wrong business, his aberrant behavior governed by almost certifiable parameters.

William Francis Gibbs came aboard
for a visit as Commodore Anderson's
retirement approached. The renowned
naval architect and the vessel's
second master were staunch friends.
(Charles Anderson Collection)

Pages 166–173: Interior views of *United States* from a United States Lines deck plans brochure. (Michael Jedd Collection)

Opposite: First class ballroom. "The indirect lighting of the dramatic ceiling dome casts a soft glow on exquisite panels of carved glass depicting undersea flora and fauna . . . pale gold leaf walls enhance the room's deep red and creamy white appointments . . . glass top tables . . . oval dance floor . . . music by Meyer Davis—all for memorable evenings at sea."

Left, top: First class suite. "Spacious rooms, luxurious furnishings, and unusual facilities for passenger comfort characterize the handsome suites of the Upper and Main decks. Large living rooms adjoin generous bedrooms, and each suite also includes two or three full baths and trunk room, with 'climate control' air conditioning in every room. By simply pressing a button, the passenger also has the added luxury of piped-in music."

Left, bottom: First class stateroom. "Spacious and pleasing in their proportions, all First Class staterooms provide every comfort . . . full length mirrors, dressing tables, and bathrooms with tub and/or shower and toilet. Individual thermostatic control of air-conditioned ventilation ensures every passenger's personal comfort."

Opposite, top: First class Dining Saloon. "A beautiful setting for dining in the grand manner with the huge symbolic sculpture *Expressions of Freedom* on the central wall, bright red chairs, snowy linen, gleaming silver, and sparkling china. The world-famous cuisine is both American and Continental and features specialities from five continents, Kangaroo tail soup . . . caviar from Iran . . . Scotch grouse in season . . . thick American steaks . . . Crepes suzettes."

Opposite, bottom left: First class smoking room. "Rich autumnal views make this one of the most attractive of the twelve public rooms for First Class passengers. Two-toned leather chairs and sofas covered in hand-woven fabric invite relaxation. And of particular interest—the huge Mercator projection of the continents showing variations of time at different longitudes."

Opposite, bottom right: First and cabin class theater. "This delightful theatre seats 352. Hand-woven stage curtains

with their gay pompons create a festive atmosphere. Vertical paneled walls assure good acoustics while thick carpeting and molded-for-comfort chairs enhance the pleasure of viewing pre-release films daily. Complete equipment and lighting for stage shows too!"

Above: Cabin class dining room. "Celery colored walls, and upholstered chairs grouped around beautifully appointed tables set the delightful scene for elegant dining. Epicurean specialities from world-over are deftly served for your pleasure."

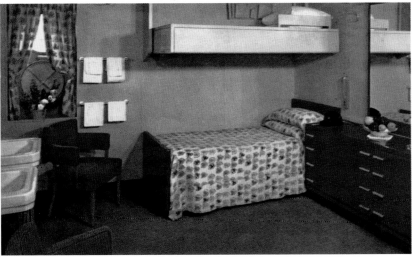

Opposite, top: Cabin class lounge. "Covered decks border two sides of this huge living room. Here, the red and gold decorative motif is one of the Old South highlighted by a large mural depicting New Orleans street scenes. This attractive theme is further carried out in ornamental Vieux Carre iron work, and a mural of the Mississippi and its tributaries. There is a stage at one end of the room, and a dance floor for evening dancing to the rhythms of the Meyer Davis orchestra."

Opposite, bottom left: Cabin class stateroom. "All the comforts of home! Beds have deep inner-spring mattresses and individual bed lamps. Matching bedspreads and curtains are fire-resistant as well as attractive. Incidentally, all furnishings in the entire ship are fire-proof or fire-resisting. Every Cabin Class stateroom has its own private shower and toilet."

Opposite, bottom right: Cabin class stateroom. "Typical in its spaciousness and functional ingenuity, this cabin includes all those little details which passengers so often look for . . . tall closets, roomy dressers, full length mirrors, world-wide telephone service, and wall-to-wall carpeting of deep pile."

Left, top: Cabin class smoking room. "This gaily decorated room has curved walls which show of the bright harlequin curtains. The hand painted mural over the bar features Early American jugs and bottles. The room, of course, is air-conditioned like every other space on the *United States*."

Left, bottom: Swimming pool. "The decorative signal flags above the pool actually spell out 'Come on in, the water's fine.' Swimmers and spectators can lounge on comfortable chairs under gaily striped awnings. Off the pool area are dressing rooms, massage rooms, therapeutic baths, and a fully equipped gymnasium."

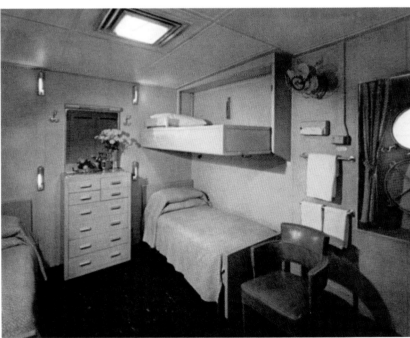

Opposite, top left: Tourist class library. "The quiet pleasures: relaxing in a soft armchair, reading a good book from the well stocked shelves, or taking a few moments to send off a letter to a friend at home. A subtle combination of soft blues and greens predominates here."

Opposite, top right: Tourist class theater. "Modern, spacious and acoustically perfect, the Tourist Class theatre seats 199. Light walls, green chairs, and wall-to-wall carpeting create a most attractive setting for viewing pre-release films."

Opposite, bottom left: Tourist class stateroom. "Attractiveness and comfort . . . that's the happy combination in all Tourist cabins . . . coordinated furnishings, beds with deep inner-spring mattresses, individual bed lamps, individual climate control air conditioning, and a telephone too."

Opposite, bottom right: Tourist class lounge. "Two large alcoves of soft blue set off by rich red carpeting, and table arrangements conducive to bridge-playing and friendly conversation. In the evening, the room's central area becomes a dance floor for dancing to the Meyer Davis orchestra."

Left: Tourist class dining room. "Interesting murals of 18th Century nautical motifs brighten the walls as do the rust colored striped curtains and handsome gun metal mirrors. Meticulous service, superb cuisine prepared by master chefs, and wines from the world-renowned cellars of the *United States* will satisfy your palate's desire."

Passengers en masse inevitably conform to one of several categories. Easiest are either regulars, those devastatingly familiar with ships and the sea, or those new to shipboard, happily finding their way about the vessel and pleased with everything they discover; whether old hands or neophytes, their outlook is essentially positive.

Conversely, a few diehards are never content. There are those perennially on the qui vive for any advantage they can wangle—a better cabin, a better table, a better deck chair, a better anything. At the extreme end of that malcontented passenger spectrum are the obstreperous, the loudmouthed, the vulgar, and occasionally those with malicious intent.

Predictably, passengers' social interaction emerges after embarkation. Some are desperate for companionship, some make no friends, some are ancient, frail, and forgetful, and there always remains a prickly or antagonistic hard core. But regardless of whichever behavioral boundaries their symptoms violate, the company is obliged to make every one of them feel welcome, treating the halt, the lame, and the awful equally well.

Complicating matters was the sensitive business of tipping. Lavish shipboard tips have always been an inveterate American indulgence; it has been said that the word *tip* originated in nineteenth-century America, a riverboat acronym derived from "to insure promptness." While Yankee passengers routinely rewarded stewards and stewardesses lavishly, many other nationalities refuse to part with a penny more than their fare. To level the playing field these days aboard internationally patronized cruise ships, mandatory tipping charges are deducted from every passenger account daily, to be shared proportionally among the crew. But in the 1950s no such automated monetary harvest was ever instituted. Tipping remained voluntary, dependent on nationality and largesse.

Whether tippers or no, all passengers, in first class especially, were fawned over. Indeed, according to crewspeak throughout every class aboard every vessel, two ironclad rules obtain: passengers are *never* wrong and a negative response to any request, no matter how outlandish, is taboo. Senior personnel on board, in league with management

In January 1964, Commodore John Anderson brought *United States* alongside Pier 86 without tugs, the first of four separate occasions when he achieved that remarkable objective.
(Charles Anderson Collection)

ashore, were determined to please everyone who embarked, whatever their inbuilt prejudices.

Back when no airborne alternative existed, everyone had to cross by ship and showbiz names frequently adorned transatlantic passenger lists. Indeed, very few vessels crossed without a star or two on board; most behaved impeccably and said little.

In the early 1950s, when an airborne alternative *did* exist, dozens of memorable personalities flocked aboard *United States* regardless, from ex-presidents to politicians, from film directors to debutantes, from democrats to dictators, from producers to the *prominente*, from leading men to occasionally misleading ladies. A sample roster of Hollywood, Broadway, and radio names who embarked were (alphabetically), Fred Allen, Jack Benny, Edgar Bergen (with Charlie McCarthy and Mortimer Snerd in tow), Irving Berlin, Victor Borge, Marlon Brando, Richard Burton, Joan Crawford, Walter Cronkite, Walt Disney, Judy Garland, Jackie Gleason, Cary Grant, Oscar Hammerstein II, Rita Hayworth, Alan Ladd, Burt Lancaster, Peter Lawford,

Jack Lemmon, Ethel Merman, Marilyn Monroe, Kim Novak, Merle Oberon, Cole Porter, Debbie Reynolds, Richard Rodgers, Mickey Rooney, Elizabeth Taylor, Spencer Tracy, Cornel Wilde, Billy Wilder, and Jane Wyman.

Some celebrated passengers abrogated shipboard norms. When Marshal Tito crossed, seated on either side of him in first class's Dining Saloon were machine gun–toting bodyguards. Ex-presidents sailed, including Harry and Bess Truman and Dwight and Mamie Eisenhower as well as John Kennedy and a young Bill Clinton. Also passengers aboard *United States* were Secretary of State George Marshall, Governor Thomas Dewey, and Senator Joseph McCarthy. One inveterate *United States* repeat passenger was Salvador Dalí with his wife, Gala, accompanied occasionally by his pet ocelot on a leash.

To summon up a representative passenger cross section, I am less interested in celebrities than in ordinary folk. So there follow accounts of individuals and/or families who sailed in first, cabin, and tourist as well as some company employees. These are the

dramatis personae who will strut my shipboard stage, a retrospective mixed bag of *Big U* clientele and their keepers.

Regardless of *United States*'s ability to overcome rough weather, severe sea motion remained an inevitable reality; for poor sailors, January crossings could be punishing. I am reminded of my favorite passage from Kipling's *Just So Stories*, describing a shipboard storm and how it affected small children.

When the cabin port-holes are dark and green
    Because of the seas outside;
When the ship goes *wop* (with a wiggle in between)
And the steward falls into the soup-tureen,
    And the trunks begin to slide;
When Nursey lies on the floor in a heap,
And Mummy tells you to let her sleep,
And you aren't waked or washed or dressed,
Why then you will know (if you haven't guessed)
You're "Fifty North and Forty West!"

Keep in mind poor Nursey lying "on the floor in a heap." Is she there because she has collapsed or, more likely, that for many chronic sufferers relief of sorts may (or may not) be obtained if one voluntarily seeks out the cabin floor?

One such passenger sailed aboard *United States*. Her name was Alison Scott Skelton and she endured a winter eastbound in January 1969, toward the end of the vessel's seventeen years of service. One of six crossings she ever made, Alison confessed that it is the one remaining most obscure in her memory, for some very good reasons.

Aged twenty, she had been an undergraduate at Harpur College in Binghamton, New York. Opting to spend her junior year abroad, she sailed eastbound in September 1966 aboard Cunard's *Aurelia*, a vessel packed with students. Later that fall, in the Scottish town of Drumnadrochit, she met and fell in love with forty-seven-year-old Scot Clem Skelton, abandoned her university studies, and married him. Invited to the States for Christmas with her family, she and Clem sailed westbound in November 1968 aboard *Queen Elizabeth*. Halfway across, she conceived their first child, Alasdair. (He remains, she wrote, "one of what must be one of the relatively few people to have crossed the Atlantic halfway and survived.")

After Christmas, for their return to Scotland, they requested inexpensive accommodations aboard *United States*. Clem had spent seven years as lay brother in a religious order and their cabin was booked for them by his superior, an aging Italian priest who, according to Alison, obviously still had "close family connections." Thanks to his fortuitous ties with a London travel agent, though the Skeltons paid only tourist class fare they were somehow booked into a first class cabin.

It had to be, as far as I can determine, cabin S12, the farthest forward cabin on Sun Deck, overlooking the bow. Alison recalls that they could hear the chime of engine room telegraphs from the bridge above. The cabin had access to a small balcony on which one could stand and survey the view ahead. For Clem, who had indestructible sea legs, visits to that outdoor aerie served as an exhilarating ritual several times daily. But for Alison, a bad sailor also suffering from acute morning sickness, they remained rarities.

Like Kipling's prostrate Nursey, moments past Ambrose Light Alison bedded down on the cabin floor, admittedly atop a mattress but staying as low

as possible. She remembers few excursions outdoors or even indoors to public rooms, including the Dining Saloon. Most of her transatlantic meals involved piecemeal consumption of a large delicatessen salami that she had brought on board, remnants of which she would smuggle into Great Britain. It was one of those typically oddball but compelling fetishes of pregnancy and, throughout the voyage, she consumed slices of salami carved off with Clem's borrowed penknife.

Because of her chronic incapacity, Alison remembers almost nothing about *United States* save for the fact that the vessel's interiors were, to her, somehow disappointing and cold.

My texture and colour images of the *United States* were of lots of silvery metal, as compared to the old *Queen Elizabeth* which was all beautiful golden wood everywhere. Black and white and metal—no idea if that is accurate, but that's how I remember her.

Gibbs's aluminum (which Alison, by then, may have spelled as her fellow Brits do, aluminium) obviously registered heavily. She stressed that Clem would have been a more reliable and informative *United States* chronicler but he has, alas, "sailed on."

After disembarkation into rainswept Southampton, they drove north in Clem's ancient Jaguar, staying at his friends' country houses ("more bathroom floors"), then the Royal George in Perth, and finally, marking the end of that northward progression, to their Highland dwelling, a caravan (trailer) pegged down in a windy, sheep-filled meadow on the shores of Loch Ness. Alison concluded her *United States* memoir charmingly with an incomparable Edinburghian aphorism: "Fur coat, nae knickers."

One crewman was John "Chick" Donohue. Raised in Inwood, in northern Manhattan, he had enlisted in the Marine Corps in 1958, serving extensively in the Far East. Honorably discharged in 1962, he went to work for General Motors parts division in Englewood, New Jersey. When the Vietnam War escalated, he tried reenlisting but, as he put it half a century later, "They didn't want me."

He decided to go to sea instead. As prerequisite, Chick needed a union card and, to get one, he and two friends were advised to forget waiting for months in New York's National Maritime Union hall and try Oakland out on the West Coast. Their cross-country journey was achieved by delivering a car.

Opposite: Commodore Anderson brought *United States* successfully into Pier 86 four times without tugs, due to tug strikes, for the last time on the day of his retirement. On that occasion, it was raining, and reporters gather on the bridge for a final glimpse of the master. Famed NBC television newsman Gabe Pressman completes an interview in the downpour. (Charles Anderson Collection)

Out there, contacts paid off. The manager of the New York Giants' clubhouse, a friend of Chick's father, passed along a West Coast connection. He told Chick by telephone to go to Oakland's union hall and tell port agent Frank that "Eddie Logan had sent him." However reminiscent of speakeasy days his words did the trick.

He obtained a seaman's card and a post as food handler on a cargo vessel called *East Hills* bound for the Far East. She was a broken-down old tub, repeatedly losing power. But Chick had his precious union card, he enjoyed shipboard, and he was paid $300 a month; automatic overtime happened frequently and, even better, wages were doubled in the war zone.

Returning to New York, he had his card bumped up and underwent retraining in a new National Maritime Union building that had just opened on Eighth Avenue. Abandoning food service, he joined the black gang and found a berth aboard Moore-McCormack's *Brazil* as a wiper, the engine room's lowest rank. He cleaned the interior of boilers, a filthy and unpleasant job.

Back in New York, after upgrading, he was given the title "fireman, water tender, oiler," job qualifications that existed separately at that time *only* aboard *United States*; on all other American merchant ships, the three were combined to describe

one man. So in December 1968 Chick Donohue joined *Big U* for a year as a fireman.

He was assigned a cabin with six bunks and always worked the 8 to 12 A.M. watch. He spent very little time in his cabin and did not get to know any of its other occupants because they all worked different shifts. Chick got off from his morning watch by 11:30 and, after lunch, spent another four hours on duty.

Chick made one fortuitous friend on board, a Belfast Irishman named Dezi O'Malley, who had worked for Cunard White Star before transferring to the U.S. Lines. Thanks to his Cunard training, he was appointed senior waiter at the commodore's table.

Dezi and Chick would get together for a drink after their afternoon watch, buying illegally obtained beers. Their supplier was one of the richest crewmen on board, a steward nicknamed Panama. He was a heavy man in his fifties with one blind, or at least damaged, eye. His job was mopping Times Square, as it was called, the athwartship crossover intersecting with Broadway, the main crew alleyway. British seamen invariably christened their main thoroughfare after Liverpool's Scotland Road; not surprisingly, Americans favored Broadway.

At the intersection of Broadway and Times Square was fire station no. 27, where a fog hose hung in a red case. Inside that same red case was Panama's illicit whiskey stash. Elsewhere, he stocked beer, chilled in ice-filled fifty-five-gallon drums. Cans of Schaefer cost crewmen 30 cents though cans of imported Heineken were, for some bizarre reason, a nickel cheaper.

Panama restocked every time the ship returned to New York. Chick regularly saw Schaefer delivery trucks drive brazenly onto the pier and park. Each wheeling a trolley stacked with cases of beer, the driver and a sidekick would embark and trundle them along Broadway to Times Square. There, they were paid in cash by waiting Panama. There was never any problem; apparently, longshoremen had been bribed to turn a blind eye.

Just as interesting as their drink supplier was their routine dinner. There were several crew messes where Chick could have eaten but, early on in his friendship, he did better. When they got off duty at midnight, Dezi suggested a meal together. "What would you like?" he asked Chick.

"What have you got?"

"Anything you want. I have friends in the galley and can order whatever I want." His job at the

Below and opposite: Every one of Commodore Anderson's tug-free dockings prompted a rash of congratulatory messages, both written and telegraphed. In February 1957, U.S. Lines president John M. Franklin dispatched the below. On the same occasion, a letter from the Waldorf Towers conveyed the Windsors' compliments. And a final farewell from his most celebrated passengers reached Anderson on January 31, 1964. (Charles Anderson Collection)

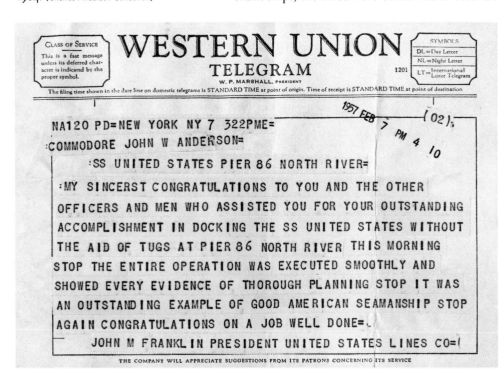

captain's table rewarded him unofficially but regularly with the first class menu's most lavish offerings. So each evening Dezi and Chick feasted on caviar, steak, foie gras, lobster, or whatever they fancied; Chick never reentered his mess again.

On one crossing, Spencer Tracy and Rita Hayworth were a sub rosa couple, occupying one of the smaller suites on Main Deck, M65 and M67. The two cabins shared a connecting door. Their steward, an Irishman, occasionally joined Dezi and Chick for a beer. It was he who told them that he had to make up only one bed of the four between them; the other three were never slept in. I sailed with Chick again recently and he tells me he is now working as a sandhog on the Second Avenue subway.

John Getz was born in York, Pennsylvania, in 1948. Having retired from his career as a television engineer, he is presently an independent travel agent—John's Travel Cruises—living in a condominium with his wife, Jan, in Asheville, North Carolina. We were their fellow passengers aboard *Ocean Princess* in the summer of 2011 and he told me that his father, John Getz Jr., MD, had been a Department of Public Health physician with whom he, his mother, and two-years-younger brother Michael twice crossed aboard *United States*, sailing eastbound in 1955 and westbound two years later.

After spending John's earliest years in Jacobus, Pennsylvania, the Getz family moved to Tompkinsville on Staten Island, location of the Quarantine Inspection Station for inbound steamers headed for New York. As the Public Health Department's medical officer, Dr. Getz boarded every one of those anchored liners repeatedly, sorting out passenger health problems and becoming dauntingly familiar with the interiors of every ship arriving in port. When advised that he and his family were being transferred for European duty to the U.S. consulate in Palermo, Sicily, his choice of carrier was quite naturally *United States*.

As a thrilled seven-year-old anticipating his first crossing, John remembers that every stick of Getz furniture had to be crated. They also had to pack all belongings from their rented Staten Island house: clothes, shoes, books, pictures. Everything was loaded inside stout, barrel-shaped cardboard containers with metal lids. The only clothing the family kept out was what they would need for the crossing, stuffed into suitcases. The day before they

Waldorf Towers
New York, 22, N.Y.

February 26th 1957.

Dear Commodore Anderson,

The Duchess and I were sorry not to see you again before we left your ship on Sunday, to congratulate you on the superb docking operation you performed without the assistance of tugs.

We watched every phase of the intricate seamanship involved with the greatest interest and admiration.

Hoping you will have better weather on your next voyages, and looking forward to sailing with you again April 18th.

With our kind regards,

Sincerely Your's

Edward

Commodore John W. Anderson U.S.R.D.
S.S. "United States"
United States Lines Pier 86
New York,   N.Y.

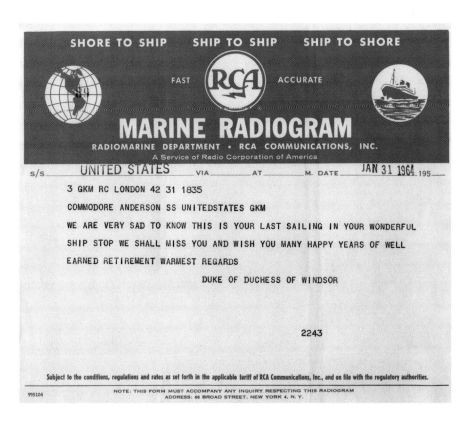

SHORE TO SHIP   SHIP TO SHIP   SHIP TO SHORE

FAST   RCA   ACCURATE

MARINE RADIOGRAM

RADIOMARINE DEPARTMENT · RCA COMMUNICATIONS, INC.
A Service of Radio Corporation of America

s/s UNITED STATES   VIA____ AT____ M. DATE JAN 31 1964 195__

3 GKM RC LONDON 42 31 1835

COMMODORE ANDERSON SS UNITEDSTATES GKM

WE ARE VERY SAD TO KNOW THIS IS YOUR LAST SAILING IN YOUR WONDERFUL

SHIP STOP WE SHALL MISS YOU AND WISH YOU MANY HAPPY YEARS OF WELL

EARNED RETIREMENT WARMEST REGARDS

DUKE OF DUCHESS OF WINDSOR

2243

Subject to the conditions, regulations and rates as set forth in the applicable tariff of RCA Communications, Inc., and on file with the regulatory authorities.

995104   NOTE: THIS FORM MUST ACCOMPANY ANY INQUIRY RESPECTING THIS RADIOGRAM
ADDRESS: 66 BROAD STREET, NEW YORK 4, N. Y.

John Getz Jr., MD, his wife, Josephine, and their sons, John, aged seven, and his brother, Michael, five, pose proudly on *United States*'s deck in mid-ocean. Playtime with the boys—Josephine Getz organizes a shuffleboard tournament and Dr. Getz supervises yet another swimming party down in the pool, alternating with visits to the flying bridge. Kitted out in party hats, gala dinner in the first class Dining Saloon works its customary magic; though neither boy has a dinner jacket, both sport bow ties. (John Getz Collection)

sailed everything—crated furniture and that host of cardboard barrels—was picked up by moving vans at government expense and transferred into Manhattan. Labeled NOT WANTED ON VOYAGE, those belongings were embarked into *United States*'s after baggage hold.

The Getz family was accommodated in two adjoining first class cabins, the location of which neither John nor younger Michael can recall. But one place that both boys remembered with the utmost pleasure was what he and the crew called the Monkey Island, a railed observation lookout located atop the bridge. What John found astonishing was that not one of their fellow passengers had heard of it, let alone used it. He and Michael spent hours up there with their father, holding on for dear life as *United States* streaked across the Atlantic.

They also enjoyed their first class dining table for four where the boys devoured plate after plate of spaghetti bolognese almost exclusively. Neither of them was troubled by seasickness and they would swim, sometimes twice daily, with their father in the first class pool. John remembers the stainless steel vertical baffles at either end that absorbed the water's motion, preventing it from sloshing over the margins.

The only Getz who disliked the crossing was their mother. Josephine had suffered an attack of polio as a teenager, which left her slightly lame in one leg. For her, progress across often sloping decks was challenging.

Their first European station was Palermo, where Dr. Getz's duties included conducting physical exams for Sicilians seeking to emigrate. John remembers little about either the journey south or their nine months of Palermo schooling. Because of the consulate's largely American staff, the boys were enrolled in a special English-language school.

The greatest Sicilian disappointment for both boys was their failed attempt to re-create America's Halloween trick or treating. Dressed in costume and carrying bags for anticipated loot, they were driven by their mother and father from house to house. But so much time was consumed by parental chitchat that the tempo of candy accumulation, legendary in the States, proved glacial.

After nine months in Sicily, the Getz family moved to Paris when their father was transferred to the embassy's staff. Classes in a French-speaking school were as disastrous as Palermo's Halloween. John recalls spending a fortnight in tears before his parents relented and agreed that Josephine would home-school the boys throughout their Parisian year. After completion of Dr. Getz's two-year tour in both Palermo and Paris, the family possessions were again crated and packed for westbound passage home aboard *United States*.

Their embarkation coincided with a medical quandary. As they clambered off the boat train in Le Havre's Gare Maritime, John and Josephine Getz were horrified to see that their eldest son had broken out unmistakably with a chicken pox rash,

presumably contracted from an infected Parisian chum; later, Michael caught it as well.

Though as a public health physician Dr. Getz was obliged to acknowledge his children's condition, he chose not to. Instead, he covered John's head with a blue French beret, turned his coat collar up, and rushed him to the cabin. There both boys remained for the next five days. I suggested to John that their cabin steward surely would have noticed chicken pox spots on the children's faces but either he did not or, he surmises, perhaps they had been disguised by their parents.

However you slice it, two chicken pox victims were on board and, once the vessel departed Southampton for New York, there was no way to get them ashore. Had Dr. Getz passed on news of his children's contagious disease to the ship's surgeon, the invalids would have been isolated in *United States*'s hospital. By the same token, keeping them in their own cabin achieved the same purpose.

The identical treatment—strict isolation—is used to forestall today's rampant norovirus, a gastrointestinal infection that plagues nearly every contemporary cruise ship. At its worst over winter months, norovirus can spread like wildfire to hundreds of passengers aboard the same vessel; brief but strict cabin confinement is the only means of combating it.

Eight years after the Getzes westbound crossing, I faced a similar dilemma while working as production stage manager for the tryout of a Broad-

way-bound play called *A Sign of Affection*. Our first booking was Washington's National Theatre and, together with the rest of the cast, I stayed at the Willard Hotel.

Suddenly, I came down unmistakably with mumps, a childhood affliction somehow hitherto avoided. I faced the same predicament over which the Getz family had agonized: acknowledge or conceal? Luckily, I had an excellent assistant who could handle daily rehearsals and performances. The company manager agreed that I should remain in my hotel room for the duration, eating room service food and concealing swollen jowls beneath a scarf whenever waiter or chambermaid appeared.

The mumps receded and we pressed on to Philadelphia's Walnut Street Theatre. After an indifferent fortnight's business the producers closed the show. My mumps eerily duplicated the Getzes' chicken pox ordeal.

I spoke with Anthony Sander, a South African chief surgeon aboard *Ocean Princess*, on which we sailed up Norway's coast in July 2012. When I told him the Getz story, he was surprised. Even five minutes' "face time," as he called it, between either son and another passenger would have involved instant contagion. He knew nothing about the *United States* nor when it had sailed. But the only possible exception to disclosure Dr. Sander might have countenanced was if the sailing had been a wartime one, just prior to the German invasion of France. Otherwise, he agreed that Dr.

Above and opposite: Four Gore young standing with their mother at the railing as *United States* steams past New Jersey. From left to right: Carolyn, Mary Jane, their mother, Betty, and the two younger boys, Bill and Glenn. The image was passed along by Glenn's in-laws. Posing yet again at another railing with their father, Dr. Herschel Gore. The photograph was obviously taken later in the crossing because Carolyn is not only holding a balloon, she is sporting a souvenir sailor hat. (Alan and June Swan Collection)

Getz had been delinquent in not disclosing his boys' highly communicable infection.

Another Public Health Service doctor, Herschel Gore, MD, took his wife, Betty, and their four children aboard *United States* in July 1967. Just like the Getz family, their crated household goods and hold luggage had preceded them to Manhattan, days before they embarked on a train from their hometown of McLean, Virginia.

They arrived in New York and spent several nights at the Henry Hudson Hotel on West 57th Street before ordering a taxi that carried them to Pier 86. The family's European destination was Athens, where Dr. Gore had been assigned as medical officer attached to the U.S. consulate, replacing, he had been advised confidentially, a Greek predecessor who was to be dismissed for accepting bribes from immigrants that would get them U.S. visas despite disqualifying infections. Of the four Gore children, the oldest was Mary Jane, aged nine; next oldest was seven-year-old Carolyn. The two younger boys were Bill, aged five, and Glenn, who was three.

Mary Jane wrote me recently, introducing her informative memoir: "It was the lap of luxury for our rather modest-means family, and a trip I will never forget. . . . I couldn't wait to get on the ship and explore."

The keenly anticipated day finally arrived. The Gores boarded alone, with no visitors to see them off and, because it was a beautiful day in high summer, clustered at the railings to enjoy departure. All four children were kitted out with matching Braniff Airways bags slung from their shoulders; Mary Jane remembered that hers was stuffed with comics and copies of *Tiger Beat* magazine.

They threw colored paper serpentines distributed by deck stewards. One fellow passenger nearby was a young woman in floods of tears, waving impassioned farewells to her fiancé on the pier. Dr. Gore did his best to console her, helping her hurl one of the family's serpentines to the young man so that they could each hold an end before it was parted by departure. Mary Jane thought it "a bit sad to watch all the streamers break as we made our wayout to sea." She and her siblings were riveted by the sight of the fragile paper link connecting the lovebirds finally sundering forever.

Serpentines or streamers were commonplace features of every New York sailing back then but they have not survived contemporary ecological strictures. In a word, they pollute; once thrown and discarded they degenerate into litter that fouls both vessel and pier. Crew and longshoremen alike had to sweep them up after every departure.

As *United States* continued steaming down the North River, passengers wearing life jackets were mustered on deck for boat drill. Herschel and Betty told their children to remember the number and location of their lifeboat so that, in the event of an emergency, they could assemble there without failure. Dire parental warnings about the *Titanic* catastrophe were imparted. And there came over the loudspeaker the same cautionary that always used to be broadcast by a bridge officer aboard every vessel departing New York: "Will the mothers of small children please make sure that they keep *both feet* on the deck at all times."

That wise dictum is, alas, no longer part of current passengers' boat drill litany. After the ship passed through the Narrows, Dr. Gore pointed out the Public Health Service Hospital, where he had been stationed for four years.

The Gores were accommodated in two first class cabins, an outside for the parents and the boys and, nearby, a smaller inside for the two older girls. Mary Jane and Carolyn slept in two lower bunks while the upper ones remained empty. One evening in her cabin, Mary Jane felt slightly unwell, not seasick but suffering the aftereffects of some bug contracted in New York. After her family went down to dine without her, she summoned the night steward and ordered a restorative milkshake as well as a Coke. The former was free but, since the latter involved a charge, she remembered how it had annoyed her father.

"Luxury's lap" notwithstanding, Mary Jane felt that the ship's staircases seemed steep and the corridors narrow. She wrote, "I thought it would be more spacious, like a hotel on land."

Regardless of that rather sophisticated evaluation from a nine-year-old, she relished the facilities available for children. She recalls, incorrectly, a children's pool and children's gymnasium whereas neither existed; both were adult facilities. What she *did* remember accurately and with great fondness was the Children's Playroom up on Sun Deck.

She and her siblings spent hours there. As their mother, Betty Gore, wrote me, articulating what is, perhaps, the credo of every shipboard parent's concern about their potentially wayward broods: "My daytime hours were spent keeping an eye on the children and hoping they were behaving themselves."

The ship was inevitably crowded during summers because so many families booked on the vessel. And whereas adolescents roamed untended in disparate packs, their younger siblings flocked dutifully to the Children's Playroom.

Mary Jane and Carolyn learned new games, one of them jacks, as well as the novel card games slapjack, war, and go fish. Provided on demand were endless root beer floats and lots of paper, crayons, paint, and brushes for drawing or painting. Late every afternoon, special children's entertainment was laid on, sometimes a magician or a comic musician, including one who somehow managed to hold in his mouth no fewer than, by Mary Jane's astonished count, five toy trombones and trumpets *at the same time*. Children's films were also screened each afternoon, a provision that Mary Jane pronounced in retrospect as "the apex of civilization." On another occasion, she attended a screening of *The Flim-Flam Man*, new that year, starring George C. Scott and Sue Lyon, patently not a film for minors. But as the oldest, Mary Jane was allowed to watch it with her parents in the grown-up cinema.

Their evening highlight was first sitting dinner although the first class menu's consistently lavish fare

quickly overwhelmed the children. Having traveled repeatedly aboard ocean liners with my four children, I well recall the indifference or even deep suspicion the young reserve for adult gastronomy.

Their two stewards obviously knew passenger children better. One lunchtime, after the table's younger occupants had been surfeited yet again with too many sophisticated dishes, the senior man announced that he knew exactly what the children craved. As though rehearsed, his subordinate fed him a line: "What *do* they want?" to increase the tension. Only then did the first man sing out loudly, *"Peanut butter and jelly sandwiches!"* A tableful of young Gores erupted in cheers, to their parents' dismay and embarrassment.

Most of the time on deck, high summer notwithstanding, it was cold and windy. Mary Jane remembers seeing outdoor pools in use but, in fact, none existed; open air pools were rarities on the North Atlantic. But she watched people playing shuffleboard and noticed how those reading or dozing in outdoor deck chairs were swaddled in blankets by solicitous stewards.

Mary Jane loved strolling the decks after dark, watching stars overhead and marveling at those incredible twin stacks towering into the night, no less than an expanse of heaving Atlantic visible in every direction. On the family's last morning at sea, her

father stood with her at the starboard rail, pointing out the Breton coast as they proceeded apace up-Channel to Cherbourg.

The children's loudest dining room cheer since the peanut butter debacle greeted delivery to the table of flaming Baked Alaska, a thrilling dessert parade climaxing their gala dinner. Although Mary Jane never forgot that Baked Alaska, she has not had another one since. "Must make a note to myself," she wrote, "to have another Baked Alaska—maybe with *my* kids, who are now 21 and 19!"

The Gores disembarked from *United States* on July 17 and spent a week in Paris, where Herschel was assigned for a stint at the United States embassy. Then they flew to Rome for a week's holiday before pressing on to Athens, where they took up residence in a charming house in the suburb of Kissifia.

Four years earlier, in April 1963, a young couple in their twenties from Philadelphia, Vic and Mimi Mather, embarked aboard *United States* for an eastbound crossing. I encountered the Mathers aboard *Queen Mary 2* over the summer of 2012. Experienced and enthusiastic passengers these days in retirement, they are saddened by heightened post–9/11 security that has so eroded the evocative image of traditional sailings. Their 1963 *United States* crossing was Mimi's first and she still recalls fondly the pleasure of a festive cabin sendoff, courtesy of Vic's stepmother.

She joined them on board bearing Champagne, flowers, and friends for a classic celebration, admiring their cabin and toasting the voyage. There were only a few celebrities on board—Salvador Dalí (with or without his pet ocelot) as well as Debbie Reynolds and her husband Harry Karl.

Though Mimi had never crossed before, her husband had already sailed transatlantic on both *Queens* and on *Andrea Doria*. Frequent and enthusiastic passengers these days, in the early sixties Mimi suffered chronic seasickness. The Mathers' shipboard routine had, perforce, to accommodate that unhappy-making susceptibility. They slept late, extending the night shortened by eastbound's advancing clocks, and ate no breakfast, either in the Dining Saloon or from trays delivered by their cabin steward. Instead, mornings were passed supine, either in bed or in adjoining deck chairs along the Promenade Deck, shrouded in steamer rugs and relishing views of unsettled sea and sky.

They soon learned to be in place by 11:00 A.M. because that was distribution time for steaming cups of bouillon, delivered by congenial deck stewards, complete with ritual Saltines. Even aboard Cunarders, registered in a country famous for its biscuits, the humble Yankee Saltine holds uncontested sway as unrivaled bouillon accompaniment.

It was, alas, a rough crossing and both Mathers remembered with unease one stupendous roll when *United States* leaned so precipitously to port that they, seated on the starboard side, suddenly saw nothing but sky. The moment the roll reversed, dramatically, clouds were replaced by tormented ocean. Almost hysterically, their neighbors clutched the arms of their deck chairs, remarking on that spectacular gyration. More similar ones followed on that roll-filled morning.

The Mathers bestirred themselves for lunch at a table for two in A Deck's Dining Saloon. Vic, blessed with reliable sea legs, ordered regularly from the choicest areas of the menu, but Mimi's perennial queasiness was such that her daily meals all the way across were restricted to chicken or cheese sandwiches. Though pressed by their steward, she repeatedly if regretfully declined every other option: caviar, steak, lobster, Dover sole, Crêpe Suzette, even Baked Alaska; anything rich she avoided.

After lunch, the Mathers spent afternoons in the cinema, seeing a succession of not very good films, followed occasionally by games of teatime bingo in the Ballroom. One day, Mimi managed to fill her card with all the numbers and still recalls the chorus of audible groans from rival players that greeted her triumphant "*Bingo!*" outburst.

One film she never forgot was *Donovan's Reef*, starring John Wayne and Lee Marvin. Its most distressing footage was an interminable episode aboard a vessel that was rolling even more severely than the one on which she was confined. The combination of the two motions—one actual, the other cinematic—was so devastating that poor Mimi abandoned the cinema and staggered back to the cabin. Vic filled her in later on the plot's outcome.

Their entire crossing, alas, was bereft of almost every conventional shipboard pleasure. Because of perpetually rough seas, the Mathers never swam, never strolled the decks, and never danced to Meyer Davis's infectious orchestrations; instead, books, bingo, bouillon, and bad movies filled their days.

Vic's profession was broker for his family's insurance firm, Thomas Stephens. It had both

Philadelphia and London offices, and he planned to spend two months in London before sailing home aboard *America*. To that end, they occupied a suite at the St. James Hotel in Buckingham Gate for what struck them both as "the exorbitant rate of $16.50 per diem"; given the present ruinous cost of London hotels, it seems a retrospective steal. At that same hotel today, now called the Taj, $16.50 will get you only a shrug.

Regardless, their London tenancy was cut short: Vic's obligation to attend a summer session with the National Guard scheduled for June sent them flying home early.

In fact, identical National Guard duty the following summer saved not only their own but also their newborn daughter's life. Up at 5 A.M. one June morning for that year's first day of duty, Vic smelled smoke in the corridors of their two-story Philadelphia apartment house. He roused Mimi and the baby as well as every tenant. The fire department arrived but, because the hydrant near their building had been struck by a car and turned off the night before, firemen had to await the arrival of longer connectors. As a result, by the time the flames could be quelled the building and their apartment, including everything they owned, went up in flames. Although firemen did salvage Mimi's engagement ring from the rubble, nothing else survived. She had only a nightgown and overcoat to her name. But as she wrote long after the fact, "Those memories are better off forgotten! We were young and the young are very resilient."

Nine-year-old Scott Glasscock sailed aboard *United States* on Friday, August 4, 1961; the vessel would arrive in Cherbourg and Southampton on Wednesday, August 9. As an only child, his shipboard adventures were quieter and essentially lonelier than the Gore family's multiple-sibling muster but Scott was a resourceful young man and made his own amusement on board.

He and his parents were New Yorkers, his father a lawyer. Although his mother was an experienced traveler, that *United States* crossing was both father and son's first venture abroad. Glasscock père was a staunch Anglophile and couldn't wait to savor Great Britain's architecture and countryside.

They had booked in cabin class. Scott, who is today both a lawyer and an actor, retained his family's itinerary; as a result, unlike every other passenger I interviewed, he knew his cabin number perfectly. All cabin class accommodations were located toward the after end of the vessel. Theirs was on the penultimately lowest level the class occupied, aft on the starboard side. Cabin A-115 lay at the end of a short jog to starboard off the alleyway, past inside cabins A-111 and A-117.

Neighboring outsides A-115 and A-119 had exterior views, thanks to a single porthole directly in line with the cabin's entry. There were four bunks in toto (uppers and lowers), as well as a private bathroom with shower. Two sinks occupied the after wall. Scott slept in one of the uppers. During the crossing, he finished two successive paperbacks, one about Geronimo, the other a biography of President Eisenhower. That was the extent of Scott's transatlantic reading save for mandatory perusal of the ship's newspaper.

Their cabin porthole, he claims, was equipped with a window seat and curtain although nothing of the kind appears on the deck plan. When not reading, he spent hours perched just inside that porthole, imagining he was driving a locomotive across the ocean, which seemed to him only a few feet below. Because of the vastness of the Atlantic and the impact of passing waves, he felt that "we were rushing through it." Sometimes he would spy ships in the distance, all of them anonymous freighters. For the most part, the seas were not especially rough and, in any event, all three Glasscocks were good sailors.

Scott remembered little about their cabin steward, probably because they never ordered breakfast from him but trooped each morning forward along A Deck, across the Main Foyer, and into their Dining Saloon.

Scott found the vessel fascinating and explored it thoroughly. Since cabin and first class shared the cinema aft on Promenade Deck, whenever he attended a film he could exit effortlessly into first class when it ended. He negotiated another surreptitious first class entry by slipping beneath a barrier. Scott found he could wander unimpeded throughout the vessel; well dressed and well behaved, he was never questioned or returned to cabin class.

Scott made a point of collecting U.S. Lines swizzle sticks, souvenirs for every enterprising young passenger that could be picked up in the Smoking Rooms of every class. They had spread-winged eagles atop them in one of three colors: blue for first, red for cabin, and clear for tourist. The fact that Scott amassed such a large haul of all three colors

On Friday morning, August 4, 1961, the Glasscock family from Short Hills, New Jersey, arrived at Manhattan's Pier 86 for an eastbound crossing aboard *United States*. From left to right: nine-year-old Scott, the couple's only child; his father, James A. Glasscock, a lawyer at Milbank, Tweed, Hope & Hadley; his mother, Adelaide Boze Glasscock. Although father and son are crossing for the first time, Mrs Glasscock was an experienced transatlantic traveler. (United States Lines)

Near right: After leaving their luggage in their cabin class quarters, the Glasscock family attended lifeboat drill. After it was over, still wearing their life jackets, father and son "clown" for the camera and Adelaide Glasscock immortalizes the moment. (Scott Glasscock Collection)

Far right: Scott's father is photographed at the rail by his son in mid-ocean. A dedicated Anglophile, he was immensely looking forward to his first sight of Britain's countryside during a fortnight's tour of the British Isles in a rented car. (Scott Glasscock Collection)

On their last night before calling at Cherbourg, all three Glasscocks don paper hats to enjoy a gala dinner in cabin class's Dining Saloon. Perhaps by design, their steward Taylor was not included in the photograph; Adelaide Glasscock felt he was more than *"un peu déclassé."* (United States Lines)

As *United States* entered the port of Southampton that summer afternoon, Scott and his parents were out on deck. Scott saw they were about to pass two vessels: farthest away was 1959 *Rotterdam* but the closer two-funneled ship defies identification. (Scott Glasscock Collection)

bore witness to the ease with which he could penetrate with impunity *United States*'s class barriers.

Once, he also penetrated alien country. Investigating a crew stairway, he suddenly realized that it was leading somewhere as interesting as it must be forbidden. But no one stopped him as he descended deeper and deeper into *United States*'s lower regions. Rising up the metal staircase before him was an increasingly deafening roar, emanating from the engine room.

Suddenly, Scott stopped, intrigued but apprehensive. More than half a century later, he remembers saying to himself firmly, "Well, I should probably not be here." Regretfully, he "chickened out" and remounted that obviously restricted descent.

The waiter at their three-seated table in the cabin class Dining Saloon was named Taylor, an African American whom Scott's mother felt was rather too casual. Mrs. Glasscock was a heavy smoker, and whenever she put a cigarette in her mouth Taylor would flip out his Zippo with a flourish and light it. That was acceptable but, when any of his clients stopped eating, Taylor also had a habit of merely pointing at their plates quizzically for confirmation that they were finished.

Mrs. Glasscock had both a bachelor's degree from Sweet Briar College and a master's in French from Columbia. Prewar, she had sailed aboard *Normandie* and, after the war, led travel groups to Europe. Having crossed in first class on many celebrated liners, she found Taylor more than a little déclassé. Because of her extensive shipboard background, Scott's mother had fashioned the family's itinerary, employing *Fielding's Travel Guide to Europe*.

Truth be told, Scott led a rather solitary existence. There was, of course, a cabin class Children's Playroom where a get-together for young passengers was offered. Though he attended, he did not meet anyone he particularly enjoyed or remembered. He never swam in the pool, yet another facility shared with first class.

The entire family did attend one evening of horse racing in the Main Lounge, just aft of the Children's Playroom. Before departing New York, a family friend had presented Scott with a stack of 50-cent coins so he could place bets on his own. What makes shipboard horse racing suspenseful was that to get over one of the jumps required the lady passenger rolling the dice to throw a double. Often, the lead horse, a probable shoo-in paying great odds, might be stalled at a fence awaiting

that elusive double while the field caught up relentlessly. Sadly, Scott never won any race and never played bingo, either alone or with his parents. He tended, by and large, to retire early while his father and mother danced in cabin class's Main Lounge. Given his dedication to "drive *United States* like a train" through the cabin porthole, it seems curious that adventurous Scott never found his way to the Monkey Island atop the bridge, a splendid vantage point that would have enabled him to experience *United States*'s tumultuous open-air progress firsthand.

When it reached Cherbourg early on the morning of August 9, the vessel was already docked by the time Scott woke up. He hung over the rail, watching passengers and cargo going ashore. Later that day, the Glasscocks took the boat train from Southampton and booked into London's Waldorf Hotel. There followed an extensive UK tour in a rented Ford Consul as far north as Scotland's Fort William. On August 25 they drove back to London, flew British European Airways to Paris's Hôtel Bradford, and raced home to New York four days later via Pan American Airways.

The film that Scott most enjoyed on the crossing was a zany black-and-white comedy about World War II. Near film's end there was a scene where the comic lead, playing a GI, was intent on sabotaging a threatening German howitzer. Straddling the huge gun barrel as though it were a horse, he shinnied up to the muzzle and lowered a substantial explosive charge down the barrel on a cord. But that's all Scott could recall. Despite his detailed memory about everything else aboard *United States*, he drew a rare blank on both his favorite film's name as well as its explosive finale.

On July 16, 1959, Chicagoans Florence Frank and her sixteen-year-old daughter Yvette embarked aboard *United States* for an eastbound crossing. Florence's husband was not with them. As a printing machinery dealer, he could not take months off from his business; moreover, Yvette confided, her father did not care much for travel anyway.

Florence Frank had grown up a British subject and immigrated to the States some years earlier. Now she was returning to visit her parents in the United Kingdom, introducing them to their granddaughter for the first time. They would be away from home for much of the summer.

It was Yvette's first crossing. The two Franks had booked in cabin class and shared a four-berth cabin with two congenial lady teachers. Although Yvette could not recall her cabin number, she says that there was plenty of room for four occupants in what she describes as a "very large and comfortable" space.

By great good fortune both Yvette and her mother kept shipboard diaries. Shipboard diarists on crossings are as rare as world cruise diarists are commonplace. During many world cruises, I have noted that almost all my fellow passengers keep meticulous diaries. But crucial pages tend to be left blank: whereas they wax lyrical about every port—information available in countless guidebooks—they recount little or nothing about intervening sea days. For maritime historians researching those diaries years later, invaluable shipboard snippets from the mid-twentieth century would have been as welcome as they are, sadly, nonexistent.

But Yvette Frank's diary, its pages dutifully filled throughout two *United States* crossings, remains a splendid and unique account of a teenager's days at sea, replete with names and adventures. For adolescents, shipboard turns into an endless chiaroscuro of introduction, encounter, chatter, crushes, disappointments, harmless peccadilloes, and, always, shared excitement. Admittedly, Yvette started, slowly.

July 16—Embarked on SS *United States* at noon. At lunch met a friend, Ardis, from my B'nai B'rith Club in Chicago. In evening went to Tourist Class, played Bingo.

Because Ardis and her mother were booked first class, it enabled Yvette to join them for occasional meals. The next day, she is off and running.

July 17—Played shuffleboard with Ardis, swam and went to gym—met many boys. In evening, met another girl and went to Tourist Class. Met 3 more girls (5 of us now). Having so much fun.

Whereas Ardis offered access up into first, "another girl" rewarded Yvette with easier access down to tourist. The diarist also includes a pointed aside, that "Mom wrote 'raining.'" The contrast between the daughter's frenetic activities and her mother's prosaic meteorological documentation remained a constant.

July 18—Alice (one of my new friends) and I walked on deck and all around ship. Had dinner at the Gala dinner with champagne, hats, and balloons and wore a formal dress. Watched Danny Kaye movie *Five Pennies* and then went to lounge and danced and drank until 3:00 A.M.

For that same day, recalls Yvette, "Mom wrote 'raining.'" On one of her two crossings, Yvette apparently dined twice in first class, once among a group of privileged passengers at Commodore Anderson's table.

Florence seemed not at all distressed that her daughter had essentially abandoned her down in cabin class's Dining Saloon; rather, she was thrilled that Yvette was having the time of her life experiencing first class, admittedly without authorization.

The next day, Yvette spent some makeup time with Florence.

July 19—Relaxed at pool with my Mom. Alice and Roberta (another new friend) and I played shuffleboard. After dinner, went into First class and then to our lounge in Cabin class, where we danced and drank. Had so much fun!

For the same day, her mother's diary read "raining" and "sunny." Yvette stayed up so late that she slept until 1 P.M. the following day.

I wondered if Yvette had sufficient elegant dresses for evenings in first class. She told me that she was traveling with a "huge wardrobe" so there was apparently no shortage. Despite repeated illicit intrusions, she encountered no problems waltzing in and out of first. Several times, she sat out on deck in a first class deck chair, always wearing a head scarf because of constant winds.

Thanks to her almost nightly forays into first, Yvette became notorious throughout cabin class's public rooms. She remembers that every time she entered the Main Lounge the band leader struck up a few bars of "My Kind of Town," pointed musical reference to Yvette's hometown, Chicago.

Her shipboard idyll ended, as it always must, with disembarkation in Southampton. She never saw or heard from those shipboard acquaintances again. After she and her mother had spent two weeks in the UK they flew to Israel for another fortnight before returning to Naples by steamer. A quick tour of Italy and France followed before they reembarked aboard *United States* in Southampton for a westbound crossing on September 3, which proved rougher but sunnier.

Again, Yvette's diary entries provide a detailed recap.

September 3—Embarked on SS *United States* from Southampton. Met Libby, Freddi, and Debbie. We sat together in the Cabin class lounge all evening, sailed at 12:00 A.M. and watched from the deck as we left Europe.

Yvette Frank, aged sixteen, and her mother at lifeboat drill, leaving New York aboard *United States* on July 16, 1959. Yvette is the young lady on the left. Her mother, two people behind her, carries a large white purse and is wearing a head scarf. (Florence Frank and Dr. Yvette Frank Greenspan Collection)

The bill from CIT Travel Service Inc. in Chicago reveals the cost of their shipboard transportation for the summer—a round-trip on *United States* in cabin class and also accommodations aboard motor vessels *Enotria* and *Messapia* for passage to Israel and back to Naples. Then mother and daughter traveled by train from Naples for some Italian sightseeing before reaching Paris and then Cherbourg for their westbound return. (Florence Frank and Dr. Yvette Frank Greenspan Collection)

CABLES: ITALCIT   TELEPHONE: DEarborn 2-5334-5

CIT
Travel Service, Inc.   Nº   7399
333 NO. MICHIGAN AVE., CHICAGO 1, ILL.

                                                    DATE
TO ___ Mrs. Florence FRANK ___ June 15, 1959
       Miss Yvette FRANK

RE: Steamship Passage –
     Eastbound: July/16/1959 s/s United States to Southampton
                 Cabin Class – A-51/1-2
                                    $260.00 p.p. ... x 2 .... $ 520.00
     Westbound: Sept. 4, 1959
                 s/s United States from Le Havre
                 Cabin Class – B-141/3-4 $277.50 $ 555.00
                              " 5.75 tax ... x 2 .... $ 11.50
     **Embarkation previous evening
     Sept. 3, 1959

RE: Aug/7/1959 MV Enotria Bringisi/Haifa$126.00 plus $9.00 tax $ 270.00
     Aug/18/1959 MV Messapia – Haifa/Naples $126.00 plus $9.00   " 270.00
                                             Total: $1,626.50
                                             Less Deposit   - 400.00
                                             Balance Due: $1,226.50

XB

Walking companionably along the pier at Le Havre, Yvette and a friend are about to rejoin westbound *United States*. (Florence Frank and Dr. Yvette Frank Greenspan Collection)

Far left: Diarist Yvette settling down for some sun time aboard *United States*. Booked in cabin class, judging from the position of the number 2 funnel behind her, she has not yet elevated herself effortlessly into first. (Florence Frank and Dr. Yvette Frank Greenspan Collection)

Near left: Although not wearing a bathing suit, Yvette, on the left, sunbathes in her deck chair. Sunning next to her and dressed for swimming is one of dozens of her shipboard contemporaries. (Florence Frank and Dr. Yvette Frank Greenspan Collection)

Pages 193–200: United States Lines
deck plans for the SS *United States*.
(Michael Jedd Collection)

Opposite:

Bridge Deck, Sports Deck, and
Sun Deck at the top of the vessel.
At the forward end of Sun Deck is
cabin no. S-12, in which seasick Alison
Skelton bedded down for her 1969
eastbound (see page 177). At Sport
Deck's forward end was tourist class's
topmost lookout with benches to
either side. A dog kennel complex also
occupied Bridge Deck.

Promenade Deck was first class's
busiest thoroughfare. Extending
forward was the Cinema (shared with
cabin class), the Smoking Room, the
Entrance Foyer to outer decks. Then
the Special Restaurant and its Navajo
bar, the Ballroom, first class's main
staircase, and the Observation Lounge.
First class ended and tourist class
began with its 200-seat Cinema,
Library, Card Room, and Main Lounge.
Tourist cabins and public rooms
descended from there.

Upper Deck started aft with cabin
class's Main Lounge, surrounded by
enclosed Promenades; forward to port
was their combined Writing Room/
Library, and to starboard the Children's
Playroom. Forward of that, Upper
Deck reverted to first class suites, separated amidships by inside servants'
cabins. Forward, the deck's final
slice incorporated tourist class cabins
as well as their Novelty Shop and
Hairdresser amidships.

During the following two days the pace quick-
ened.

September 4—Went to movie theatre with Freddi and
Libby and saw *It Started with a Kiss*. Met 2 guys on the deck
and played shuffleboard with them. After dinner, went to
lounge and played Bingo. Girls were seasick but I went to
the movie theatre again to see movie for the second time.

September 5—Boy, what a rough night. Scared stiff! Woke
up about 9:20 and stayed in sun till lunch and then went to
show and saw *That Kind of Woman* with Tab Hunter. Af-
terwards, stayed on deck till 6, got dressed for Gala Dinner.
Went down to Tourist and met a boy, Bob. Came back to
Cabin, and met a Mr. Greer from First class. Danced with
him and he is very nice.

As her social whirls unfold, some unusual reve-
lations: that the rough night frightened Yvette
and—the only reference in any of my passenger recalls—mention of actual sunbathing on a *United
States* deck. And who was the anonymous "Mr.
Greer" from first class? Yvette confessed that she
could not recall his first name at all.

September 6—Met Libby, stayed on deck and played
shuffleboard until 4:00 P.M. Went to see movie *It Happened to Jane* (not very good). Went swimming. In evening,
I went to First class, had dinner, and danced with about 5
boys and talked a great deal. Left First class and went to
Tourist class and Cabin class lounges and danced with Smiley, a boy I met playing shuffleboard.

More friends, more fellows, and yet again continual case of passage between classes in both di
rections.

September 7—Sunbathed on deck with Libby and other
girls. In the afternoon, went to see a movie, *A Private's
Affair*. Played the races with all my friends and won $5.50.
Danced with Smiley.

The proximity of North America's coastline in
early September obviously produced more warm
weather.

The diary pages reprise Yvette's giddy onboard
paseo to perfection. Her final entry indicates that
the second crossing was ending, reducing the diarist to tears and exhaustion.

September 8—Got up at 6:00 A.M. with only five hours sleep.
Saw the Statue of Liberty and here I arrive in America, my
home. After customs, my father, brother, sister-in-law and
young niece met us as we disembarked. And PICKED US
UP in New York. I was so happy I cried. We disembarked
and went to the motel and showed the gifts and then went to
the Empire State Building and out to eat and then to rest.
Am so tired. Spent day sightseeing in New York.

Yvette's father had left his company's office over
Labor Day weekend and been driven east by his
son in a capacious Oldsmobile to pick up his wife
and daughter. After one whirlwind New York day,
the reunited Franks headed west, driving for two
days home to Chicago.

Although Gibbs had designed *United States* as
a potential troopship, she was never formally converted. The closest it came was that (happily
aborted) Joint Chiefs' flap while she was fitting
out. However, she did transport many American
armed forces personnel and their families stationed in Germany home by sea. One such dependent was young Stephen Wassner, aged
eleven. I sailed with him aboard *Queen Mary* 2 in
the summer of 2012 and he told me he had traveled
aboard *United States* on January 20, 1961, voyage
no. 216 westbound.

In fact, it was not his first crossing because he
had sailed eastbound with his family in 1951 at the
age of one. But when his father, by then Major
William R. Wassner, stationed at Frankfurt's
Rhein-Main Air Base, received orders transferring
him to Oklahoma's Tinker Air Force Base, he was
told that he and his family would be eligible for
first class passage home aboard *United States*. The
Wassner party included Wassner's wife, Amelia,
and two children, nine-year-old Daphne and
Stephen, newly eleven; in fact, embarkation occurred just two days after his birthday.

Once aboard, they were delighted to find that
they had been assigned a suite on Upper Deck. Although none of the family can recall its actual
number, the fact that their spread included two
separate bedrooms as well as a central sitting room
identifies it without question as a suite, one of fourteen on board. Stephen suggested that it was located across from the empty "Presidential Suite."
In fact, not directly across from it because there
were two back-to-back banks of inside cabins in
the center of the vessel separating the grander quarters lining the hull. But he claims that their steward gave the Wassners a sub rosa tour of that unoc-
cupied Presidential Suite.

Stephen's memory triggers controversy among
Big U buffs who insist that no such Presidential
Suite existed. Although several former White
House occupants—Trumans, Eisenhowers, Ken-
nedys, and a Clinton—embarked aboard *United
States*, no first class deck plan labeled any suite
"Presidential."

Opposite:

Main Deck aft incorporated cabin class's Main Lounge and, forward on the port side, some cabin class cabins before reverting again to first class. These larger cabins continued forward to the first class's main lobby, accessed through doors piercing the hull's sides. There were purser's desk, baggage master, chief steward, and access to the medical center, where chief surgeon and assistant surgeons were available for all three classes. At the forward end was more tourist country, including a smoking room and additional cabins.

A Deck accommodated all three Dining Saloons. Cabin class cabin corridors aft led into their own purser's office and desk but without hull entry. Across that lobby lay their Dining Saloon. Separated by a solid bulkhead, first class's Dining Saloon was entered at its forward end. Near the bow was tourist class's Dining Saloon and more tourist cabins.

B Deck had a starboard-side assemblage of tourist class cabins.

C Deck housed the pool and gymnasium, complete with treatment rooms for ladies and gentlemen. Although the deck plan indicates that the pool/gymnasium ostensibly accepted all three classes, in fact, tourist passengers were denied entry. Farther forward was a final assemblage of tourist class cabins.

Because theirs was a midwinter passage seas were rough and many passengers were seasick. Walking outdoors, both Stephen and Daphne recalled, mandated warm clothing and diligent care of sloping and almost perpetually wet decks. But the Wassner family enjoyed every moment regardless. There is one foolproof yardstick with which one can always gauge passenger enthusiasm: no Wassner missed a single meal or snack from day one through day five.

The family seemed to eat nonstop, from dawn till dusk. A tray of pastries, coffee, and juice was delivered to their suite first thing each morning. Consumption of that preliminary notwithstanding, the Wassners then proceeded to the Dining Saloon for an enormous breakfast. Then in late morning, seated on adjacent deck chairs and shrouded in steamer rugs along Promenade Deck, they drank cups of hot chocolate for the children and bouillon for their parents. Amelia Wassner states to this day that *United States* bouillon was the best she ever tasted. Then came lunch, tea, dinner, and usually a final "snack" before bedtime.

For two children who seemed to inhale food of every description, the crossing was an unalloyed delight. Having been conditioned to dinner party etiquette when the family was stationed near Washington, D.C., they were perfectly at ease with formal dining aboard *United States*. Stephen remembers dressing in what he describes as "church attire" every day: "My dad in a suit, me wearing a sport coat, my mom and sister in dresses or shirts."

The Wassners were impressed by their two extremely competent table stewards. One evening, Daphne ordered a New York strip steak, which she found hard to slice, so the waiter immediately volunteered to cut it for her. He removed the center of the steak and divided it into manageable, bite-sized portions. But he left at least an inch of meat around the plate's periphery. When Major Wassner interjected that his daughter could eat that part, too, the waiter responded that they routinely dispatched passenger steaks' outboard edges up to the kennel. But for good measure he returned to the galley and brought Daphne a second steak, just in case.

Of all the Wassners, Daphne seemed the most cognizant of the menu's possibilities. One evening, she announced excitedly that she would like Baked Alaska. Both parents objected, explaining that she was asking for a very special dish that, on a subsequent night, would be produced for the entire dining room and to please choose something else. But, having overheard the exchange, the waiters took her order regardless and, twenty minutes later, appeared bearing Baked Alaska with, as Daphne crowed delightedly, "all the frills." The Wassners shared their bounty with some grateful fellow passengers at a neighboring table.

One evening, the ship's photographer snapped a photograph of the Wassner children in evening attire, playing gin rummy at a card table in the Children's Playroom, complete with score card and accompanying drinks. The following day, the picture was posted prominently in the photo gallery and an announcement was made several times over the loudspeakers, advising passengers to be aware of "Two notorious card sharks on board."

Stephen recalls that they filled their time playing cards or other games, including shuffleboard. Daphne remembers a bowling alley on board but was not sure. She was incorrect. Bowling at sea is rare, although *France* of 1912 did have a special *le bowling* lane installed on the stern. Few if any spares, let alone strikes, were achieved aboard that notorious roller.

The children spent hours alone in the swimming pool. Few other passengers showed up because so many were seasick. There was some spectacular turbulence and, due to the rough seas, pool water sloshed back and forth. At their end of the pool, the depth would suddenly diminish to only a foot or so but, moments later, a miniature tidal wave would come hurtling back. Both children found it endless fun riding those indoor cascades. Miraculously, the water remained largely inside the pool. The remedy for the same problem aboard *America*—shortening the pool's length—never had to be implemented because *United States*'s pool was equipped with damping underwater baffles around all four margins.

The Wassners found the level of service incredibly devoted. One day Daphne lost a bracelet. Their cabin steward suggested she check with lost-and-found at the purser's desk to see if someone had turned it in but no one had. So the steward and several of his fellows searched every public room that Daphne had visited, trying to locate it. Even though Amelia assured them that her daughter's bracelet had little or no value, they persisted. It never turned up and may still be somewhere aboard *United States* as she molders at her Philadelphia pier. Good stewards, indeed *every* steward, always indulge passengers' children shamelessly, quite simply because they are reminded so poignantly of their own families in far-away homes, with whom they spend too little time.

One afternoon, the children were invited to an event in the Children's Playroom where helium-filled balloons were distributed. Next morning, before those balloons lost their buoyancy, Stephen and Daphne released them from an open deck aft and watched them dance aloft before vanishing high over the heaving Atlantic. On the festive gala evening—complete with a second Baked Alaska for the Wassner table—hats and noisemakers appeared on the tables as though it were New Year's Eve.

Stephen said he did not remember any other children on board but was convinced "there must

A photograph of Stephen and Daphne Wassner playing cards in the Smoking Room. Shortly thereafter, a cautionary announcement was circulated, identifying the two as ruthless professional gamblers on board for that crossing. (William Wassner Family Collection)

have been some." In fact, I expect there were none; January was, after all, out of season and most children, apart from those identified worldwide as service brats, were in school.

It was *United States*'s lavish dispensation of food the Wassners remembered most fondly. At their final dinner, the surfeited children asked for a hamburger but were informed by their stewards that, regretfully, the chef did not dispense hamburgers.

So their first New York meal was a hamburger. But, to parental chagrin, as they drove to Oklahoma in the Wassners' new automobile, Stephen and Daphne reverted to ordering Dining Saloon meals. Amelia remembers when they arrived in New York that, of all the clothes she had brought, she was able to wear only a single skirt, the one with an elastic waistband.

Another passenger encountered on *Queen Mary 2* that same summer was Bruce Blitz of Media, Pennsylvania. Rather than first or cabin, Blitz traveled exclusively in tourist. At the age of twenty-three, he had completed two *United States* round-trips, the first in June 1967. Armed with a Eurail pass, he sailed eastbound and spent his summer traveling all over the continent before returning home in the fall. He repeated the procedure the following year. Each of his *United States* round-trip fares was $550, the lowest on board.

I asked him what tourist class *United States* shipboard was like. He was accommodated in an inside cabin shared with two strangers at the bottom of the ship. Tourist class cabins were spread along the starboard side of B Deck (crew were accommodated to port) and also in the forwardmost portions of C and D decks.

Every tourist cabin had two sinks as well as lower berths that converted to sofas by day. Bathroom and bathing options lay down the alleyway. Their open deck space was forward on Promenade Deck, outside the main lounge. Forward of that, down on Upper Deck, was a barbershop, beauty parlor, and the Children's Playroom. A small—the smallest—Meyer Davis orchestra played in the class's Main Lounge for dancing each night.

Even though it was summer, the weather was cold on every one of Bruce's crossings. Perhaps understandably, he recalled little about food. Tourist's Dining Saloon was tiled in red and white with maroon-colored chair upholstery and bright white walls. Emblazoned atop every menu was a breezy suggestion: "You could satisfy your palate's desire from the favorite hamburger to *paté de foie gras*."

He sat at tables full of strangers and, on his first crossing, found only one man with whom he had any enjoyable conversation, but he did occasionally chat with others encountered out on deck. Despite those somewhat barren surroundings it was, he reminded me, for only four nights and five days.

Although Bruce's cabin was low in the vessel, it was not noisy. But he did remember there was some sort of nocturnal machinery that went on and off; he could hear it out in the alleyway, not loud but certainly audible. I asked him if he ever went swimming. Never, he replied. Tourist class was denied access to the pool.

His passenger list boasted no celebrities. The only one he encountered was Peter Noone, a twenty-year-old rock star from Manchester in the UK, one of Herman's Hermits. Noone was traveling cabin class and Bruce managed to spot him once briefly but, because of class barriers, only from a distance.

In 1966, New Yorker Jessica Weber had just graduated from the Parsons School of Design and been awarded a combined Parsons and New York University decorating degree. She was refused admission to the Yale School of Design because there were very few openings for women in those days. So, unexpectedly, her summer of 1966 was free of obligations.

Her mother, Tamar, happened to know an agent who booked shipboard entertainers from an office in Manhattan's Brill Building. He told Tamar that United States Lines was looking for somebody to look after groups of first and cabin class children aboard *United States*. Jessica had a cousin whom her mother thought might be a good candidate, but when she heard about Yale's refusal Tamar wondered if Jessica might qualify instead. She could play guitar and had a good singing voice.

Jessica had sailed on only one other vessel, Cunard's second *Mauretania*, sixteen years earlier. After her husband died, widowed Tamar had taken her two children, Jessica and her younger brother, Mark, on a Caribbean cruise. Interestingly, to market those voyages in the UK, the company routinely promoted them as "West Indies Sunshine Cruises," guaranteeing rain-weary Brits seagoing days of subtropical warmth.

Now, there might be an opportunity to sail again but this time aboard *United States*. Jessica went for her Brill Building interview, well aware that she was being auditioned for personality and presentability in addition to musical ability. Everything went well, the interview was a success, and she was given, in effect, a perfect job for the entire summer of 1966.

She would make four round-trips on *United States*, and she would be paid, in cash, $125 per voyage. (Aboard ocean liners, a voyage is a round-trip, eastbound and westbound combined.) Before departing New York each time, she was given sealed envelopes containing prepaid tips (she never knew for how much) for her cabin and dining room stewards. She was accommodated in cabin B4 for all four voyages, a first class inside with attached bathroom. The cabin steward was a young Englishman, working to earn enough money so he could marry his sweetheart back in England.

Jessica never wore a uniform but dressed in her own clothes. Her working schedule involved two hours spent each morning with cabin class youngsters—from 9:30 to 11:30 A.M.—and from 2:30 to 4:30 P.M. with another batch from first. Her headquarters was the Reading and Writing Room just off the Observation Lounge but she was cautioned that the children had to be quiet so as not to disturb adult passengers.

On that first crossing she was supplied with only one game of checkers and some jigsaw puzzles. So Jessica had to play perennial Pied Piper, taking long files of children out on deck and parading all over the vessel as she and they sang. In fact, she sang so much that she nearly lost her voice.

Back in New York, Jessica insisted to her superiors that decks of cards and board games had to be provided for her charges as well. They were produced for the remaining voyages and she was able to amuse the children with games for part of the session and not be required to sing herself speechless and, incidentally, out of a job. In fact, she found that she could handle six games of checkers at once, setting up boards and opponents at tables while she ran around the room, keeping one move ahead of successive shifts of half a dozen opponents.

Apart from those morning and afternoon gigs, a total of four hours each day, Jessica's shipboard time was her own. Though technically a crew member, she sailed in first class quarters and enjoyed first class perks. She ate breakfast, lunch, and dinner during first sitting in the first class Dining Saloon, in company with one of the ship's singers. She could order whatever she wished but, although she always loved the caviar, she felt the menu was somewhat provincial, lavish but predictably limited. I think she was right. America's popular palate in the 1950s was scarcely adventurous, especially as perceived retrospectively by the dedicated foodies that most New Yorkers seem to have become.

Jessica had a splendid time-off bonus because, by 1966, *United States* was conforming to *America*'s itinerary. She disembarked in Cherbourg as the ship proceeded without her to Southampton and Bremerhaven. Thus, Jessica spent two nights in Paris in the midst of all four voyages. She always booked a seat in tourist class's boat train carriage to Paris, partly because it was cheaper and partly because she enjoyed being with people her own age for a change. When the vessel returned to Cherbourg, she would reembark, get back to work, and sail home.

Love reared its head. During her first eastbound, Jessica met a fellow passenger named Claude Levy. A young French professor of American literature, he'd been studying in the States and had so enjoyed his time there that he wanted to extend it by sailing home aboard *United States* rather than *Liberté*. Jessica and Claude fell for each other and she used to see him nonstop during each Parisian stay.

Jessica did not drink at the time so all her pay could be saved. Since her tips were covered, she had no expenses. She was tipped only once, presented with a five-dollar bill by an American colonel whose three children she had kept happily amused. In sum, for an adventurous young guitar-strumming New Yorker, it had been a dream job. Jessica Weber stayed with design and today heads her own eponymous firm in New York, happily married to an artist named Alan Peckolick.

Many Gibbs & Cox employees not only crossed occasionally aboard *United States* but also made the trip down to Newport News for the annual November drydocking, supervising maintenance work on the vessel's infrastructure and machinery. One of the most interesting was Walter Bachman, who joined the company in 1937 as a novice and retired as vice president and chief engineer in 1970.

He was a short man who, starting in the early 1940s, suffered from psoriatic arthritis, which meant he walked with a slight limp; he also suffered an occasional stammer. Regardless, he was imbued with incredible engineering talent. He grew up in the small rural town of Nazareth, Pennsylvania, where he became an Eagle Scout and was elected president of his high school class.

After graduation, he went to Lehigh University in nearby Bethlehem. Equipped with a master's degree in 1935, he obtained his first job with Federal Shipbuilding and Drydock, located on Kearny Point, New Jersey, alongside the Hackensack River. Organized in 1917 as a subsidiary of United States Steel, it served as the center of U.S. Navy destroyer construction for years.

Bachman's stay there was brief. The following year he was loaned by Federal to Gibbs & Cox; his wife, Betty, used to joke with friends that Walter's "loan" was lifelong.

His salary throughout his tenure until retirement in 1970 was never very generous, though William Francis Gibbs once remarked: "It is the opinion of many that Walter Bachman is easily the best and foremost marine engineer in the world today. If modesty be a fault, he can plead guilty."

His daughter-in-law Molly came from Concord, Massachusetts. She recalls that she and Van Bachman, Walter's oldest child and only son, had decided they wanted to get married in 1962. At the time, both her future parents-in-law were abroad, sailing home via *United States*. When they landed and were told of the plan, it turned out that the wedding weekend they had selected coincided with *United States*'s—and Walter Bachman's— scheduled visit to Newport News. As Molly lamented in a letter to me, "I found myself in competition with her . . . and she was much bigger than I was!" But, thankfully, the matter was resolved and the wedding proceeded mostly as Van and Molly had planned. She added, "How the *United States* fared that year, I do not know, but I did all right, tying a knot that has held for fifty years."

Gibbs & Cox had a company yacht called *Weather*, commanded by Norwegian master Reidar Christiansen. A former shrimp boat, she had been purchased and redesigned in Florida. Sturdy rather than sleek, she was about 50 feet overall, twin screwed, with a cabin that slept three. Installed in the vessel were additional fuel tanks that increased its potential range as far as Bermuda.

Walter was promoted to the post of Gibbs & Cox chief engineer in 1938 as a replacement for

ailing Henry Meyer, a brilliant Dutchman who had occupied the position before him. Although Short Hills, New Jersey, is today reputed an elegant suburb, the Bachmans lived there modestly, their house a remodeled three-car garage on a quarter acre. Walter owned a simple, basic car but in fact, Van recalled, his father hardly drove anywhere, only to the railway station for his weekday commute. Once he exited his train on the North River's west bank, he would cross by ferry and then walk all the way to Gibbs & Cox at 21 West Street.

Van's physical description of his father is revealing: "My father, though only about five-foot-four, was determined, intelligent, and well informed about almost everything. He said little but said it well, was highly respected, and had, despite his stature, a commanding personality. He also had a very genuine modesty, which was perhaps connected with a resigned and somewhat mournful view of the world." This conjures up an image of a man of enormous prestige, skill, and knowledge who nevertheless resigned himself to feeling somehow as emotionally restricted as his physical stature.

Whatever the Bachmans' financial limitations, they booked passage regularly across the Atlantic, sometimes on *United States* but also on other vessels, including *Queen Mary*, *Mauretania*, *Ryndam*, and *Parthia*. The family always traveled in cabin rather than first class and never exceeded Walter's stringent one-month vacation allotment.

For *United States*'s maiden voyage, Bachman embarked alone but, later that year, he booked again with his entire family. En route to cabin class, when their steward heard the name Bachman, he escorted them immediately to first. But the family adhered to cabin class for meals and entertainment. Van recalls that his father was "surprised and greatly moved by this kindness." In fact, the upgrade was organized on board; shoreside probably never knew about it.

A day into the crossing, the Bachmans received a written invitation for cocktails with Commodore Anderson. Walter suggested to his wife that this was not a compliment but a "left-handed invitation," that the master had invited several couples, including them only as what he branded a "perfunctory afterthought." Betty insisted they go anyway and found that they were the only invitees. Once again, Bachman was surprised and flattered.

The first Newport News drydocking since the maiden voyage took place on December 17, 1954,

Herewith, 21 Wayside, the Bachmans' modest dwelling in Short Hills, New Jersey. It had originally been made over from a three-car garage and was comfortable if occasionally crowded inside. The building's lot was only a quarter of an acre. (Van Bachman Collection)

similar to the occasion that would conflict with Van and Molly's wedding plans. The vessel returned to no. 10 Shipway and was maneuvered over the keel blocks. Then the shipway was drained. More steam was required from yard boilers to keep the vessel warm against winter's cold. Walter Bachman supervised all the necessary work.

One thing preoccupying him was the need to correct propeller shaft weardown on each of four shafts. Rudder weardown had to be corrected as well. Also needing attention were the Powell Pressure Seal Bonney valves; their steam as well as their disc assemblies all had to be modified and refashioned.

Sometimes, if the need arose, shipyard workers had to be brought to New York to complete repairs scheduled in between the vessel's arrival and departure times. Such was the case in the spring of 1957 when a fifty-man team from Newport News was dispatched to New York to repair blading on turbine numbers 1 and 4.

Two banks of cabin class cabins were assigned them: riggers and drivers on B Deck, machinists and all others on A Deck. Scheduling was tight as all cabins had to be empty by noon on April 1 because

passengers would embark the following day. Prominently posted inside each cabin was a notice: IT IS REQUESTED THAT EXTRA CARE BE TAKEN TO PREVENT UNNECESSARY SOILING. Senior Gibbs & Cox personnel were assigned first class cabins up on Sun Deck.

Hot meals were organized: breakfast between 0700 and 0900 hours and dinner between 1630 and 1800 hours in cabin or tourist Dining Saloons. In addition to those seated occasions, two lunches were laid on as well, one at noon, the other at midnight, which took the form of individual box lunches.

On another occasion, repairs were required on *United States*'s number 3 low pressure turbine. Once again, a work team was dispatched by bus and truck from Newport News. They reached the pier at 2 P.M. and watched the vessel dock (without tugs, as it happened) at 3 P.M. The turbine's top casing was raised at 1:30 A.M. in the middle of that night. It was discovered that in the seventh stage of the afterflow, at the very back end of the turbine's rotor, a single blade had been lost. Repairs and replacement were completed by 8:30 A.M., the casing blades faired, a damaged sealing strip reinstalled,

and the casing cleaned and resecured. By 0230 hours on Friday repairs were complete and Bachman was able to sign off triumphantly "with complete satisfaction."

In between those frequently grueling disruptions, Walter's simple home life continued. He loved gardening and puttering around in old clothes. No television set appeared until one was inherited from his mother-in-law in 1959. Walter installed it in their unheated garage; to watch it, one sat in the car. In the late 1960s he gave Betty a bedside television for Christmas. Van's seven-year-younger sister Bonnie and he watched the unwrapping in "shocked silence," as though their mother were being introduced to hard drugs.

As retirement approached, the Bachmans became less attached to Short Hills. Walter and Betty bought a cottage at Eze-sur-Mer in the south of France; yet again, "tiny" was the word that Van used to describe it.

Walter's affliction with psoriatic arthritis intensified. Though incurable and extremely debilitating, he never complained. Van remembers that after one family picnic his father wanted to lie down for a nap, but the arthritic pain in his neck was so

bad it took him fully half an hour to get his head down to rest.

A subsequent automobile accident paralyzed his legs, arms, and diaphragmatic musculature; he learned to breathe by using his intercostal muscles instead. Even so, a breathing tube had to be inserted down his throat, which made speech impossible.

Most remarkable to his family was how gallantly the man endured what proved a terminal illness. The nurses were amazed at his cheerful resilience. He suffered for three months before his life ended. So died one of Gibbs & Cox's most brilliant engineers.

A man who toils today with the United States Conservancy is fellow U.S. Marine Dan McSweeney. He was drawn to the task as a long-cherished means of getting close to the memory of his father, who died when his only son was eight.

The first Dan McSweeney came originally from Cork. His father, a mason, had immigrated to Glasgow where he married and produced eight children. As they grew, they were all desperate to break free of the family's crushing poverty. Dan's sister Jane remained at home and one brother studied for

Top left: The Bachman family poses for a group photograph in September 1958. (*from left to right*) Walter Bachman, his younger child, Bonnie, his wife, Betty, and their seven-years-older son, Van. (Van Bachman Collection)

Top right: Walter Bachman poses alone. A brilliant engineer, he was a short, modest man, who suffered for years from the debilitating and painful effects of psoriatic arthritis. (Van Bachman Collection)

the priesthood. But another brother, Terry, became a Royal Marine and the rest of his siblings managed to spread their wings, immigrating to Canada or Australia, sometimes working aboard ships.

During World War II, Dan found work aboard a succession of merchant vessels, steaming from Great Britain to Australia, Latin America, and later Archangel in Russia. He also signed on as a steward aboard *Queen Mary*. After VJ Day, he resigned from Cunard White Star and went to work in London as a variety artist manager for actors and singers. There he met his first wife, an actress named Louise Maud. They were married for only two years before he was offered a job with United States Lines, courtesy of a resourceful British expat named Nancy Swan, who owned a bar on Twelfth Avenue near Manhattan's west side piers. It was she who sponsored Dan McSweeney's U.S. residency. Louise Maud was to have followed him to America but decided she'd rather stay in the UK. Their brief marriage ended in divorce.

A full decade after starting work aboard *United States*, Dan McSweeney met Carmen Martinez, a Puerto Rican beauty, on the platform of Times Square's subway station. She and her friend Dali were headed for the Lorelei restaurant and club in Manhattan's German quarter. By pure happenstance, Carmen happened to ask Dan for directions to the shuttle that would get them to the east side.

For McSweeney, it was love at first sight; for Carmen, that accidental encounter inaugurated an adventurous and rewarding liaison with a man she thought of as a "classy gentleman" boasting a Scottish accent that, initially, she could not always comprehend. Once, she asked him in all innocence what his first language had been. Dan was so amused that he often told the story at family gatherings.

They were married two years later. Considerably younger than Dan, Carmen became his devoted wife and bore him two children: Danya, a daughter who would be killed in a car accident aged eighteen, and then Dan, her younger child and husband's namesake.

Like Chick Donohue's meal ticket Dezi O'Malley, also a Cunard-trained steward, Dan's *Queen Mary* credentials obtained him an immediate United States Lines posting, first aboard *America* and a year later in *United States*'s first class Dining Saloon, where he remained for years.

Right, top: Dan McSweeney during the early 1950s at the beach. At the time, he was serving as a steward in *United States*'s first class Dining Saloon. (Dan McSweeney Collection)

Right, center: A portrait photograph of Carmen Martinez at the time Dan McSweeney, circa 1962, encountered her in Times Square's subway station and fell head over heels in love. (Carmen McSweeney Collection)

Right, bottom: Steward Dan McSweeney's crew card at the time of the vessel's withdrawal in September of 1969. At the time, he was serving as a library steward. (Dan McSweeney Collection)

FORM D-39-G	**S. S. UNITED STATES** UNITED STATES LINES, INC.		VOYAGE NUMBER
	CREW PASS and MUSTER CARD		
Article No. 710	Rating: CC LIBRARY STWD		
Name DANIEL mcSWEENEY		Room No. 216A	
Fire and Emergency Station: BOAT STA. #19 ASSIST & INSTRUCT PASSENGERS			
Abandon Ship and Boat Station #19 DIRECT & ASSIST PSGRS INTO BOAT			
		Department Head	

Dan McSweeney's New York hegira was no mere quest for employment. It was a fully life-changing decision. He became an American citizen and he and Carmen settled in Weehawken, New Jersey, in an apartment that boasted a view of his moored ship across the Hudson at Pier 86. Like his fellow crew members, Dan was immensely proud of *United States*, its size, splendor, and speed. The ship dominated his later life and, because of that, his son became inextricably involved with her restoration as she lies moored in Philadelphia. The vessel serves as an imperishable link with the father he too faintly recalls and, effectively, the symbol of "a lifelong search for meaning."

As a first class dining room steward, Dan met and served many notables, including the novelist Somerset Maugham, widowed Madame Chiang Kai-shek, the inventor of penicillin Sir Alexander Fleming, as well as film stars Sean Connery, Judy Garland, and John Wayne.

One passenger he wished he had *not* served was a notorious figure from American headlines in the early 1950s. Dan made an admittedly negative comment about Senator Joseph McCarthy to a couple at one of his tables. The next day, the male passenger to whom he had made the remark showed up in Marine Corps uniform, plastered with ribbons and medals. Only then did McSweeney realize to his horror that the passenger was, in fact, the notorious Wisconsin senator Joe McCarthy himself.

A happier dining room encounter during another crossing was with a British lady passenger who sat at a table for two by herself. Conscientious steward that he was, Dan made a point of chatting her up. The woman enjoyed his overtures and looked forward to her steward's enrichment of her solitary breakfasts, lunches, and dinners. He later discovered, to his surprise, that the lonely woman was a lady-in-waiting to Her Majesty Queen Elizabeth.

On one occasion, Dan was delayed reembarking in Southampton by a train that was late reaching the port from London. He arrived at the Ocean Dock after *United States* had sailed but was instantly taken aboard a tender that chased the ship down Southampton Water and got him safely aboard, up a Jacob's ladder and through an open port door. Carmen told me that her husband was so liked and respected by his fellow crew members that, even though late for the ship, he kept his job.

Many *United States* crewmen tried making money with extracurricular sidelines. McSweeney somehow obtained a supply of cut-rate gold Rolex wristwatches, which he sold to fellow crew members; a Chinaman down in the laundry was an early customer. Dan had become an amateur jeweler as a youngster in Glasgow and he loved dealing in jewelry. In New York, he made contacts along 47th Street's diamond district and, over the years, bought and sold jewelry for many crew clients.

When the vessel was abruptly laid up in 1969, McSweeney, who had first embarked in 1953, still needed four years' maritime employment to qualify for his twenty-year National Union of Seamen pension. After taking a cookery course, he obtained work aboard freighters, serving happily in a succession of merchant ship galleys. Dan McSweeney, former steward, variety artist manager, and *chef de rang* aboard *United States*, turned his hand effortlessly to yet another newfound talent. His final job was as night watchman in a West New York, New Jersey, building; the job included an apartment.

One vivid memory came from young Dan. His father was so fascinated by ships that for one of the first Operation Sails, he and Carmen hosted a daylong party in their West New York apartment with its capital North River view. The three McSweeneys and their guests watched entranced as the parade of tall ships passed upstream before them.

Shortly after that memorable day, the McSweeny family—both Dans and Carmen—moved from West New York to East Stroudsburg, Pennsylvania. And it was there that a diagnosis of stomach cancer ended Dan McSweeney senior's life.

David Fitzgerald, now retired in Weehawken, served aboard *United States* in the purser's department from her first trials until the vessel's withdrawal in 1969. Long before then, he achieved the rank of chief purser.

Son of a *Washington Post* sports editor, David was born in 1924 and educated at the Devitt Preparatory School on Connecticut Avenue in the capital. Just before Pearl Harbor, the young man tried enlisting in both army and naval air corps but neither would accept him because of a slight vision impairment in his right eye. However minor, it forever prevented him from qualifying as a pilot.

So he signed up instead with the Maritime Administration and was dispatched to Sheepshead

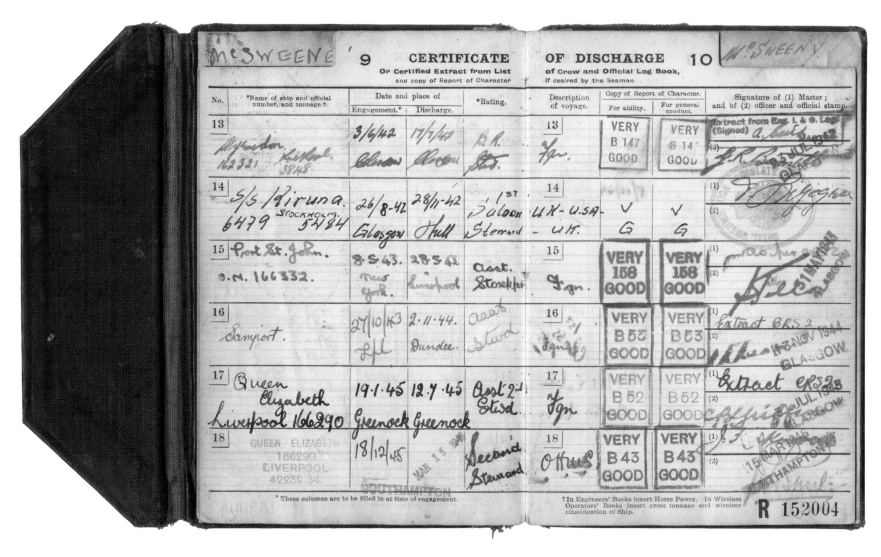

Pages 9 and 10 of Dan McSweeney's Certificate of Discharge from Britain's Merchant Navy, which lists all his Cunard voyages from 1937–1951.

(Dan McSweeney Collection)

Bay in Brooklyn. In the 1940s there was a maritime training establishment there as well as a Coast Guard station. After graduation, he was reassigned, against his wishes, to undergo medical training at Baltimore's Public Health Service Hospital.

Welcome parental intervention: Charlie Hand, one of his father's old newspaper buddies, had become a vice president of United States Lines. Thanks to his intercession, David was transferred from Baltimore to Port Arthur, Texas, where fleets of wartime cargo vessels were under construction.

He signed on as assistant purser aboard *Cape Palmas*, a C1A diesel vessel, which took him to New Orleans and thence throughout the South Pacific. David got his sea legs handling payrolls, monetary transactions, and victualing. The Swedish master, Oscar Johnson, a former bosun

promoted to captain, was "a bit of a boozer and tough guy with not much kindness in his heart." Regardless, the eighteen months David sailed under his command served as invaluable shipboard apprenticeship.

After returning to California, David was anxious for European service and signed on the cargo ship *George Verity* for another eighteen-month tour. Her master, Captain W. H. A. Mills, *did* have "kindness in his heart" and became a good friend. Both Mills and Fitzgerald would later be assigned to United States Lines.

Before then, however, David attended both Washington University and then American University graduate school, immersed in courses about labor relations, a field of study the company considered vital for pursers. Postwar, he was assigned to *Marine Flasher*, a larger passenger/cargo

SS UNITED STATES

ship that, among other chores, delivered one consignment of British war brides to the States.

Fitzgerald requested assignment to SS *America* where he served as junior assistant first class purser. (Although neither he nor I knew it at the time, we were inadvertent shipmates for a March 1947 westbound.) In command was Captain Harry Manning, the colorful figure with a checkered career at U.S. Lines. Fitzgerald would stay aboard until February 1952, when he was delighted to be seconded to Newport News for assignment to nearly completed *United States*.

Among a host of other chores, he and fellow assistant pursers had to devise a different means of embarking passengers aboard the new flagship. For United States Lines, it was an entirely new ball game. Extraordinarily, when *America* took on passengers, they never surrendered tickets on the pier; apparently, the company considered it "rude to ask for them." David and his team updated that procedure, collecting tickets on the pier so that a passenger manifest could be more quickly assembled.

That "team" to which Fitzgerald was assigned were, to a man, World War II veterans, old hands, compared with whom he felt utterly green. But he learned by watching and listening carefully. For starters, he learned almost at once to detect which colleagues were mere hangers-on—just marking time—as opposed to those who were really, as he put it, "earning their pay."

Of all the jobs aboard ocean liners, it is in the pursers' department that many lessons must and can only be learned on the job. Apart from intense study of labor relations, there was no other formal training; neither diploma nor degree existed. Pursers tend no machinery that drives or navigates the vessel. They deal instead with the vessel's sometimes fractious human cargo, and they had to learn, essentially, by doing, doing that involved astute and incessant observation.

Fitzgerald recalls *United States*'s trials well, an exciting and emotional outing. Everyone aboard was anonymously dressed in civilian clothes and he talked on the stern with another apparent civilian whom he discovered later was the admiral commanding the Third Naval District. Another trials friend was someone already familiar from the *America*, the chief engineer Bill Kaiser, an entertaining man he much admired.

Contrary to public acknowledgment, there was some noisy vibration echoing near the stern,

originating from the baggage hold. Decking for the space was made up of removable aluminum planking. When the space was unused, those panels were easily dislodged, producing a continuous, penetrating rattle. During those trials, all luggage brought on board was destined for cabin use only. Because no reporters, Maritime Administration members, or U.S. Lines personnel brought hold baggage, the rattle of those loose aluminum panels was unceasing. Once in regular transatlantic service, of course, with an accumulation of passenger hold baggage stacked atop them, the racket was quelled. It bore out the same noise phenomenon produced by coal wagons ashore. From time immemorial, they were noisiest when empty; once filled, they became silent.

Following the second trials against those pronounced headwinds, Fitzgerald had no contact whatsoever with the reporters who remained on board; he was, he recalled, "working my tail off." But one interesting thing that he did notice during passage north was that the journalists preferred taking meals in the cabin rather than first class Dining Saloon. It had blue walls, highlighted by Michael Lantz's aluminum sculptures, with chairs upholstered in green leather. Somehow, the press contingent found the space more appealing than the red seating and loftier ceilings of first class's Dining Saloon. It became, curiously, a common passenger predilection as well. Throughout the vessel's life, the comforting appeal of cabin as opposed to the stuffier formality of first was consistently remarked.

One of David's recurring special passengers was Joan Crawford, married at the time to her fourth husband, Alfred Steele. She always dispatched two cases of the special brand of vodka she preferred in advance. He would put them in storage until the Steeles' embarkation.

David knew Dan McSweeney well. He described him as an entertaining man, always smiling with sometimes loose dentures but very popular with passengers. An African American steward once confided to Fitzgerald that anyone who had undue influence in the National Maritime Union was known as a "blue eye." The first class Dining Saloon had its share of blue eyes, a kind of ex–Cunard White Star mafia that was not above trying to shift stewards around so that an incoming pal could take his place and, coincidentally, his job. Fitzgerald found out that McSweeney was being set up to be elbowed out. He immediately sent a signal to his old master and friend Captain Mills at company headquarters, requesting that Dan's post be saved. It was, forthwith.

Among crewmen who ran little side businesses were not only McSweeney's Rolex trade and Panama's beer and whiskey concession down on Broadway. Others established shipboard baseball or numbers pools. Chick Donohue used to smuggle home Church's shoes from England every fortnight, selling them to fellow crew members or New Yorkers ashore.

Once, just after he had disembarked from *United States* and was walking east, a customs inspector with a badge stopped him between Eleventh and Twelfth Avenues, ordering him to return to the ship. What had caught his eye were Chick's glistening new shoes. "Are those contraband?" he demanded. Chick played dumb. "What does that mean?" He was let go but learned to be more careful.

Fitzgerald hosted his own table, customarily at first sitting in first class's Dining Saloon. He always invited attractive people, sometimes a half dozen college girls. It made for socially demanding evenings, invariably a round of cocktails before dinner and sometimes dancing afterward.

Meyer Davis, together with the late Eddy Duchin (he succumbed to leukemia in 1951, survived by his talented son Peter) and Lester Lanin, led America's most famous and sophisticated dance bands. Small wonder that U.S. Lines booked Davis to provide music aboard *United States*. Every evening at sea throughout the vessel, four separate Meyer Davis orchestras played. The largest, complete with two violinists, performed in the Ballroom during cocktails. Those two violinists and some side men would later play in the musicians' gallery in first class's Dining Saloon, a balconied elevation above the space's elegant central section. Gibbs had put a smaller musicians' balcony aboard *America*.

It would be duplicated aboard the fifth *Rotterdam* that the Holland America Line entered into service in 1959. That vessel's musicians' balcony precipitated what could have been a hideous accident. The vessel encountered a severe storm that dislodged the piano; it fell over the railing, pulverizing a table and its chairs down on the dining room floor. By good fortune it happened late at night when the space was deserted.

Two additional, progressively smaller Meyer Davis bands would play elsewhere each night, in the Main Lounges of both cabin and tourist class. Overall, there were, David Fitzgerald told me, about fifteen musicians aboard and they worked very hard and long hours. In addition to those orchestral players, there were a couple of independent pianist/vocalists as well.

As the 1960s progressed, class ructions became commonplace. What David described as "left-wing" passengers in tourist class, feeling discriminated against, demanded first class privileges and perks. David summoned the vessel's master-at-arms, asking him to point out to the miscreants that their demands would and could not be met. Fitzgerald made a point of recording the names of those troublemakers to ensure that they could never again buy another ticket.

For the limited number of *United States* cruises, class restrictions were relaxed. First and cabin were united into one cruising class while tourist was given over entirely to entertainers and cruise staff. There were outings to Dakar and also Rio de Janeiro. The vessel's shipwide air-conditioning was a huge plus on those subtropical voyages; nothing even remotely like her had ever tied up at those ports before.

A final passenger glimpse comes thanks to Arthur McClean, who happens to be Molly Bachman's first cousin. A teenager from Little Rock, Arkansas, he crossed twice with his parents, Arthur and Louise McClean, in the summer of 1958. They sailed eastbound on July 26, returning on August 14, which happened also to be his fourteenth birthday. Louise was his father's second wife and he was the only child of that marriage. Two older half siblings were already, as he put it, "in the workforce" and hence unable to participate.

The young man, a devotee of ocean liners as well as an enthusiastic builder of model ships, was thrilled to embark aboard *United States*. The vessel's name and fame resonated with Little Rock inhabitants because much of her aluminum came from Arkansas's bauxite mines. Arthur McClean Sr. was not only a banker, he was a lumber merchant as well. So he, for one, was not necessarily pleased about the absence of wood on board.

His son shared a cabin with his parents in both directions, one on Upper Deck and the other on Main Deck, which he described accurately as first class's "major residential decks." Between crossings, the McClean family had allowed a busy fortnight abroad encompassing two destinations, the Brussels world's fair and a sightseeing tour of the United Kingdom. Shortly after leaving the port, they passed inbound *Queen Mary* heading for New York, her white superstructure tinged prettily pink by the setting sun.

Arthur McClean's overriding passion was bridge. Finding another passenger couple that could play at his and Louise's level was supremely important, a search he began immediately after embarking. As a shipboard lecturer, I am painfully aware of bridge addicts because they never attend my talks, seldom abandoning the bridge table before nightfall, if then. If McClean père failed to find sufficiently skilled opponents on board, his son told me that his dad was almost equally happy with "a good Perry Mason whodunit."

Young Arthur was a keen walker and spent much of every morning strolling along both the enclosed promenades as well as around the open decks. A persistent olfactory memory of both crossings was the smell of new paint; *United States*'s deckhouse walls, he remembers, were forever being touched up.

After dinner, he and his parents would often go to the Ballroom for horse racing. Thanks to his recall of those evening sessions, we understand that *United States* apparently followed the example of Cunard White Star: uniformed bellboys were assigned the task of moving the six wooden horses as the dice dictated, imparting an apropos maritime flavor.

Though Arthur does not recall winning, he made a cogent observation: "In today's era of nightclub floor shows and casinos, it's hard to believe we were willing to settle for such tame stuff but we were."

He is quite right. Fifties' shipboard with its focus on horse racing and/or bingo on alternate evenings was admittedly "tame" yet, at the same time, it tells us a great deal about the willingness of passengers to suspend shoreside sophistication for simpler and more innocent pastimes in mid-Atlantic.

Every afternoon, young Arthur haunted the cinema. Some of the films he enjoyed had not yet been released in stateside theaters. He also loved seeing British movies for the first time, to which no Little Rock theatrical chain was apparently attracted. While Arthur Junior found it exhilarating that there was no admission charge, he heartily lamented the absence of popcorn.

And then—shades of nine-year-old Scott Glasscock, who would embark three years later: "My idea of happiness was to sit in the porthole cubbyhole and watch the ocean go by."

What a telling coincidence, that two young *United States* passengers of comparable age were riveted by the sight of the ocean through a cabin porthole. Young Arthur found "the flank turbulence and breaking waves" a compelling sight that kept him entranced for hours. He saw few other ships and not one marine mammal but he did take note of the ship's tumblehome, that pronounced outward slope of a vessel's hull as it approaches the waterline.

Not only familiar with abstruse shipbuilding terminology, young Arthur was also an avid model maker. Thanks to his passage aboard *United States*, he was able to correct an error perpetrated by Revell, America's most popular modeling firm. The company always bragged that its plans were based on actual ships' drawings, unlikely for *United States* because of Gibbs's security. But when comparing his Revell model with the vessel on which he was sailing, Arthur found a minor anomaly: there were two, rather than one, staircases descending from the after end of Sun Deck. When he got home, he wrote and told Revell's CEO of the error.

Also like Scott Glasscock, Arthur McClean was a solitary adventurer. He disliked the pool, feeling it too small and chilly, and never ascended to the Monkey Island. But somehow he did find his way forward to the forepeak. Clutching the jack staff, Arthur leaned over the bow and watched the vessel's cutwater "break the waves like a hot knife through butter"; he found it an amazing sight.

He had to hold on for dear life. Wind pressure on *United States*'s bow at speed, even allowing for the protection of the raised enclosure surrounding him, was like nothing he had ever before experienced. He remembers turning around and seeing the vessel's bridge screen and funnels, watching wisps of wind-dashed smoke curling around them.

Patently, young Arthur was in crew rather than passenger country and it surprises me that the officer of the watch neither spotted the intruder nor sent anyone to remove him. Yet after visiting laid-up *United States* in November 2012, I understood why not. The bulwark protecting the bridge was not only very high but also substantial, the vertical deflector incorporated into its construction bending the wind stream straight up. I am over six feet tall and yet, standing on the bridge with the vessel at rest, found that inspecting the forepeak was not easy. So I think it probable that even an alert officer of the watch would not have spotted Arthur. Obviously, when *United States* traveled at speed, wind impact on the bridge had to have been daunting.

For Arthur's birthday on his return, the ship's confectioners prepared the most elaborate cake the McCleans had ever seen. It was largely chocolate, made up of fourteen contrasting layers—one for every year of Arthur's birthday celebration?—each with a slightly different color and flavor. He and his parents were delighted that it lasted for the entire crossing.

Their table for three was among the side ones situated under the Dining Saloon's two outboard lower ceilings. They noticed a family of four who ate in the taller central section at whatever hour they chose, using a table apparently reserved for both sittings. They asked their waiter the family's name and were told that it was John Jacob Astor VI, the son of millionaire John Jacob Astor who perished aboard *Titanic*. As a United States Lines shareholder, he was given special status and perks on board.

Another of the McCleans' fellow passengers on that westbound crossing was the celebrated comic pianist Victor Borge. Young Arthur remembers seeing him being interviewed and photographed on deck as the vessel approached New York.

Arthur's actual last sight of *United States* occurred a full year later from a considerable distance. He was near the end of a westbound crossing aboard *Queen Elizabeth*. Where the tracks of inbound vessels converge as they near Ambrose Channel, he spotted *United States*, paralleling their course, picked out prettily as she headed into the setting sun. The stance of her profile and the tall stacks were gloriously enhanced by that late afternoon's golden light.

Had Arthur known it, very early next morning, William Francis Gibbs would in all likelihood be driven by his chauffeur down as far as Brooklyn to enjoy the earliest possible sight of his beloved vessel's return to New York.

There can be no more apropos finale for this chapter documenting *United States*'s glory years.

United States departs from New York one summer afternoon in the early sixties. History buffs are often less interested in the passing ships than the profile of downtown Manhattan. The World Trade Towers are conspicuously absent. (Charles Anderson Collection)

CHAPTER TEN

WITHDRAWAL AND LAYUP

LINER UNITED STATES IS BEAUTIFUL, FAST, POWERFUL, AND BROKE.

—*New York Times* headline, September 21, 1969

Opposite: An aerial view of Manhattan's West Side piers, taken on the morning of September 11, 1966. From top to bottom—*Constitution, United States, France, Raffaello,* and first *Queen Elizabeth.* It seems an appropriate commemoration of the last great ocean liners that linked Europe with North America by sea. (The Port of New York Authority)

The year 1969 was scarcely kind to shipping anywhere in the world. The U.S. Navy's submarine

USS *Scorpion* sank in May; ninety-nine officers and men lost their lives. That same month, aboard recently retired *Queen Elizabeth*, a crewman was killed in a fall down an elevator shaft. In August, on the far side of the globe north of Sydney, the freighter *Noongah* capsized in a storm. Of her twenty-four crewmen only two survived.

In early September, USS *Intrepid* ran aground off Jamestown; although there were no casualties

S.S. UNITED STATES
GRAND PACIFIC CRUISE 1970
JANUARY 21, 1970
55 DAYS

PANAMA CANAL
PITCAIRN ISLAND
NEW ZEALAND
AUSTRALIA HONG KONG
JAPAN HAWAII
SAN FRANCISCO MEXICO

UNITED STATES LINES

Right: Still on the drawing board for *United States*'s immediate future was an extensive maiden Pacific cruise in 1970 that would deliver her to San Francisco, New Zealand, Australia, Mexico, and Hawaii. Alas, it would never happen. (Michael G. Jedd Collection)

Opposite: *United States* departs Newport News Shipyard on June 16, 1970, bound for indefinite layup at the Norfolk International Terminal. Ironically, it was only days short of the eighteenth anniversary of the vessel's formal delivery on June 20, 1952. (Newport News Shipbuilding Collection)

and the vessel was freed after two hours, it was nevertheless a worrisome episode. Aboard another carrier, USS *Lexington*, fire broke out in the boiler room as she lay in dry dock at Newport News. Two months later the tug *Marjorie McAllister* disappeared off Cape Hatteras, drowning all her crew.

In New York, after seventeen years in service, *United States* stopped sailing after completion of her four hundredth crossing. Three planned voyages had already been canceled: a sixteen-day Christmas cruise to Madeira, Tenerife, and Saint Thomas; a world cruise scheduled for January 21, 1970, which would have dispatched her through the Panama Canal for the first time; and one of her transatlantic round-trips to follow. It was common knowledge that on many of her 1968 and 1969 crossings, crewmen outnumbered passengers three to two but iron-clad labor contracts forbade any manning reductions.

The vessel had a new owner; the conglomerate Walter Kidde and Co. had taken over United States Lines. Although Edward Heine, the company's executive vice president, insisted that the previous year's gross revenues of $18 million were identical to those of 1952, expenses, he acknowledged, had "sky-rocketed": "We just can't make a go of it because of the high costs and the airline competition."

Deployment of hundreds of jet aircraft had reduced airfares with draconic finality. A transatlantic airline seat was now priced at exactly *half* what it cost to book even the least expensive tourist class cabin. "*United States* will remain in layup status indefinitely," was Heine's gloomy prognosis. She was retired down to Norfolk.

Joseph Curran, head of the National Maritime Union, wrote in a column for the NMU's house organ, "We are going to have to make some sacrifices … in order to keep the passenger ships sailing."

Pickets were already in place at four piers in New York Harbor, two in Port Newark as well as Piers 76 and 86 on Manhattan's west side. They were members of the Staff Association of America, a small union representing pursers only; United States Lines had employed a total of thirty-five of them.

New York's mayor John Lindsay sent a letter to President Nixon, telling him that although New York port services generated municipal income of approximately $25 million annually, a federal subsidy

was still necessary. His request was rejected. The House Committee on Merchant Marine and Fisheries scheduled hearings about passenger ship operations for February 1970.

In truth, millions of federal dollars were being lavished elsewhere. At the same moment as *United States* was withdrawn, a remarkable new transportation modus enjoyed flawless operation. Apollo 12 had just lifted off from the Kennedy Space Center on Florida's Merritt Island, ferrying a second astronaut trio to the moon. They were en route only four months after historic Apollo 11, when Neil Armstrong, Buzz Aldrin, and Michael Collins had pioneered man's first touchdown on the lunar surface, implementing Armstrong's unforgettable "... one giant leap for mankind."

As American rockets roared triumphantly into space, American shipping was ruthlessly curtailed. *United States* was not the only U.S.-flagged vessel laid up. All three ships of American Export Lines—*Constitution*, *Independence*, and *Atlantic*—had also been withdrawn from service. Bracketing a deserted Baltimore pier were *Argentina* and *Brazil*, also deserted. The only American flags seen along the East Coast flew from the yardarms of *Santa Rosa* and *Santa Paula* as well as aboard four Grace Line cargo/passenger vessels trading between the States and South America. All six of those laid-up ships, incidentally, had been designed by William Francis Gibbs.

A *New York Times* editorial in the Sunday edition of November 16 was headlined GOOD-BY TO THE "BIG U." A final bleak paragraph summed things up: "The future belongs to the containerized cargo ships, the oil tankers and other ungainly automated workhorses, plus a handful of foreign registry luxury liners. The sun has set for glamor on the sea lanes."

Gibbs had died on Wednesday, September 6, 1967, at the age of eighty-one, before *United States*'s withdrawal. Had he lived two more years, the premature end of his great ship would have distressed him acutely. It came only seventeen years after the maiden voyage, as though a trusted and still promising employee had been arbitrarily retired in early middle age. What had to be factored in was the impact of jets whisking passengers across the North Atlantic in hours rather than days. That rapacious but apparently irresistible aerial alternative would finally doom every ocean liner in turn save one, Cunard's giant *Queen Mary 2*.

William Francis Gibbs did not die in harness as he had predicted and hoped. He was confined for the last months of his life in Manhattan's Roosevelt Hospital, suffering from heart trouble. "A lanky man of somber mien and ascetic habits," read his obituary in the *New York Times*.

He was buried in a Princeton cemetery. Immediately adjacent to his grave rests the body of his younger brother, Frederic, who died on September 16, 1978. Inseparable in life, they remain so in death as well.

Opposite and above: On July 24, 1996, *United States* is towed into Philadelphian waters. As seen from shore, the vessel is proceeding upriver. Tugs push her against her initial berth, identified as the Packer Terminal. Seen from the bow, *United States* is secured. Later, she would be transferred to her present and final mooring at U.S. Navy Yard Pier 82. (David Pike Collection)

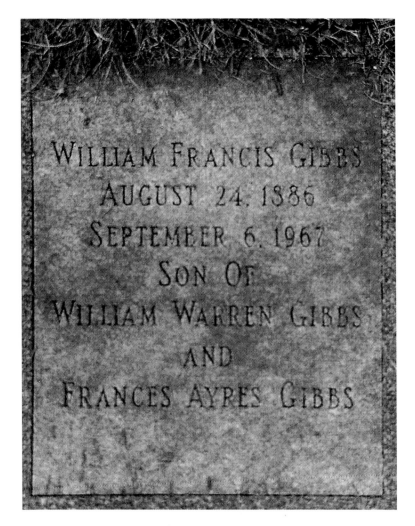

WILLIAM FRANCIS GIBBS
AUGUST 24, 1886
SEPTEMBER 6, 1967
SON OF
WILLIAM WARREN GIBBS
AND
FRANCES AYRES GIBBS

FREDERIC H. GIBBS
APRIL 12, 1888
SEPTEMBER 16, 1978
SON OF
WILLIAM WARREN GIBBS
AND
FRANCES AYRES GIBBS

Above: The graves of the Gibbs brothers in a Princeton cemetery. William died first, in 1967; his younger brother, Frederic, lived until 1978. (Michael G. Jedd Collection)

Opposite: This bronze bust of William Francis Gibbs was sculpted by Malvina Hoffman in 1954. When he sat for it, Gibbs kept his glasses on and the sculptor has reproduced them prettily. (Photograph by Theodore Piccone; Susan Gibbs Collection)

Vera Gibbs sold the Fifth Avenue apartment and moved permanently to their Rockport getaway on the Massachusetts coast. She died there on January 27, 1985, and the house was subsequently sold.

I have, in both epigraph and text, quoted William Francis Gibbs at length. It is difficult to think of a single comprehensive remark that characterizes and encapsulates his persona but perhaps the following comes close. One day when he was aboard *United States* while she was being fitted out, he took a well-earned but momentary break with a similarly exhausted colleague. On vessels fitting out, because there is neither bed, sofa, nor even chair on which to collapse, the two men were resting by lying flat on deck in an anonymous cabin somewhere inside the hull. Their ears were still assaulted by the racket of construction and they stared up at naked steel above.

It was then that Gibbs suddenly proclaimed, "Boy, don't we have fun!"

His words can be interpreted in two ways, either a sarcastic observation on the demands of his profession or, more likely to my mind, a heartfelt cri de cœur. Revealed is a rarely exposed stratum of—what else?—unadulterated joy behind that too-often forbidding facade. Beneath exterior armor lurked cogent sensibility.

"Boy, don't we have fun!" They might have been the same words chuckled to Frederic as the brothers raced on a fire engine to a Philadelphia blaze, as they struggled to extinguish burning *Leviathan*, as they laid the keel for *America*, as they jointly solved the problem of a misplaced column in Gibbs & Cox's model shop, as they designed and christened *United States*, or as they swept giddily past Bishop Rock.

At heart, both remarkable Gibbs brothers were as sensitive as they were skilled.

CHAPTER ELEVEN

DERELICTION AND REPRIEVE

"In Quiet Darkness, a Liner Slowly Dies"

—Washington Post article, by Donnel Nunes

*She is worth keeping. This ship is an iconic part
of American maritime history and if there's any chance at all
that she can be saved, we should take that chance.*

—"Gerry" Lenfest, philanthropist

Laid up *United States*, moored alongside Philadelphia's Navy Yard Pier 82.

(Michael G. Jedd Collection)

Currently, United States *languishes alongside Philadelphia Navy Yard's Pier 82. Three years ago,*

I was aboard a small schooner drifting along the slip beneath her starboard side. The formerly sleek black hull rearing overhead is scarred and, in late afternoon's slanting sunlight, suffers from what naval architects call "starved horse syndrome," the noticeably inward indentation of steel plating between frames. For reasons unknown, the end of a large I-beam protruded grotesquely through a gaping midships porthole.

Instead of rusting, her aluminum funnels were flaking. Regardless, from down at sea level, the stance of those stacks was as potent as ever, their staunch rake radiating the vigor of Gibbs's design. That profile still compels, conjuring up the dazzling performance *United States* delivered for seventeen triumphant years.

Conventionally, moored vessels are at temporary rest, marking time between voyages. During those mandatory pauses in their workaday lives, passenger ships disembark one set of passengers and welcome aboard replacements, the lifeblood of every ocean liner since shipping companies began. Also while they are in port, crews must load provisions, refuel, and complete countless ongoing maintenance chores.

Ocean liners used to remain inactive and unmoving for a night or more. Before World War I, coal-fired vessels' port stays were longer because bunkering consumed thirty-six hours, depositing a gritty pall of coal dust on every open deck and interior space. It had to be cleaned up before anything or anyone else could be embarked.

Today's cruise ships gulp hundreds of tons of oil in a few hours from port tankers moored alongside. Sometimes they take on freshwater as well, throbbing through oversize blue hoses connected to pier mains. As a result, they almost never remain in port for more than a day: mooring before dawn, by dusk they are gone.

But whatever the duration of their downtime, the vessel's seagoing capability remains reassuringly in evidence. Smoke tendrils hover above stacks, muttering blowers and ventilators indicate that circulating systems are operating, condenser outlets aboard steam-driven hulls emit periodic cascades, and echoing everywhere is the persistent *ching-ching-ching* of hammered steel, that in-port sound track betraying every crew's unceasing battle against the demon rust.

Aboard moored liners in the old days, the ship's cranes, released from horizontal tethers, would be elevated above holds. Once hatch covers had been retracted, steam-driven winches would loft hold baggage ashore. Wardrobe trunks, retrieved from cabins by stewards, had been wheeled on deck and dumped atop spread cargo nets. Crewmen would gather up the net's corners and attach their looped appendages to a crane's hook so that netted luggage bundles could be lowered to the pier.

Mail, every liner's most profitable cargo, was delivered to the pier more speedily. Hundreds of sausage-shaped mail sacks, manhandled up from below, were already stacked near the vessel's flank. The moment she moored, they were dropped down a vertical canvas chute suspended over the side. Whizzing down, they thumped onto the pier in mountainous accumulation.

At the same time, balanced atop spattered paint tenders beneath the bow, crewmen daubed out spots despoiling half-lowered anchors. On the pier, crewmen wielding long-handled paintbrushes touched up rust streaks or scars. High above, promenade deck and public room windows were hosed off and squeegeed.

Today's cruise ships are tended by bustling forklifts. They dart everywhere, first withdrawing pallets of provisions from open refrigerated containers delivered to the pier days earlier. Once those foodstuffs have been inspected and occasionally tasted by food-and-beverage personnel, the forklifts thrust them through open ports in the ship's side for consignment by onboard forklifts to the lowest decks' provision rooms: legs of lamb, haunches of beef, boxes of poultry and bacon, hams, joints of pork, dozens of egg cartons, crated vegetables and fruit, gallons of milk and yogurt, stacks of butter, flour, and, always, hundreds of gallons of bottled water. Buttressing that comestible influx are hard goods from company warehouses—carpeting, pillows, mattresses, towels, dusters, brooms, mops, crated machinery for the engineers, and cartons of computer parts and supplies for the purser.

The primary commitment of every vessel's port call, however, is the aforementioned turnover of clientele. Having been delivered to their terminal port, those ending their passage forsake now familiar cabins and public rooms to their sometimes jet-lagged replacements.

Opposite: Carrying the requisite flashlight, the author waits to board through the vessel's deteriorating flank. Farther forward, Susan Gibbs, granddaughter of the vessel's naval architect and chair of the *United States* Conservancy, stands at the extreme right of another group of visitors. On board, she confers with the author. (Michael G. Jedd Collection)

The forklift swarm copes with luggage of the shorebound. Vanished wardrobe trunks have been supplanted by ubiquitous wheeled suitcases that, rainbowed with color-coded tags, are systematically stockpiled inside the pier shed. Once they have been located by porters and stuffed into buses' open luggage compartments, their owners will become fellow bus rather than ship passengers, trundled to the nearest airport.

Whatever the era and whatever the vessel, moored ships convey an unmistakable aura of waiting, of imminent departure, ready to exchange port grime for the sea's clean, windswept embrace. Once cables have been slipped and the vessel undocked, only an empty pier remains.

But there is not a flicker of life either aboard or anywhere near *United States* today. She seems frozen, somehow disassociated from time, enduring a twilight of indifference and abandonment. A plague of rust disfigures once peerless white-painted upper hull strakes and superstructure. Rigged the width of the wheelhouse windows, bracketed by stars and stripes, is a rumpled banner: SAVETHEUNITEDSTATES.ORG.

The vessel is utterly deserted. There are no passengers, no visitors, no crew, no master, no bridge officers, no engineers, no pursers, no medical or shore staff, no master-at-arms, no longshoremen, no watchmen—nobody. Her capacious reefers, unrefrigerated, are empty. So too her fuel tanks. What seem like miles of blue hawsers infest mooring decks fore and aft, some secured around bollards, with tangles of others cast aside.

Every interior, whether public room, suite, cabin, or backstage crew country, has been stripped. Furniture, curtains, carpets, hangings, paintings, those useful cutaways that once helped lost passengers find their way are no more. Melted lead that once flowed in the print shop's Linotype has long since chilled into solidity. The vessel's only occupants are gulls, perched indifferently along funnels and railing, despoiling everything with their droppings.

On November 10, 2012, my wife Mary and I were asked by Susan Gibbs, William Francis Gibbs's granddaughter and chair of the *United States* Conservancy, to tour the vessel, a rare and privileged invitation. One fellow enthusiast who accompanied us for yet another visit was Charles Howland, CBS's *60 Minutes* coproducer. An old friend and Manhattan neighbor, Charlie is an inveterate *United*

Above and opposite: The empty first class Promenade Deck. Without walls, only ghostly cabin outlines remain; evidence of a bathtub betrays first class. Gibbs's overscale portholes indicate the Special Restaurant's Navajo bar, soaked with rainwater.

(Michael G. Jedd Collection)

States collector and authority. There could be no more invaluable guide. He warned us to dress warmly—*United States*'s 'tween decks can be glacial in fall or winter—and to bring flashlights, spare batteries, and cameras.

Driving through the chain-link fence that cordons the vessel, I was pleased to note that the I-beam I remembered protruding through the starboard side porthole has gone. We assembled beneath the vessel's port side along Pier 83 with *United States*'s rusted and flaking port flank rising above. B Deck's forward crew gangway door was open and we entered a dark foyer, festooned with paint shreds flaking from deckhead and bulkheads. Only after each of us had signed a release form were we directed to a claustrophobic spiral staircase where, via flashlight, we ascended two levels

to Main Deck, renouncing crew for passenger country.

Over the years, Mary and I have toured dozens of passenger vessels moored in shipyards all over the world, either new ones fitting out or old ones undergoing renovation. On either those pristine newbuilds or temporarily idled working vessels there is always light, noise, and frenetic activity, invariably accompanied by deafening rock-and-roll broadcast for the workers' entertainment. Despite the mess and the racket, the heartening prospect is of ultimate completion, of emergence into something finished or improved, hulls girt for either maiden entry into or welcomed return to service.

Aboard *United States*, the very reverse obtains: no noise, light, or activity, only silence, darkness, and desertion. Portholes admit a pale wash of daylight

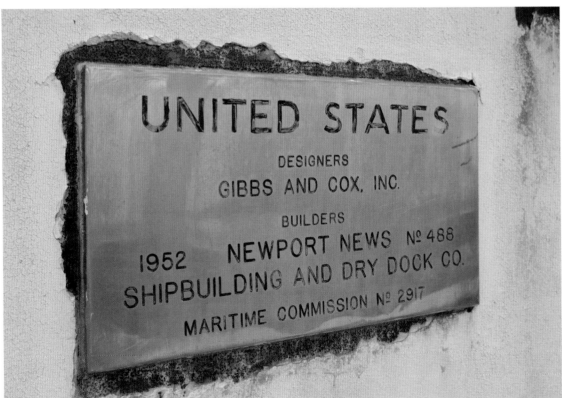

Right: The author pauses to chat with
fellow maritime historian Steven
Ujifusa. *United States*'s builder's plate
is still in place outside the bridge.
(Michael G. Jedd Collection)

and, occasionally, rainwater. Despoiling steel decks along several alleyways, we splashed through puddles. Hundreds of linoleum tiles, soaked and liberated from steel decking, have been washed out of ordered alignment and redeposited randomly. Ballroom, Dining Saloons, Lounges, and Smoking Rooms in every class are empty. The famed Special Restaurant is scarcely recognizable. Its bar, with Gibbs's pioneering outsize portholes still in place, occupies the starboard side across from it.

Far below, out of sight and unvisitable, are the engine rooms. Ironically, Gibbs's cloistered yet now moribund secrecy therein has been retained; clusters of those once zealously concealed engine room dials register noncommittal zeroes. Every element of machinery, so carefully crafted and wrought, lies silent; stilled turbines, drained boilers,

and cold furnaces remain linked by miles of empty steam pipe.

The necessary work that was undertaken in Odessa in 1992 removed the half million tons of asbestos—Marinite was the manufacturer's brand name—that had originally insulated every cabin wall as well as lagging her engine room piping. Asbestos removal is a demanding job but Russian workers were prepared to undertake it without wearing the same cumbersome hazardous-materials clothing that is obligatory in the West. By the time the *Big U* was towed back, all her cabin partitions had been excised down to deck level, leaving only outlines of their original configuration.

Everything one surveys has been reduced to what seems an overscale blueprint: here the doorway, there a bathroom outline, indicating tub or

Inside, conventional bridge furnishings have vanished: wheels, chart lockers, signal flags, compasses, LORAN, telegraphs—everything save the inclinometer, which, against all odds, remains. (Andy Hernandez Photograph)

shower according to class, their emergent truncated piping plugged with spouting gobbets of plastic. Without intervening walls, one can survey acres of identical cabin areas, repetitious vistas of surreal desolation.

Because passenger alleyways were covered with linoleum rather than carpeting, the flooring occasionally bears traces of its original class identification. First class's gray background was decorated with repeats of large red discs, each roughly two feet in diameter. Cabin class alleyways were indicated by paler discs with three orange/red hashmarks and tourist with two hashmarks. On landings at the summit of each stair flight, names of existing decks are still legible.

Up on the bridge everything has gone. Engine room telegraphs, the ship's wheel, and that welter of sophisticated machinery that once defined *United States*'s brain stem—depth indicators, dials and gauges of every description, LORAN, chart racks, signal flag holders—have all been removed. Curiously, the only item remaining is the mercury-filled glass crescent of the vessel's inclinometer, still bolted in place atop the projection before which the wheel was once mounted.

In 1978, after nearly ten years of layup, an extended episode of activity began for *United States*. Enterprising Seattle and Hawaii developer Richard Homer Hadley purchased the vessel for $5 million. His scheme was to convert her into a floating condominium. Investors would become members of what he dubbed his Cruising Society, rewarded with an annual fortnight's voyage in their cabin of choice, the total number of which represented, incidentally, only 15 percent of the vessel's transatlantic occupancy. Though fares were pegged officially at $200 per day, members would be awarded a 60 percent discount in return for a twenty-year commitment.

The vessel would sail exclusively between California and Hawaii, and Hadley planned some ambitious warm-weather renovations, including three open-air pools, an on-deck tennis court, and, below, seven new restaurants. Flying the Stars and Stripes, retired but rejuvenated *United States* would not have incurred the restriction of foreign-flag ships that Congress's Jones Act prohibits from calling at only American ports; for instance, non-American-flagged vessels en route home from Hawaii must divert momentarily to the Mexican

Opposite and left: The Conservancy's banner is draped across the bridge front. Toward the forepeak, bollards wrapped with blue hawsers and chains secure the vessel to the pier. The author is interviewed while standing on the vessel's port after docking bridge.
(Michael G. Jedd Collection)

port Ensenada before disembarking their passengers in Los Angeles.

Unfortunately Hadley did not succeed and found himself mired increasingly in debt. The number of condominium investors was too sparse, and his renovation costs had somehow soared from $125 to $200 million. A hastily assembled consortium of banks designed to refinance the venture did not materialize.

To implement his Cruising Society's faltering financial health, Hadley decided to sell off the vessel's furnishings and fittings. In October 1984, a weeklong auction organized by Guernsey's Auctioneers proved a chaotic if clean sweep. Posses of dealers, collectors, and fans, some of them past passengers and enthusiasts from all over the country, converged on *United States*. All furniture and furnishings went under the hammer. Every deckchair was snapped up, as was the ship's wheel, bell, and whistles. So, too, all her china, glassware, cutlery, lamps, tables, beds, blankets, sheets, pillows, carpeting, bedspreads. Everything sold and the vessel's interiors were picked clean.

Hadley may have temporarily resolved his financial shortfall but, in the process, he had disposed of the very furniture and furnishings essential to the viability of his condominium dream. In any case the auction was only a stopgap. Finally, his mortgage holder demanded repayment of $5.7 million principal and interest owed and he found he was unable to pay even pier rental. Hadley filed for bankruptcy protection under Chapter 11.

The ship was sold at auction to Fred Mayer and a Turkish colleague; later they were joined by Edward A. Cantor of Linden, New Jersey, who shortly thereafter became the sole owner. Cantor paid $2.6 million for the vessel in 1992 and it was he who arranged for the vessel's round-trip tow for removal of her asbestos. Her original destination had been Turkey but it was the desperation of Russia's Odessa workforce that changed the locale, agreeing to tackle asbestos removal.

Edward Cantor died suddenly shortly after the vessel's return to the United States and, on April 15, 2003, Norwegian Cruise Line bought the vessel from his estate; it also purchased *Independence* for Hawaiian service. Norwegian Cruise Line was determined to transform *United States* into a modern-day cruise ship, not just shuttling between California and Hawaii but voyaging all over the world. The company had started assembling stacks of plans and drawings.

Opposite: In June 1992, on a misty morning near Cape Henry at the entrance to Chesapeake Bay, a Richmond doctor took this photograph of *United States* under tow, en route for Odessa. (Henry Willett Collection)

Reminders of *United States* today.
In place atop Rent-a-Tool headquarters
in Revere, Massachusetts, one of
United States's whistles has been
mounted for twenty-five years. Occasionally, the company's president Steve
Williams sounds it, deafeningly.

(James Giammatteo Photograph)

Then, in May 2006, Star Cruises, based in
Malaysia, bought Norwegian Cruise Line. Tan Sri
Lim Kok Thay, the successful cruise line's CEO,
announced that his company's next project would
be full restoration of *United States* flying the American flag. Alas, one trap ensnaring American-
flagged vessels is that only American officers and
crew may be employed. All very well on bridge,
deck, or engine room but less so in dining saloon
and cabin. Unionized American stewards do not
have the same dedication as hungry third-world
personnel. American Samoa served as the only and
patently inadequate manpower resource for recruiting cabin staff. Aboard resurrected *Independence*, her funnels daubed with Hawaiian greenery,
there was continual labor unrest. Unionized men
who had learned their jobs on an initial cruise saw
no reason to rebook for successive exhausting tours.

Once it was discovered that it would cost more
to put *United States* back in shape than to build an
entirely new vessel, Norwegian Cruise Line abandoned its planned conversion. Nothing came of Star
Cruises' plan either, and by February 2009 the company started looking for a buyer. It declined a bid
from a scrapyard and in July 2010, thanks to a $5.8 mil-
lion gift of H. F. "Gerry" Lenfest, a Philadelphian
philanthropist, the *United States* Conservancy, under
the chairmanship of William Gibbs's granddaughter
Susan Gibbs, was able to buy the vessel.

A retired U.S. Navy Reserve captain, Lenfest
was the son of a naval architect who had designed
components of the original vessel. He is a staunch
supporter of its preservation.

One wonders, if Hadley's "cruising society" had
succeeded, would it have ensured *United States*'s
survival? The question has no simple answer. Installation of Hadley's warm-weather structural
refinements—seven restaurants, three outdoor
pools, and an on-deck tennis court—would have
fundamentally altered the vessel. *United States*

would have segued into a slower, hobbled ship, no longer the remarkable ocean liner that had captured the Blue Ribband forever, which would have negated, in effect, her singular historic distinction.

Conventionally, naval architects anticipate that their vessels will achieve success whatever service they undertake. But Gibbs had been locked into a highly restrictive bind. *United States* had been custom-built for the navy, her speed and capacity designed for swift conversion into trooper or hospital ship. Yet at the same time, of survival options that would later be essayed, it seems, in honest retrospect, that Hadley's attempt, although unsuccessful, was perhaps the most imaginative.

United States's only remaining options are either the scrapyard or preservation as a museum, exhibit, and/or hotel. But Lenfest's lifesaving grant represented only a daunting preliminary. The hundreds of millions of additional dollars required to

turn the vessel into a viable attraction alongside represent a huge financial challenge.

Preserving ocean liners is an expensive undertaking. Witness the problems of the first *Queen Mary* in Long Beach, *QE2* in Dubai, and *Rotterdam* in Holland. The combined costs of renovation, docking fees, fire and liability insurance, hiring and maintaining requisite staff is mind-boggling. Apparently, either New York, Philadelphia, or Miami is in the running as possible waterfront sites for the future but, as of the moment, no hard and fast commitments have been made and hence no action can be taken. The vessel continues in protracted limbo, her hull rusting, machinery inoperable, and stripped interiors in need of drastic rejuvenation.

I hope fervently, as do all Americans proud of William Francis Gibbs's achievement, that the Conservancy can and will succeed. Future generations, large numbers of them inveterate cruising passengers, will doubtless flock aboard a preserved and restored *United States*, the Gibbs brothers' final and unquestionably most memorable creation. To do so, however, they will be among the host of Americans asked to help defray the enormous expense involved.

No one can estimate the sum total of that budget, no one can envision the demanding complexities of completion. As it has for so long, the vessel, together with its challenged Conservancy, waits.

Left: Probably the last surviving artist who designed items for *United States*'s interiors is Mira Jedwabnik Van Doren, shown here with the author in her studio apartment on Manhattan's West 57th Street. In 1950, as a talented young Polish enamelist, Mira Jedwabnik designed a series of handsome Smoking Room tables that seemed to reflect the night sky. One of them stands in front of her and her husband John's drawing room fireplace. (Greg Shutter Collection)

BIBLIOGRAPHY

Braynard, Frank O. *By Their Works Ye Shall Know Them* (New York: Gibbs & Cox, 1968).

———. *Lives of the Liners* (New York: Cornell Maritime Press, 1947).

———. *The Story of the Leviathan*, volumes I–VI (New York: South Street Seaport Museum, 1972).

———. *The Big Ship* (Newport News, VA: The Mariners' Museum, 1981).

Brinnin, John Malcolm. *The Sway of the Grand Saloon* (New York: Delacorte Press, 1971).

Fox, William A. *Always Good Ships* (Virginia Beach: The Donning Company, 2011).

Griffiths, Denis. *Power of the Great Liners* (Hitchin, UK: Patrick Stephens Limited, 1990).

Hughes, Richard. *In Hazard* (New York: New York Review Books, 2008).

Kludas, Arnold. *Record Breakers of the North Atlantic* (London: Chatham, 2000).

Miller, William H. *S.S. United States* (Hitchin, UK: Patrick Stephens Limited, 1991).

Mylon, Patrick. *The White Star Collection* (Stroud, UK: The History Press, 2011).

Newton, Jim. *Eisenhower, The White House Years* (New York: Doubleday, 2011).

Pedraja, Rene de la. *The Rise and Decline of U.S. Merchant Shipping in the Twentieth Century* (New York: Twayne Publishing, 1992).

Tazewell, William. *Newport News Shipbuilding, the First Century* (Newport News, VA: Newport News Shipyard, 1986).

Ujifusa, Steven. *A Man and His Ship* (New York: Scribners, 2012).

Watson, Milton H. *U.S. Passenger Liners* (Hitchin, UK: Patrick Stephens Limited, 1981).

Zerbe, Peter. *Die Grossen Deutschen Passagierschiffe* (Hamburg: Imperator, Vaterland, Bismarck, Nautik Historie Verlag, 1999).

A group photograph of the entire waitstaff and supervisors of *United States*'s first class Dining Saloon. Dan McSweeney is seated at the far right-hand table by himself. (Dan McSweeney Collection)

INDEX

Page numbers in bold refer to illustrations.

advertising, 21, **22**, 53, 94, **130**, 138, **167**
Afghanistan, 19
aircraft carriers, 78, 83–84
Air Force, U.S., 82–83
airline competition, 218
alcohol, shipboard, 46, 48, 54–55, 129
Aldrin, Buzz, 221
Alexanderson, John, **162**, 164
Allegro, 29
Alshain, USS, 121
Ambrose, John Wolfe, 122
Ambrose Channel, 54, 121–22, **122**, 214
Ambrose Light, 125, 131
America, SS, 11, **12**, 31, 56–65, **57**, **59**, **60**, **65**, **66**, 71–79, 84, 90, **94**, 96, 106–7, 138, 142, 202, 204, 208, 211–12, 222; christening of, 60; in conversion to USS *West Point*, 65, **68**; maiden voyage of, 61, **67**; postwar reconversion of, 71, **72**, **73**, **74**
American Bureau of Shipping, 47
American Steel Foundries, 45
Amerika, 31
Anderson, John W., **145**, **146**, **148**, **158**, **161**, **162**, **163**, 164, **165**, **174**, **177**, 189, 205
Andrea Doria, 22, 184
Apollo mission, 221
Arcadia, 22
architecture, naval, 11, 26–28, 34, 41, 60, 77–78, 90, 93–94, 113, **165**, 226, 236–37
Arctic, 136
Argentina, 221
Armstrong, Neil, 221
Army, U.S., 19, 69, 122
Arnold, Henry "Hap," 83
Arosa Kulm, 127
art deco, 38, 94
artificial reef, 29
artwork, restoration of, 73
asbestos, removal of, 231
Astor, John Jacob, 214
Astor, John Jacob, VI, 214
Athens, 184
Atlantic, **136**, 221
atomic bombs, 82–83
Augustus, 22
Australia, 208
Australis, **76**, 77

Bachman, Walter, 204–7, **206**, **207**
Bachman family, 205–7, **207**, 212
baggage tags, **120**
Baker, Newton, 38
Ballin, Albert, 34
Baltic, 136
Baltimore, Md., 221
banana boats, 29
barges, 34, 38, 51

Baskerville, Charles, 73
Battle of Britain, 61
Baudelaire, Charles, 114
bellboys, 213
Berengaria, 39, 46, 90
Bernard, W. J., 43
Bishop Rock, 122, 125, 127, 131, 222
Blewett, William E., Jr., 88
Blohm & Voss shipyard, 34, **34**, 39, 41
Blue Ribband, 11, 39, 114, 122, 125, 129, 131, 136, 138, 237
"booze cruises," 54
Borge, Victor, 214
Boston Navy Yard, 36, 42, 47, 60
Brazil, 221
Bremen, 22, 34, 39, 94
Brest, France, 36–37, **37**
Brinnin, John Malcolm, 39, 239
Brooklyn Bridge, 122
Brunel, Isambard Kingdom, 26
bunkbeds, 69
Burrow, Edwin, 130

Cadwalader, Emily, 29, 31
campaign slogans, 17–18
Campbell, Donald, **145**
Campbell, Malcolm, **145**
Canada, 30, 208
Canberra, 21–22
Cape Henry, Va., 43, 109, **234**
cargo ship construction program, 78
cargo vessels, 29, 82, 178, 210–11, 221
Caribbean, 62, 113, 203
Carp, Sam, 25
Cassier's Magazine, 26
celebrities, 47–48, **158**, **161**, 175, **178**, 192, 203, 209, 211
Central Park, 114–15
Chandris, **76**, 77
Cherbourg, 128, 184–85, **187**, 188, **191**, 204
Chesapeake and Ohio Railways, 43
Chesapeake Bay, **234**
Chiang Kai-shek, Madame, 209
Chicago, Ill., 192
Chota Peg (dog), **148**
christenings, **5–9**, 60, 100–106, **103**, **105**, **107**
Christiansen, Riedar, 206
Christy, Howard Chandler, 48
Churchill, Winston, 18
Chusan, 22
cigarette lighters, **152**
Cleveland, Mrs. Grover, 26
Clinton, Bill, 175, 192
Coast Guard, U.S., 44, 65, 117, 210
Cochrane, Edward L., 109
Cochrane, Mrs. Edward L., 103
Cold War, 18–19
Collins, Edward, 136, **136**, 138
Collins, Michael, 221
Collins Line, 136, **136**
Colorado, USS, 48

communism, 19
Congress, U.S., 39, 47, 54, 73, 97, 136; *see also* House of Representatives, U.S.
Connally, Lucille, 103, **103**, **105**, 106–7
Connally, Tom, 103
Connery, Sean, 209
Constitution, U.S.: Eighteenth Amendment to, 54; Twenty-first Amendment to, 48
Constitution, USS, 82, 113, 217, 221
Contact! (Morris), 17
Conte di Savoia, **22**, 39
contraband, 212
Cooper, Gary, **161**
Cove, George E., 129
Cox, Daniel Hargate, 28
Cramp, William, 26
Cravath, Paul D., 30
Crawford, Joan, 211
crew card, **208**
crews, 12, 41–42, 46, 65, **126**, 128, 133, 177, 182, 226
Cristoforo Colombo, 22
Cronican, Frank, 114–15
cruise ships, 21–22, 36, 55, 61–62, 77, 181, 226, 236
Cuba, 47, 109
Cunard, Samuel, 136, **136**
Cunard White Star, 21, 22, **22**, 26, 39, 41, 53, 59, 61, 85, 113, 136, 138, 143, 178, 208, 211, 213
Curran, Joseph, 218
customs inspection, 212

Dalí, Salvador, **158**, 175, 184
dancing, 55, 96, **173**
Daniel, Margaret Truman, 118, 120, 125, **151**
Daniels, Josephus, 28
Davis, Meyer, 128, 133, **173**, 212
dazzle paint scheme, 37, **37**, 69
Delaware River, 26
Denmark, 61
Depression, 18, 48
Dewey, Thomas E., 18, 113, 175
Dion, John, 65
Dirigio, 106
DND (Do Not Disturb) door signs, **124**
dockworkers, 60
Donohue, John "Chick," 177–78, 208, 212
Donovan's Reef (film), 184
Doolittle, James, 83
Dorothy, 43
doughboys, 36–38
Dubois, Georges, 128
Duchin, Eddy, 212
Duquesne, Frederick "Fritz," 62

Earhart, Amelia, 106
East Hills, 178
Eisenhower, Dwight D., 18, 175, 192
Eisenhower, Mamie, 175, 192
Eisenstaedt, Alfred, 106
Ellis Island, 36

El Vale, 34
emigrant carriers, 22, 77, 180
Emmet, William Le Roy, 27
Empire State Building, 192
employment, ocean liners and, 203–14
Empress of Ireland, 30
England, 22, 208
Enterprise, USS, 83
entertainment, shipboard, 55, 58, 96, **173**, 183, 213
espionage, 62
Esso Raleigh, **65**
Europa, 22, 34, 39, 94
Evans, Chester A., 117

Federal Bureau of Investigation (FBI), 62
Federal Shipbuilding and Drydock, 205
Ferguson, Homer, 43, 47, 60
ferries, 117, 131
Ferris, Susan, 78
Ferris, Theodore, 78
fireboats, 29, 42, 117
Firefighter 1, 29
Fitzgerald, David, 209, 211
Fitzgerald, Ted, 133
flappers, 55
Fleet Week, 121
Fleming, Alexander, 209
Florida, 127
flotillas, 117, **119**, 131, 209
Forrestal, James Vincent, 82–83
Forrestal, USS, 83
France, 61, 181, 207
France, 22, 39, 61, 85, 138, 202, 217
Frank, Florence, 188
Frank, Yvette, 188–92, **190**, **191**
Franklin, John M., 78, 96–97, 103, 118–20, 131, 133, **178**
Franklin, Mrs. John, 120
Franklin, Philip, 28, 34, 103
Freeport, 34
freighters, 29, 34, 65, 127, 185, 218
French, Vickie, 114
French Line, 53, 61, 71, 94, 125

Garland, Judy, 209
Gedney Channel, 26, 122
Gedunk stations, 70
Genoa, Italy, 22
George Verity, 210
George Washington, 31
George Washington Bridge, 121
Georgic, 59
Germany, 181, 192
Gestapo, 65
Getz family, 179–80, **180**
Gibbs, Christopher, 30
Gibbs, Francis, 30
Gibbs, Frederic, 22, 25–31, **25**, **29**, 34, 78, 88, 118, 128, 221–22, **222**
Gibbs, Susan, **226**, 227, 236
Gibbs, Vera Cravath Larkin, 30–31, 222

Opposite: *United States* under construction at Newport News Shipbuilding, looking aft on December 5, 1950. (Newport News Shipbuilding Collection)

Gibbs, William Francis, 11, 22, 25–31, **25**, **29**, 33–34, 45, 58–61, 77, 81, 83, 88, 90, 94, 96, 99–100, **105**, 106–7, 109, 113, 118–19, 122, 125, 128, 131, 133, 135, 138, 164, **165**, 205, 212–14, 221–22, **222**, 237
Gibbs, William Warren, 26
Gibbs & Cox, Inc. (Gibbs Bros. Inc.), 28–31, **29**, 34, 38–39, 41–44, 46–48, 51, 58, 77–78, 84, 93, 96–97, 114, 118, 204–7, 222
GI Bill, 18, 90
Gifford, Walter, 130
Gilbert, Charles, 163
girl scouts, **158**
GIs, 69, 73, 142, 188
Giulio Cesare, 22, 94
Gladstone Dock, Liverpool, 36
Glasscock family, 185, **186**, **187**, 188, 213
Gleason, Jackie, **161**
Goodrich, 117
Gore family, 182–84, **182**
Grace Line, 11, 29, 90, 96, 221
Grattidge, Harry, 129
Great Britain, 26
Great Eastern, 26
Great Western, 26
Greece, 77
Guerrier, Albert, 128

Halsey, William F., 83
Hamburg, Germany, 34, 39, 41
Hamburg America line (HAPAG), 31, 34, 36, 89
Hand, Charlie, 210
Harding, Warren, 48
Harris, Mrs. Basil, 60
Hartley, Herbert, 47, 48
Hayworth, Rita, 179
Heine, Edward, 218
Herald Tribune, 57
Himalaya, 22
Hoboken, N.J., 12, 31, 34, 36, 38–39, 42, 48
Holland America Line, 22, 65, 212
Homeric, 39
Hopkins, A. L., 43
Hornet, USS, 83
horse racing, 188, 213
Horton, Dulcie, 118, 120, 125
Horton, John, 118, 120
Hottelet, Richard, 65, 68
House of Representatives, U.S.: Merchant Marine and Fisheries Committee of, 114, 221; Un-American Activities Committee of, 25
Howland, Charles, 227
Hudson River, *see* North River
Hughes, Richard, 121, 239
Huntington, Collis Potter, 43, **43**

Iberia, 22
Ile de France, 22, 38, 94
immigrants, 54, 58, **76**, 142, 182, 188, 207, 208
immigration restriction act, 39, 54
Imperator, 89–90
Independence, 221, 236
Indian Ocean, 22
Ingham, USS, 65, 67
In Hazard (Hughes), 121, 239

interior design, 38–39, 73, 96
International Mercantile Marine (IMM), 27, 28, 34, 43
Intrepid, USS, 117, 218
Intrepid Sea Air and Space Museum, 117
"Invitation au Voyage, L'," (Baudelaire), 114
Iran, 19
Iraq, 19
isolationism, 61, 65
Israel, 189
Italis, 77

Jacob Christensen, 29
James River, 106
Jamestown Bay, 88, 114
Japan, 65, 83
Jazz Age, 52–55
John Ericsson, **148**
Johnson, Louis, 82–84
Johnson, Oscar, 210
Jones, John Paul, 113
Journal of Commerce, 47
Just So Stories (Kipling), 176

Kaiser, William, 47, 99, 109, 113, 125, 131, **145**, 211
Kane, John R., 81
Kaplan, Elaine, **92**
Karl, Harry, 184
Kelley, Frank H., 65–67
Kennedy, John F., 18, 175, 192
Kennedy Space Center, 221
Keyes, Mrs. Arthur E., 103
King, Ernest J., 83
King, William, 163
Kinney, Eugene, 29
Korean War, 19, 82, 83
Kuwait, 19

labor strikes, 73
Lake Champlain, 102
Land, Emory Scott, 25, 58
Land, Mrs. Emory S., 60
Lanin, Lester, 212
Larkin, Adrian, 30
Lasker, Albert, 42, 47, 48
Latin America, 208
Lee, Bill, **73**, 77, 90
Lee, Howard E., Jr., 90
Lenfest, H. F. "Gerry," 225, 236–37
Leonardo da Vinci, 22
Leviathan, SS, 11, 29–31, 32–51, **45**, **48**, **51**, **53**, 106, 129, 222
Leviathan, USS, 11, 29–31, 32–51, **33**, 36, **37**, **40**, **44**, **45**, 69, 106; conversion from coal to fuel oil, 44; German sabotage of, 36; restoration of, 32–51; Spanish influenza aboard, 38
Levy, Claude, 204
Lexington, USS, 78, 218
Liberté, 22, 125, 204
lifeboats, 44–45, **47**, **53**, 58
life jackets, 182, **186**
Life magazine, 106
life rafts, 69
life rings, **19**

Lindsay, John, 218
Lisbon, Spain, 65–66
lithographers, 142
Liverpool, England, 36–37
Lloyd, Robert, 114
Lock, John, 118
London, England, 30, 185, 188, 208, 209
Long Island Rail Road, 27
longshoremen, 178, 182
LORAN (long range navigation), 73
Lowery, Frank H., 69–70
Lurline, 30

MacArthur, Douglas, 19, 38, 97
MacIver, David, 136
magnetic mines, 62
maiden voyages, 61, **67**, 99, 117
mail service, 22, 39, 129, 136, 226
Maine, 109
Maine, 113
Majestic, 39, 41
Malolo, 29–30
Management Engineering magazine, 30
Manning, Harry, 58, **73**, 94, 106–9, 120–21, 125, 127, 129, 131, 133, 164, 211
Marckwald, Dorothy, 73, 96
Marine Corps, U.S., 36, 65–66, 83, 209
Marine Flasher, 210–11
Mariposa, 30
Maritime Commission, U.S., 25, 58, 61, 66, 78, 99, 109, 114, 133, 209, 211
maritime historians, 12, 58, 133, 189, **230**
Maritime Service, U.S., 107
Marjorie McAllister, 218
Marshall, George C., 97, 175
Marvin, Lee, 184
Mather, Vic and Mimi, 184–85
Matson Line, 11, 29–30
Maud, Louise, 208
Maugham, Somerset, 209
Mauretania, 26, 39, 47–48, 203, 205
Maury, Matthew, 122, **122**
Maxtone-Graham, Michael, 58
Maxtone-Graham, Mr. and Mrs., 58
Maxtone-Graham, Peter, 58
Maxtone-Graham, John (author), **226**, 227–28, **230**, **233**, **237**
Maxtone-Graham, Mary, 227–28
Maxwell, Elsa, **146**
McCarthy, John F., 34
McCarthy, Joseph, 175, 209
McClean, Arthur, 212–13
McDonald, Eugene, 29
McLean, Arthur and Louise, 212
McSweeney, Carmen Martinez, 208–9, **208**
McSweeney, Dan, 207–12, **208**, **210**, **239**
McSweeney family, 207–8
merchant vessels, 78, 82, 178, 208
Mergenthaler, Ottmar, 142
Merrimack, 113
metallurgists, 88
Mewès, Charles, 41, **51**
Meyer, Henry, 205
Michelangelo, 22
Mills, W. H. A., 210, 212
Mizpah, 29

model boats, 114–15, 212–13
Monterey, 30
Morgan, J. P., 27–28
Morgan Line, 34
Morris, Jan, 17
Moscow, Russia, 61
Mothersill's Seasick Remedy, 54
murals, 96, 163–64
Murrow, Edward R., 65
museums, 117, 122, 163

Nagasaki, Japan, 83
Nantucket, Mass., 29
Naples, Italy, 189
National Guard, 185
National Maritime Union (NMU), 177–78, 211, 218
National Union of Seamen, 209
nautical school ships, 106, 127
naval architecture, 11, 26–28, 34, 60, 77–78, 90, 93–94, 113, **165**, 226, 236–37
Navy, Royal, 26–27, 48, 58
Navy, Soviet, 29, 84
Navy, U.S., 28–29, 36, 47, 62, 65, 68–71, 77–78, 82–83, 97, 99, 107, 117, 205, 236
Nazis, 65
Neotex, 94
New Orleans, Louisiana, 210
Newport, 106
Newport News Shipbuilding (NNS), 12, **25**, 31, 42–44, **45**, 57–58, 60–61, 65, **65**, 68, 71, 81–85, **81**, 90, 93, 97, **97**, 100, 107, 204–6, 211, 218
New York, N.Y., 22, 26, 29–30, 34, 36, 48, 54, 58, 78, 109, 113, 118–19, 125, 127, 131, 182, 188, 192, 204, 206, 213
New Yorker, The, 30
New York Harbor, **12**, 34, 38, 47, 68, **117**, 121–22, 218
New York Times, 82, 117, 138, **148**, 217, 221
New York World, 33
New York World's Fair, 61
Nieuw Amsterdam, 22, 34, 39
Nixon, Richard, 18, 218
Noonan, Fred, 106
Noone, Peter, 203
Noongah, 218
Normandie, 27, 34, 39, 59, 61, 71, 94, 188
norovirus, 181
North Korea, 19
North River (Hudson River), 120–21, 182, 205, 209
Norway, 61
Norwegian America Line, 59
Norwegian Cruise Line, 236
nuclear weapons, 19, 82

"O Captain! My Captain" (Whitman), 135
ocean liners: employment on, 203–14; preservation of, 237
oceanographers, 122
Ocean Princess, 179, 181
oil tankers, 221, 226
Olympic, 39, 59
O'Malley, Dezi, 178, 208
Orcades, 22

Opposite: *United States* in dry dock at ship-way no. 10 during construction, June 18, 1951.

(Newport News Shipbuilding Collection)

Oriana, 22
Orient Lines, 22
Orion, 22
Orontsay, 22
Orsova, 22
Oslofjord, 59

Pacific, 136
Palermo, Italy, 180
Palm Beach, Fla., 29
Panama Canal, 22, 27, 62
Panamax, 85
P&O/Orient Lines, 22, 77
parades, 117, 127, 131, 209
Paris, France, 180, 184, 188
patriotism, 17, 30–31
Patroller, HMS, 58
Peake, James, 44
Pearl Harbor, Japanese attack on, 29, 61, 65, 83, 113, 209
Peckolick, Alan, 204
Peninsular & Orient (P&O) Line, 21, 22
Pennsylvania Railroad, 27
Perry, 117
Pershing, John J. "Black Jack," 38
Peters, Ralph, 27
Philadelphia, Pa., 26–27, 29–30, 209; Navy Yard at, 221
picket boats, 83
Pier 86 (New York City), 17, 17, 48, 65, 117, 120–21, 155, 174, 177, 182, 186, 209, 218
piers, 17, 34, 38–39, 42, 48, 61, 68, 117, 218, 221
Pike, David, 94
port calls, 155, 226
Portsmouth, Va., 65, 68
President Roosevelt, 106
Pressman, Gabe, 177
Prohibition, 46, 48, 54–55, 129
propellers, 92, 93
pursers, 211, 218

Queen Elizabeth, 22, 39, 61, 69, 85, 94, 113, 129, 133, 136, 177, 214, 217–18
Queen Mary, 11, 22, 27, 39, 61, 69, 85, 94, 103, 113, 125, 127, 129, 136, 143, 155, 205, 208, 213
Queen Mary 2, 94, 184, 203

radio training station, 107
Raffaello, 22, 217
railroad networks, 27, 43
Red Sea, 22
reefers (refrigerated containers), 226
Rent-a-Tool, 236
Revell model boats, 213
Rex, 22, 39
Reynolds, Debbie, 184
Riddington, William, 162, 163
Riggelsen, Jakobus and Wilhelmine, 152
Ritger, Marcus, 72
Ritz-Carlton restaurant, 41, 46, 48
Robertson, Ben, 67
Rockport, Maine, 9
Rome, Italy, 30, 184
Roosevelt, Eleanor, 60
Roosevelt, Franklin D., 18, 57

Rotterdam, 22, 187, 212
Royal Princess, 55
Runciman, Viscount, 130
Ruser, Hans, 34
Russia, 19, 83, 208
Ryndam, 205

St. Louis, 26, 29
St. Paul, 26
Sanchez, Jorge, 109
Sander, Anthony, 181
Sandy Hook, N.J., 26, 34, 43, 122
Sandy Hook Pilots Association, 122
Sanitation Department, New York City, 118
Santa Ana, 65
Santa Paula, 96, 221
Santa Rosa, 96, 221
Santa Teresa, 65
Saturnia, 94
savetheunitedstates.org, 227
Savorona, 29, 31
Sawyer, Charles, 97
Scorpion, USS, 218
seamanship, standards of, 136
seasickness, 54, 133, 184, 189, 192, 201–2
Secret Service, 118
security, post-9/11, 83, 118, 184
September 11, 2001, terrorist attacks, 19
Sequoia, 29
Shelldrake, Westpoint Leslie, 69
shipbuilding, 22, 26, 41, 77; see also naval architecture; shipyards; shipyard workers
Shipping Board, U.S., 28–29, 34, 42, 47
Shipping Control Committee, U.S., 28
shipping lines, 11, 22, 29–31, 34, 59, 77; see also ships: British; specific lines
ships: British, 22, 39, 61, 77; Dutch, 22, 34, 65, 187, 212; French, 22, 38, 53, 61, 71, 94, 125, 136; German, 11, 18, 22, 29, 31, 34, 36, 39, 46, 94; Italian, 22, 39, 94, 127, 184; Norwegian, 29–30, 59, 61
Shipyard Bulletin, 84, 100, 106
shipyards, 26, 29, 34, 34, 36, 39, 41–43, 47, 60, 77, 88, 221
shipyard workers, 59, 81, 84, 90, 99, 99, 206
shrimp boats, 205
Siegler, Erwin, 62
signal flags, 171
"Sinews of Peace, The" (Churchill), 18
60 Minutes, 227
Skelton family, 177
small craft, 117, 131
Smith, Constance, 96
Smith, Edward J., 122
Smith, William W., 99
Smyth, Urquhart & Markwald, 73, 96
Snyder, Fred, 117
Snyder, John, 118
Southampton, England, 128–30, 133, 164, 185, 187, 188–89, 204, 209
South Korea, 19
South Street Seaport Museum, 122
space race, 18
Spanish influenza, 38
Sputnik, 18
Stalin, Joseph, 135

Star Cruises, 236
Statendam, 39
Staten Island, 51, 65, 117, 179
Statue of Liberty, 43, 122, 192
Stedman, Giles C., 61, 65
Steele, Alfred, 211
Steinway, Theodore, 94
Stevenson, Adlai, 18
Stigler, Franz, 62
Storstadt, 30
style paquebot (steamship style), 38, 39
sunken ships, 65
supercarriers, 82
Supreme Court, U.S., 48
surveyors, 47
Swan, Nancy, 208
Sydney, 22, 77

Tacey, Steve, 76
Taft, Robert, 18
Tagus River, 67
tall ships, 209
Taylor, David W., 28
telegrams, 47, 113, 118, 177, 178
terrorism, 19
Thermopoulis, Pete, 145
Tilberg, Robert, 94
Tilberg, Tomas, 94
Time magazine, 77
Times (London), 131
Tissot, Charles Lin, 144
Titanic, 113, 122, 182, 214
Todd Shipyard, 42
Tokyo, Japan, 83
Topila, 34
tourists, 54, 61, 177–92, 201–4
Townsend, David, 138
Tracy, Spencer, 179
transportation history, 18, 26, 106
travel diaries, 189
Treasury Department, U.S., 65
Tromp, Maarten, 47–48
troopships, 11, 29–30, 36, 43, 48, 58, 65, 67, 78; see also Leviathan, USS; West Point, USS
Truman, Bess, 118, 151, 175, 192
Truman, Harry S., 18, 82, 151, 175, 192
Tuckahoe, 117
Tucker, John, 117
tugboats, 30, 34, 37, 42–44, 103, 107, 117, 131, 218, 221

U-boats, 67, 106
Ujifusa, Steven, 133, 230, 239
Ulster, 34
uniforms, 162, 163
United States, postwar, 18–19
United States, SS, 11–12, 17, 26, 31, 47, 59, 61, 84, 100, 113, 119, 122, 126, 128, 129, 134–216, 145, 155, 217, 221, 228, 228, 230, 231, 233, 234; brochure for, 130, 167; building of, 81–97, 86, 89, 92, 192, 237, 241, 242; christening ceremony of, 100–106, 103, 105, 107; cutaway of, 195–98; deck plans for, 193–94, 199–200; departure trials of, 109–14, 109, 114, 245;

Duck Suite on, 96, 110, 143, 146; final voyage and layup of, 218, 221, 225; Gibbs brothers on, 25, 118–19; interior of, 110, 165, 169, 171, 173; jobs aboard, 203–14; lifeboat drills and, 186, 190; maiden voyage of, 17, 18, 117–33, 117, 124, 131, 133, 205; needlepoint of, 135; passengers on, 21, 161, 174–92, 191; sunbathing on deck and, 192; tug strikes and, 177
United States Conservancy, 226–27, 233, 236–37
United States Steel, 205
"upholsterart," 38
U.S. Lines (U.S. Mail Steamship Co.), 29, 31, 34, 39, 48, 58, 61, 65, 66, 77–78, 82, 93–94, 96–97, 103, 106–7, 114, 117–18, 129–31, 138, 143, 178, 178, 185, 203, 208, 210–11, 218

Van Doren, Mira Jedwabnik, 96, 237
Vaterland, 11, 18, 29, 34, 34, 36, 46, 89
vendors, 44–46
Versailles, Treaty of, 39
Vesta, 136
veterans, 18, 211
Vietnam War, 19, 67, 177
visas, U.S., 182
Volstead Act, 54
voyages, maiden, 61, 67

Walker & Gillette, 42
Walter Kidde & Co., 218
war brides, 113, 211
War Production Board, 78
Warrington, USS, 117
Washington, 58, 106, 138
Washington, D.C., 19, 28, 34, 42, 58, 61, 65, 70, 78, 97, 103, 109, 201
Washington Post, 209, 225
Wassner family, 192, 201–3, 201, 202
Wayne, John, 158, 184, 209
Weather, 205
Weber family, 203–4
Wendell, Raymond, 164
Weser Yard, 39
Western Union, 118
West Point, USS, 58, 65–71, 68, 71, 130, 142; in reconversion to America, 71–77
West Virginia, USS, 43
Whitman, Walt, 135
Whitney, William C., 43
William Cramp & Sons shipyard, 26, 29
Williams, Steve, 236
Willis, Douglas, 125, 127
Wilson, Woodrow, 36, 54
Windsor, Duke and Dutchess of, 96, 142–43, 145, 146, 178
Woodward, John, 82, 88, 103
World War I, 29, 34, 48, 69, 90, 94, 226
World War II, 11, 28, 59, 61, 67, 70, 83, 106, 188, 208, 211
Wright, Wilbur and Orville, 26
Wyman, Jane, 161

yachts, 28–29, 31, 117, 205
York, Lewis, 164

Opposite: The *United States* stack, May 14, 1952. Overleaf: Sea trials, June 10, 1952; navy destroyers USS *John D. Weeks* and USS *Cogswell* sail in the background. (Newport News Shipbuilding Collection)

The forward wall of first class's
Smoking Room shows the Mercator
projection surmounted by a decorative
frieze of all the world's time zones.

(Newport News Shipbuilding Collection)